WHERE THE RUBBER MEETS THE ROAD
with **GOD**

Praise for
Where the Rubber Meets the Road With **God**

"A knock out punch for Jesus if there ever was one! Jack Alan Levine's book is the Heavyweight Champion of the World when it comes to Christians walking a life of faith with God. Let Jack be your coach, teaching you as God taught him every step of the way, so you can knock out Satan and be champion of your life. Read it and you can make certain you will wear the champion's crown of life for Christ."

NATE "GALAXY WARRIOR" CAMPBELL
3 time Lightweight Champion of the World

"Another must read from Jack Levine. I truly look forward to reading this book several times over as I did his previous book, *Don't Blow It with GOD*, which sits by my bed stand. Jack captures your attention with real-life examples and useful advice, melding sports analogies with scripture, to strengthen your relationship with Jesus Christ. As Jack will tell you, it's never too late to bring God into your life, however, you MUST stay in the game and finish strong!"

DON SILVESTRI
Professional football player, New York Jets

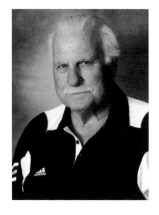 "I have coached football for over 50 years and I know the importance of a playbook and proper execution in order to be a winner. Jack's book gives you the plays as ordered by God Himself to insure we are winners for Christ. Motivational, spiritual and full of guidance and wisdom necessary to encourage, teach and discipline each of us to perform at a level that will guarantee our lives are victorious for Jesus. Like football the Christian life is all about sacrifice and teamwork, that's what equals success and championships. Jack's book offers the key to victory for every Christian looking to "go deep" for God. Get it! Read it! Study it! and then live it...the winning life for Christ."

HOWARD SCHNELLENBERGER
Legendary Pro Football and College Coach

"This book will be an immense blessing to all who endeavor to traverse life's journey with Jack. His ability to communicate authentically is truly a gift. You will gain valuable insight as Jack interprets his experiences through the filter of God's Word. The Biblical idea of God working all things for good to those that love Him and are called according to His purpose is unmistakably displayed on the stage of Jack's life. I have known him for many years and can genuinely say that there is never a dull moment with Jack Levine! If you don't want to be challenged, this is definitely not the book for you; however, if you're willing to take an honest assessment of yourself with a potential for growth then you need to read *Where the Rubber Meets the Road with God*."

ROB TAYLOR
Senior Pastor, First Baptist Church, Boca Raton, Florida

"Jack's book is awesome, spiritually speaking it ROCKS! I am recommending the book to our senior leadership as 'must reading!' I believe every Christian needs to be sure they will hear "well done good and faithful servant." Jack's done an outstanding service to Christian believers with this book. It takes what we sometimes see as being so complicated; figuring out how God wants us to live, and makes it so simple. The TRUTH in this book smacks you right between the eyes! I feel it's a wake up call for every sleeping or daydreaming Christian... to make sure they are ready to live the life God desires for them. Jack did his job writing this fantastic book, now believers everywhere need to read it and let God's spirit speak to them and work in their hearts through it. I know that's what happened to me when I read it, and I'm certain it will happen to you!"

SEAN LAGASSE
Executive Pastor, The Crossing Church, Orlando, Florida

Jack goes deeper then ever with this book. I still can't believe how God took this Jewish advertising executive and drug-using hotshot TV producer and turned him into such an on fire Christian and mighty man of valor for God's kingdom. This book brought me to a deeper understanding of God and his love for me, and has resulted in my walking even closer with God. What a blessing! Required reading for every Christian believer who wants a closer walk with God.

CARL "THE FOSS" FOSTER
Development Director, Radio/TV Host, "The Road Show" and
"The Good Sports Magazine Show," GraceFM Radio 90.3FM
Board Member of the Fellowship of Christian Athletes (FCA),
DeVos-Blum Family YMCA and Match Point Ministries.

WHERE THE RUBBER MEETS THE ROAD

with **GOD**

Your Moment of Truth

JACK ALAN LEVINE

WHERE THE RUBBER MEETS THE ROAD WITH GOD
By Jack Alan Levine

Published by Great Hope Publishing, Coconut Creek, FL
www.DontBlowItWithGod.com
www.JackAlanLevine.com
www.GreatHopePublishing.com
jack@dontblowitwithgod.com

Neither the publisher nor the author is engaged in rendering advice or services to the individual reader. Neither the authors nor the publisher shall be liable or responsible for any loss, injury, or damage allegedly arising from any information or suggestion in this book. The opinions expressed in this book represent the personal views of the author and not of the publisher, and are for informational purposes only.

Many of the various stories of people in this book draw from real life experience, at certain points involving a composite of stories. In some instances people's names have been changed in these stories to protect privacy.

ISBN 978-0-9825526-1-2 - perfectbound
ISBN 978-0-9825526-4-3 - hardcover
Library of Congress Control Number: 2010942848
Printed in Korea

The photographs of celebrities and public figures appearing in this book with the author are not meant to, and should not be construed to constitute an endorsement of this book by any of them. No endorsement is intended or implied.

Dedication

To every Christian believer who answered the call of Jesus knocking at their heart, all of whom are my brothers and sisters in the Lord. I am inspired by watching you live your lives in sacrifice and service to the Lord. I am so proud to watch you work and walk in faithfulness as you live devoted to the Lord. I am honored to be a part of the family of God with you, and so joyful as together we keep "pressing on" to live the abundant life to which our God has called us.

Thank you my brothers and sisters for your love and inspiration. I know I can walk in any church any place in the world, or sit down with any believer anywhere in the world and feel the love and fellowship of Jesus himself and know that I am among family. This is another great gift from our loving God. Thank you for your part in it. I dedicate this book to you believers everywhere and pray that it may influence you, speak to you and motivate you in such a positive way that you walk even closer with God, your Father.

Love,

Jack

Table of Contents

Foreword *by Pat Williams* xi

Introduction..xv

1: September 11—Love, Not Fear 1

2: Finishing Strong 23

3: Three Strikes, You're Out!... 41

4: Pass the Salt... 67

5: The Devil's Credit Card 87

6: Because You Said So..109

7: Pain, Pain, Go Away 125

Photo Section 141

8: You Be the Judge 159

9: Who Says You Haven't Got A Prayer? 173

10: It Happened To Me 195

11: Struggles with Sin 205

12: Are You Ready?..215

13: Rules for Holy Living..231

14: Is Less More? 249

15: Dead Man Walking 263

Ending Thoughts...280

Acknowledgments 282

Foreword

I believe that living an abundant Christian life for God and getting God's full blessings is something every Christian can achieve. Each one of us should desire to do whatever it takes to insure that happens, just like every athlete trains hard to insure he plays his best. That's why I love Jack's book.

It's down and dirty; it gets right to *Where the Rubber Meets the Road with God*. It forces you to look at what God wants of you in order to insure you will hear "Well done good and faithful servant, come and share your Master's happiness." It makes you look to yourself to see if you are *willing* to do it.

In my motivational books, I've often encouraged you to dream big dreams and build a strong foundation on which to build your dreams. I believe Jack's book provides the final piece to the puzzle for any Christian not 100% certain what they will hear from God when they get to heaven. Chapter by chapter it will teach, motivate, inspire and encourage you to be certain you will receive the prize God has in store for you. Jack exposes himself and leaves no stone unturned, as God opens up Jack for spiritual surgery. In each chapter we see God cutting away at Jack's worldly faith and replacing it with spiritual faith. As you see Jack faced with the choices of the world or the choices of God, I am sure you will see the parallels to your own life.

Don't miss out on God's best for your life. It's not too late, no matter how old you are or where you are in your life. Remember in life, as in sports and business, success is not measured at the beginning but rather the end.

This book is for Christians who are serious about God. The truths are blunt, direct and accurate. Let me say it nicely... read it and you'll have nowhere to hide! Jack is a businessman turned preacher; he is a bottom line guy who knows what it takes to get the job done.

I have 19 kids, 14 of them adopted from four foreign countries. For one incredible year, 16 of my children were teenagers at the same time, so I know a little about perseverance and God's grace. I have managed professional sports franchises and am a motivational speaker to some of America's top businessmen, so I know a little about pressure and performance.

I've written over 65 books so I know a little about how words can impact people's lives. I see people everywhere trying to make certain they are doing it right with God. But, could it be you are still not certain, still not sure you are living the life God desires of you? Read this book with anticipation and excitement and you can be sure your Christian life will be a success by God's standards. His are the only ones that matter.

Jack and I share the same desire. We both desperately want you to succeed in life and live the joyful abundant Christian life. Jack wrote this book because he wants every Christian believer to get the full reward God has in store for them. I believe you'll want to be where he is... certain that when you get to heaven you will hear "well done good and faithful servant."

Wishing you all of God's Best Blessings,
Pat Williams

Author, Motivational Speaker and
the NBA's *Orlando Magic* General Manager

Introduction

I wrote this book as a reminder for myself, so I won't forget how I want to live, what I want to accomplish, how I want to feel as I live my life now, and how I want people to remember me. This book is my moment of truth with God and I hope it will be one for you. If I follow what God has taught me in it, it will insure that I earn the best reward possible in heaven. I pray that I not just hear the "parable of the talents," but more importantly, live the lesson learned from them.

If you are a Christian, and you are not 100% certain that when you die, you will hear "Well done, good and faithful servant, come and share your Master's happiness," then this book is for you.

We all know what to do, but most of us don't do it. Why do you think many successful athletes, businesspeople, and entertainers have coaches? In major league baseball, the players have batting and pitching coaches. Why? They already know how to hit and pitch. It's because their coaches keep them focused and remind them of the important physical and mental preparation and training necessary for them to perform at their peak skill level and to be rewarded accordingly. God wants to be your "life" coach.

I believe that if you follow God's instructions, as He has allowed me the privilege of sharing them with you, you can and will be 100% certain that you will have lived your life for God. You can be certain and able to rest assured that you were a light in a world of darkness, that you were salt to a tasteless generation, and that God will bless your obedience abundantly and exceedingly more than you can ask or imagine, both in this lifetime and for all eternity. Remember, God instructs us to "run in such a way as to get the prize."

This is my second book. My first one, *Don't Blow It with God* is a primer for Christians who want to know how to grow in the Lord. I wrote this book for more mature Christians who want to make sure that where it really matters, "where the rubber meets the road," the tire marks they leave on the road to eternal life are both fruit-bearing and of lasting kingdom purpose. This book is for those of us who want to make sure we fight the good fight and win the prize! So, if you are ready, it's time to grab the steering wheel, hang on, hit the gas, and enjoy the ride. It's a fast one, but it should be the most amazing ride of your life.

See you on the road,

Jack

1

September 11—
Love, Not Fear

Not long after that fateful day, September 11, 2001 (when the terrorists hijacked airplanes and crashed them into the World Trade Center towers in New York City), I took my son Ricky and one of his pals to a Miami Dolphins game. Everybody needed a diversion back then; remember? We'd spent days frozen at a point in time that filled us with all kinds of emotion, not the least of which was fear. Every security method around the nation went into overdrive, and we struggled with fear from the outside—what if it happens again? What if there's a bomb? And fear from within—our own fear of the future, of other people, of loss.

We needed a breather, a chance to just turn all that off and tune in to something else. And so we sat in the sunny seats on an unbelievably hot afternoon, and what a great game it turned out to be, with the Dolphins coming back to win in the last five seconds. Games like that are so exciting and make you glad you stayed until the end, rather than leaving in the final quarter so you could beat the crowd out of the parking lot.

I bought bottled water like crazy at five bucks a pop. I nabbed at least six bottles before the price started going way up; the law of supply and demand was in full swing at that game. Anyway, it was so hot that we felt like we were frying, and we started pouring the water over our heads to cool off. Ricky was thirteen at the time, and he and his pal laughed hysterically. Somewhere in the third quarter, he turned to me and said, "Dad, this is the greatest game I've ever been to."

It was so wonderful, him sitting there drenched and happy with complete joy in his face. No fear of terrorist attacks. No fear of a bomb going off or some sudden destructive act. No fear of the thousands of people cheering in the heat. Ricky trusted me to take him somewhere safe. He trusted me because he knew that I loved him completely and only had his best interest in mind.

I froze that moment in my mind, that moment when my son's joyful face made such an impression on me, and I realized that I felt completely happy because of his joy. And I couldn't help but think that this must be how God looks at us when we are happy. God must be thrilled when we are happy and enjoy life, laugh, and cherish stuff rather than being fearful about what might or might not happen.

God has perfect love for us, with so many blessings He wants to give us, but we have to trust where He wants to take us in life to experience fully what He has to offer, and we have to stop fearing what a relationship with Him might mean.

Most of us have had times when fear and emotion took over our lives, whether it was September 11, 2001, or some other significant upheaval or life interruption, and our ability to think clearly was sorely tested. If you're like me, some of those times weren't necessarily perpetrated by someone else... they came, instead, by my own foolish choices that clouded my judgment and made me look and act like an idiot. I think back to a time when I was in college, and this story is either very funny or very sick, depending on your interpretation of it, but I will share it with you.

I'm sharing a time in my life I'm not so proud of, a time when I did more drugs than we need to discuss. There were rumors in 1975, my freshman year at college, that narcs (narcotic agents) were on campus, and to a person who did drugs, that was a concern. It was beyond concern; *panic* is a better word. My pals and I were terrified that we would be arrested but, go figure, we were not terrified enough to change our behavior. Anyone who could think clearly would have looked at us and said, "Hey, you want a way to stop being so terrified and worried?" Quit doing the stuff that puts you in that position. But when you're into drugs, *thinking* and *clearly* are words that don't often show up in your vocabulary together, much less in your actions.

Anyway, the narc rumors continued to grow and so did my paranoia. I suspected the security guard in our dorm because he always wanted to come up to the room and smoke pot with us. We never let him. Then, one night, all that changed, and it was no longer the security guard I feared. It was pizza.

You see, I am not what you call a regular eater (extremely picky would be a better description), and eating in college on the meal plan was hard for me. So, every night I called Domino's to order pizza, *literally* every night. So, I made my usual call to Domino's, and I was talking to the guy on the phone when he said something to me. I don't remember exactly what he said, (it was back in 1975), but I know he said something to make me think, "Uh-oh, it's them. The Domino's Pizza guys are the narcs."

In hindsight, I can say, sure, I was under the influence of drugs. But at the time I remember very clearly that it hit me dead on, as if I'd just made a great scientific breakthrough.

I hung up the phone, ran to my roommate George, and said, "You are not going to believe this, but I figured it out; it's the Domino's guys. They're the narcs, and they're on their way to arrest us. We've got to go run and hide."

George asked, "Jack, what are you talking about?"

"I think they're recording the phone calls; that's how they know who we are." Paranoia, anyone?

George said, "I'll tell you what. Why don't you go up to the third floor to Hank's room (a friend of ours in the dorm) and wait there?"

"Yeah, yeah, I'm getting out of here, no problem." I went up to Hank's room, and I was scared. I was absolutely convinced that I had figured this out. It was the Domino's guys! How obvious! They delivered the pizza, so they always saw us in our rooms partying. How could I have missed that? It had to be them; it made sense. Almost an hour went by, and I sweated. Finally, there was a knock on the door, and Hank made me open it, even though I was never more scared in my life. I opened the door and froze.

It was George. I thought, "Oh, no... he's the narc!" I couldn't decide whether to puke or run.

George just looked me dead in the eye and said, "Jack, the pizza's here."

No narc. No police. Just me sweating and shaking in my own fear and out-of-control emotions. It's true, and the lesson I learned from that experience, plus others during my lifetime, is that we can't let fear and emotion run our lives. We have to be able to think clearly and base our decisions on proper information. My story was driven by actions—choices—I knew were wrong, I knew were illegal, and I knew had major consequences. But I stayed on that path, anyway—a path that was full of fear and led to many irrational thoughts and actions.

Isn't that the human condition? We can all fall into that same pattern. It doesn't have to be induced by illegal substances. Why risk arrest when we have so many legal choices surrounding us that, if allowed, will drive our emotions crazy and cloud our thinking? I know I'm being a sarcastic. Yet we have ample opportunity to spend our lives reacting to such things as fear from the outside—the ailing economy, foreclosures, job losses, war—and fear from the inside—health crises, relationships crumbling, worrying ourselves to sickness over things we cannot control.

My pizza-paranoia story happened a long time ago, but I am sure that every one of us has a story of fear and emotions overtaking our ability to think clearly, a story that might even be unfolding as you read this book. And we have a choice—we can choose to allow our emotions to carry us or we can choose to look to God. I am glad to say that I have learned to look to God. However, I wish that was true, also, for some people I love very much.

My mother comes to mind (she is the most wonderful, caring loving mother in the world). We were talking one day. She's Jewish, and somehow, we got around to religion.

She said, "When I used to work at the hospital, this lady Nellie and I used to have lunch every day and she would open her Bible. She was very spiritual, and I saw her talking to God." Mom paused and looked at me curiously. "You're like that. You and Nellie have what I want."

I said, "Mom, you can have that!"

"Well, yeah, I know." She shrugged.

I said, "No, Mom, I mean you can have that." I got a chance to talk to her about Christ and witness to her, but even as I did that, I realized that, for some reason, she thinks this is something only other people can have, that it's not available to her, as if it's reserved for someone special. It's an odd way for a mom to look at a son. Instead of thinking I was so special that God gave me this kind of relationship, she should have thought, hey, this is my kid. I know him; he came out of my vagina; I wiped his butt for years; I raised him from an infant; and I've seen him all his life. If he can have that joy and peace through Christ, then so can I.

I tried to explain that this gift from God is not just for "some people." It's not reserved for the Nellies in the workplace. "Mom, it's just that we have Christ living inside of us, and that's what you see." But she has yet to take it.

Why? I've never figured that out, but I wonder if there isn't some sort of underlying fear about what a relationship to Jesus Christ might "do" to her friendships. She's Jewish. Many of her friends are Jewish. What would people think? What would her mom and dad think, even though they had died long ago? What would her husband (my dad) think?

You probably have people in your own life who have responded the same way. I hope you'll think like I do and promise that you won't give up on them and that you will keep praying for them.

Why? Because we don't know which one of us that person will finally respond to and, hopefully accept salvation. I take that lesson from Paul, who said in 1 Corinthians 3:6–10, "What, after all, is Apollos? And what is Paul? Only servants, through whom you came to believe--as the Lord has assigned to each his task. I planted the seed, Apollos watered it, but God made it grow. So neither he who plants nor he who waters is anything, but only God, who makes things grow. The man who plants and the man who waters have one purpose, and each will be rewarded according to his own labor. For we are God's fellow workers; you are God's field, God's building. By the grace God has given me, I laid a foundation as an expert builder, and someone else is building on it..." So, maybe I plant the seed, but you're the one there when it's time to harvest.

I've been planting seeds diligently for years now in the lives of some good friends I try to witness to.

There are three friends in particular. One of them is a raging hypochondriac. The guy is just dying of something all the time, and I'm convinced he will literally worry himself to death. He's wealthy, too, so he's got it all—the glam house, the kids, the toys, everything—but he can't enjoy any of it. He has never enjoyed his life. He always worries about losing his job, about losing his life or his kids dying, and then September 11 hit and put the guy into a serious tailspin. Of course, I witnessed to him before that day, and I used the 9/11 opportunity to talk to him again. And his reaction?

He says, "Well, you know I'm not a religious man." I said, "Yes, I know that, but this isn't about religion. It's about an individual relationship with God. It's about a one-on-one relationship between you and God. You don't have to go to church. It would be good if you did because you'd learn more, but that's not a requirement. God wants to love you."

No thumbs up or down, he just watched me, listening.

I said, "Imagine if your son or daughter ran away and never saw you again; think how you'd feel. That is how God feels about us when we don't turn to Him. He just wants to be close and help us through tough times and love us no matter what."

He still wouldn't budge. Fear of everything keeps him from enjoying the incredible blessings he already has, but until he understands who God is and the greater blessings of doing life God's way, he will not change.

Then, I have another friend who searches for happiness in money, sex, and drugs, and his entire life has been a series of searches, searching for another happy time, business deal, relationship, or trip to a casino. I've seen him in action. The guy is miserable, one of the most miserable, depressed guys I know. I love this guy so much, and I want him to be saved and to have joy and happiness in his life, but he won't stop long enough to look for real joy. Why?

This guy knows he's miserable where he is, but at least he knows what to expect. His misery might not be fun, but it's comfortable and familiar. Fear of the unknown, fear of changing his pattern by changing his focus to God, keeps him from facing up to what's at the root of his joyless life, and that's simply that he's unwilling to receive the love that God is offering.

Then, there is the third guy. He hasn't accepted Christ, but he is closer to the truth than the other two are. He gets it, he understands it, but his life is going downhill fast. He's lost a couple of businesses along with a lot of money. He also gambles, trying to find solace and numb his pain. He can't figure out why things haven't worked out for him in life. He is a smart guy and can't figure out why he just can't get it together. He's middle aged, not pleasing his father; and the guilt and shame of the family focuses on him. They consider him the black sheep of the family because, by their standards, he isn't successful. It's really getting him very depressed; yet, he won't reach out and take the gift of life God offers. Why?

This guy knows the right thing yet will not act. He's put his hope in so many things that haven't worked out. I wonder if fear of family ridicule and fear of yet another failure keep him from making a decision for Christ.

Fear. For many of us, it's the reason we avoid change, deny the truth about our lifestyles, and continue in habits that cause us pain. It's nothing new. In Proverbs 26:11, it says, "As a dog returns to its vomit, so a fool repeats his folly." Gross, huh? But think about it. I kept going back to the drugs, even when they made me look and act like an idiot. Alcoholics go back to the booze that makes them sick. Porn addicts go back to the Internet, even though it ultimately causes them so much grief and emptiness. The next time fear of change tempts you to return to your same old habits, think about Proverbs 26:11.

Fortunately, we don't have to keep returning to the same old, uh, pile of crap. Why not? Because we have a very protective God who has better things in mind for us. He says to His children, to those that believe in Him and call on His name, "So do not fear, for I am with you; do not be dismayed, for I am your God" (Isaiah 41:10). What is to fear? Things will be tough down here on earth; absolutely, they are. You will have trials, tribulations, make mistakes, (maybe even addictions) , and complications in life. Jesus even said so, in John 16:33, "...In this world you will have trouble. But take heart! I have overcome the world." Jesus said we would have trouble, so it should not surprise us. Rather, we can look to Him for help and for a better future, because if we are in a saving relationship with Jesus Christ, then we have the hope, the promise of eternity in heaven with Him, free from trials and pain. We can face our fears and our rampant emotions, and we can stop them flat out by speaking God's Word into the situation that causes us to react poorly. We can use that time to draw closer to God, but we have to *choose* to do that.

If an old habit tempts me, if I have a frightening event in my life, I can focus on the fear and the worry, which means I rely on my own strength to get me through (which failed me in the first place); that also means I'd be pushing all-powerful God to the background. Or, like a child grabs hold of his father's hand, I can grab on to God's Word and His power because my heavenly Father can take on the entire world and beat it, and more than that, He made the entire world, and He sustains everything in it.

The challenge, as the difficult situation I face unfolds, is whether I will stay close to my Father or whether I will let go and let those emotions grab hold of me again. I can't help but think back to the events of September 11, 2001, and the days that followed. Do you recall the town meetings, gatherings, and ceremonies where politicians, rabbis, priests, and religious leaders of all kinds and denominations would speak words of hope and unity? I went to one such gathering in Weston, Florida, and was amazed at how united the crowd was, and believe me, there is a lot of diversity in south Florida. There were families and individuals of every race and ethnic background. Everyone was quiet. When it was time to pray, people prayed; they waved American flags silently; and a local band played "God Bless America." I thought about how incredible it was to see the change in people, to really see people being about each other rather than about themselves. In the event's aftershock, the world didn't just say it cared about its neighbors, it demonstrated that care with acts of compassion, unity, comfort, kindness and unconditional love.

What a shame that it took a tragedy to get us focused on important things such as love, on praying for the next guy, on reaching out to the hand that's lifted up in need, regardless of what color it is. I started to wonder what would happen when the immediacy of the tragedy passed. Would that sense of community concern be pushed into the background as "normal" life returned and grabbed our attention and emotion? Would "normal" drive us back to being about our own needs and wants, drive us back to doling out help, attention, or love conditionally?

Yes. It's only natural—the natural process of the sin that we inherited from Adam. And because of that sin nature, it's inevitable.

"My sin is despicable." So said Dave, a friend of mine, in a bible study group. He wasn't talking about a specific sin, but rather about his life measured up against Christ, Christ who lived perfectly, who was tempted but didn't give in, who followed His Father's commands every step of the way, who was obedient even to the cross, even to death to fulfill His Father's mission. And Dave represented me, you, and us all by saying that, compared to Christ, "I'm despicable."

I know I am. Compared to Christ, I am the worst. I am so far away from what I should be and from what Christ is. You see, Christ never lost sight of being about others. It was His reason for being, His reason for coming to earth, and His reason for dying. He never lost sight of it, even when He breathed His last breath.

Me? Once the immediacy of a crisis passes, I lose sight of that whole community thing and being about other people, about loving unconditionally, and I go back to being about myself—and loving conditionally. God showed me my hypocrisy as I stood in that post-September 11 gathering in Weston, wondering about how "everybody else" would go back to his or her selfish ways and their conditional love.

Specifically, He helped me get clear-minded about my attitude toward two people in my life. I have a friend I've known for a long time, and this person's behavior started to change a little bit (maybe I interpreted his changing behavior incorrectly, but that was my interpretation at the time). So, I started to withdraw my friendship. I stopped hanging around with him, stopped being interested in his life. Even though he was a very close friend, somewhere along the line, I decided to ditch him. I got that attitude that says, "I'm done with this guy."

The second person was somebody I never liked. He was just an acquaintance from a shared circle of people, and I never embraced this person lovingly. As a matter of fact, I can't say that I didn't gloat at times when he didn't do well or, in my opinion, when somebody got the best of him.

What God showed me was how I just never thought these people deserved my love.

Does that ring any of your bells? Got a family member, a neighbor, a church-mate that you've labeled "undeserving of your love"?

God showed me how conditional my love was and, man, it really bothered me to see that and to see how hard and unforgiving I can be, even while thanking Jesus for being gracious and forgiving toward me. God reminded me of Jesus' words in Matthew 7:5, "You hypocrite, first take the plank out of your own eye, and then you will see clearly to remove the speck from your brother's eye." Jesus warned us that before we judge somebody else, before we look at the speck in our brother's eye, we need to look inside ourselves first.

I thought about those two friends. Who am I to judge them? Who am I to withhold my love based on my desires and my judgment, which changes daily with my emotions and circumstances? How does that kind of behavior please God and draw others to Him? God drew the plank out of my eye so I could see my own despicable sin, so I would realize how conditional my love for others is. He showed me that if I lived in an attitude of humbleness like my friend Dave when he confessed how far short he was of Christ's perfection, then I would love everybody.

God wanted me to think about that. In 1 Peter 4:7–8, Peter says, "The end of all things is near. Therefore be clear minded and self-controlled so that you can pray. Above all, love each other deeply, because love covers over a multitude of sins."

September 11, 2001, is far behind us. As I write this in 2011, the world seems once again to be falling apart. Wall Street melted down in the last few years; the world's economies are sliding down with us; and wars still rage on. Is the end of all things near? The Bible says it's not for us to know the time or day. But regardless of the specific date and hour, we are instructed to be ready for it, to be clear-minded, to be self-controlled, to pray, and to love each other deeply.

What does it mean to be clear-minded? How about this: be sober, not drunk or stoned, be focused, not distracted by the rest of the world? Self-controlled? How about knowing the boundaries God has set and living within them, whether it means dealing with your lust, greed, temper, your appetites, or your fears?

Why? So you can pray and love others.

Why is it important to pray? So you can communicate with God. God answers prayers. We'll talk about that a lot more in a later chapter. He says above all, above everything, love each other deeply because love covers a multitude of sins. Love forgives, encourages, and draws others to Jesus Christ. Love is our way of illustrating for the world who God is and what He has to offer. Love distinguishes us from what the world has to offer. If I'm not clear-minded or self-controlled, I will not be able to love others the way God calls me to.

In 1 Peter 1:22, God says, "Now that you have purified yourselves by obeying the truth so that you have sincere love for your brothers, love one another deeply, from the heart." What does it mean to have purified yourself by obeying the truth? It means you believe in Christ; therefore, your sins have been washed away, and after that happens, you can obey the truth (the instructions in God's Word). When we obey God's truth, we stop doing those impure things. And when we obey the truth of God, we will have sincere love for our brothers and will love one another deeply. As believers, then, if we don't love one another deeply, we need to look at how pure we are and whether or not we are obeying the truth. This kind of love isn't about feeling warm and fuzzy about each other. This kind of love is about serving one another and looking after one another's best interests.

Peter says in 1 Peter 3:8, "Finally, all of you, live in harmony with one another; be sympathetic, love as brothers, be compassionate and humble." Are we living in harmony, being sympathetic and compassionate? Well, yes, sometimes, when we feel like it. When I want to go out of my way to help someone or love someone, you can't find a more loving person than me. But when I don't want to go out of my way, forget it; I am nowhere to be found. So again, it just gives me a clear illustration of how conditional my love is.

How about that bit about giving all you possess to the poor? How many of us think simply by writing a check or donating time that we do someone a favor, that we score deposits into the First

National Bank of Heaven? Hey, Red Cross Relief Fund needs help. No problem, here's a check. Orphaned child? No problem! Food fund? Here's my check. Just leave me alone once you cash it.

No, God says it's about love. We should do those other things because they are good things to do, but we should do them because we are motivated by love. Love is first, and love will guide us to which actions to take. We have to stay committed and focused on what God wants, so we know how to love others. One of the things God instructs us to do is to "...hold unswervingly to the hope we profess, for He who promised is faithful. And let us consider how we may spur one another on toward love and good deeds" (Hebrews 10:23–24). Hang on to God no matter what and think about how to encourage others.

Do you spend much time thinking about how you can help your fellow believers move toward love and good deeds? Or are you like me, thinking in the moment about what's convenient or who I want to cut out of my life because I don't like how he behaves anymore? When I feel smug because a guy I never liked in the first place screwed up, guess what? I am certainly not obeying the truth; and I am certainly not loving my brother deeply; and I'm for sure not helping him on to love and good deeds. What I should be thinking about when I think of that guy and what you should be thinking about the people in your life is "How can I build up this brother? How can I help him on toward love and good deeds? How can I be more like Christ and sacrifice myself, show kindness, take the hit, turn the other cheek?"

If I need a reminder, all I have to do is look back to the post-crisis attitude of love and service that much of our nation witnessed and experienced after September 11, 2001. It comes back to being about others and not about me, to being united with one purpose. In 2001, we Americans were united in the process of grieving, comforting, and healing, but all those things changed with time. In God's economy, in His plan, it's about our being united in heart and love, so we have the fullest blessings we possibly can. Colossians 2:2–3 puts it this way, "My purpose is that they may be encouraged in heart and united in love so that they may have the full riches of complete understanding, in order that they may know the mystery of God, namely Christ, in whom are hidden all the treasures of wisdom and knowledge."

When I do things God's way, I receive the incredible blessings of knowing Christ, of gaining wisdom and knowledge. When I do things God's way, my actions will reveal my love for others. If my actions reveal something other than love, then my hypocrisy is what is seen. I cannot claim to do things God's way when what I do screams otherwise. A verse that captures this clearly is 1 John 2:9, "Anyone who claims to be in the light but hates his brother is still in the darkness." Claiming to be in the light, to be a follower of Christ, cannot coexist with hating your brother. If you really do love your brother, then your actions will reflect an attitude of love and concern and would build him up; your actions would be void of envy, rage, jealousy, anger, and the like. Loving your brother means loving "other people."

I look at God, and I say, "You have got to be kidding. Love all my brothers and sisters? Love other people who maybe aren't believers? Give me something else to do! Let's have a church workday or something, but don't tell me I have to go out there and love everybody. God, in case you haven't noticed, there are idiots out there. There are loud, obnoxious, arrogant, selfish, and annoying people out there! Some of them smell bad. Do not make me go out there and love them."

And God says, "That is exactly what I want you to do, Jack. And by the way, it might interest you to know that some other folks have described you that same way."

Me? But I'm such a nice guy. "Come on, God, I can't do that, you know me. You know every hair on my head is numbered; you knew me before the beginning of the earth; you know the perfect plan for my life; you've written my name in the book of life. You know me, God; this just isn't my area; this isn't my style. How about I go dust the pews or paint the classrooms?"

God says, "No, Jack, you will go out, and you will love others, and no, you can't do it by yourself, but you have my Holy Spirit in you. And through me, you can accomplish everything. Through me, you can even love those unlovable people. People like you."

So, I wonder, in my despicable state, how can I lift someone up in love today? What can I do today? What can you do today? What if we all respond unconditionally to God, as we did after the 9/11 crisis? God would be praised and worshipped, and we would have a perfect world. Of course, that's exactly what God wants us to do and what He tells us to do.

"A new command I give you: Love one another. As I have loved you, so you must love one another. By this all men will know that you are my disciples, if you love one another" (John 13:34–35). Think about this. God says, "As I have loved you." In the same way that God has loved me, I need to love others, and so do you.

What did God do for us? He sacrificed everything. He gave the thing that meant the most to Him, His son, put Him on a cross to die, to pay for our sins, so we could be free here on earth now and free with God in heaven later. We are supposed to love each other the same way. We are supposed to sacrifice and put other people first, to love them and care for them, cry for them and pray for them, as Jesus did for us.

And what about that last part, that everyone will know we're His disciples when they see how we love one another? Uh oh, let's turn that around—all men will know you are **not** my disciples if you don't love one another. What do others know about my relationship with God based on how I love them?

We really need to examine ourselves individually and ask, do I live as Christ has instructed me to live? Not in the "religious" way, with church rules and regulations that tell you what you must do to earn points with God. Quite the opposite—God instructs us to be joyful and to live a life of peace. Imagine if you could have all the resentment, guilt, and fear taken out of you and replaced with love, joy, and happiness. It would show. Others would see it, want it, and call on Jesus as their Lord, just as it happened to me.

I had a pastor friend, Dr. David Morgan, who has since passed away, and for years, I admired him and his family because I could always see God's joy reflected in their lives and actions. They were always happy. Their lives continually reflected God's love, grace, peace, and joy, which got me very inspired when I first met them years ago. I saw what they had, and I just had to have that peace and love flowing through me. I was willing to do whatever it took to be like that, and they taught me that it was all about seeking God's face in love and obedience. It was all about imitating him and desiring to be holy. Because of that desire, I believe I grew tremendously in my personal relationship with Jesus Christ.

The funny thing is that not everybody responds the same way. We see the joy and peace in others, and we want it, but we refuse to accept it when it's offered, like my mother and those three friends I mentioned earlier. I think about how much I love them and want them to have this gift. I think that maybe I'm too close to them. They've heard me witness to them over and over. I've done everything I can, and I will not stop trying because I don't know the day of their salvation; that's between God and them. My job is to keep going, and I will, wholeheartedly, but God has said that sometimes, a man can't be a prophet in his own home (Luke 4:24). Sometimes, we are too close to people. They know us too well; they know our flaws and our weaknesses; and they think we have no right to tell them what to believe. But guess what? My mom and my three friends probably don't know you, my reader, and one day, maybe you'll meet one of them in a restaurant, in a meeting, or on an airplane, and maybe you'll witness to them that day, and they will make the leap of faith into Christ's salvation. I hope so.

No doubt, you have people like that in your life, people who need this love God offers. Perhaps you've tried to give them this gift, and they've rejected it. Still, you want them to have freedom from living a life driven by fear and emotions, but you can't force it on them. Maybe one day, I'll meet them and be the guy who witnesses to them, and they'll respond to Christ through me, even though they didn't respond to you. That's often how it happens, but we must be out there doing it. We must be out there loving each other.

My challenge to you is to go and be witnesses. God tells us, "Do not fear, for I am with you" (Isaiah. 41:10). God is with you. He does not keep score to see how many people you convert. He's the one converting, but He often uses us to do it.

I shudder to think about how I could have stayed on the path to hell and how my fear of change could have kept me from enjoying so many blessings I never expected. I also wonder what might have been different, way back at the pizza-paranoia phase of my life, if there had been someone at the door ready to share Jesus Christ's love with me. How many more years of delighting in the Lord would I have had? To how many more people might I have passed that blessing on to?

Maybe you're fearful about sharing Jesus with others because you think it'll make you look like an idiot. Well, trust me, I know what it is to look like that, remember? So, here's what helped me. I thought about how hot it was in that Miami stadium at the Dolphin game and how that would be nothing compared to an eternity in hell. I thought about standing in front of God at some point, and one of two things would happen. Either I'd see people there that I'd influenced for Christ, and they'd be like Ricky at that football game, just having the best time and thanking me for bringing them; or I'd struggle to explain why I'd left so many others to fry in the heat of hell because I was afraid to talk to them about love. And in God's sight, that would make me the idiot!

2

Finishing Strong

Do you know any great comebacks? Not the verbal quips we sometimes think of when someone insults us, and we fire back when we want to seem so smart and witty. I'm talking about "comebacks in life."

Whether it's a famous person, an athlete, a relative, or even yourself, how did these people have the opportunity to come back? They had it because the game wasn't over. In football, they don't stop at halftime and say, "The team that's winning wins the game." No, they wait until the end. What matters is what happens at the end. Did the leading team at halftime win, or did the losing team make a comeback in the final seconds and leave everyone talking about its great finish?

My dad had a great comeback in 2006, thanks to triple bypass surgery. We had a birthday party in my home for my nephew Dylan from New York, who was turning ten. My dad hadn't been feeling well for the past year or so, and it wasn't uncommon for him to come in tired and lay down. Dad arrived at the house for the party but needed to lie down, and no one thought anything of it. I went out to buy some decorations, and my wife called.

"Get home quick," she said. "We had to call 911. Dad's having chest pain."

"Is he breathing?"

"Yeah."

"That's good." I started to pray as I drove, and my prayer was simply this: "Lord, please give him more time so he can watch his grandchildren grow up. Give him more time so that we can enjoy him more. Give him more time, Lord, most importantly, so that we can continue to witness to him and he can be saved and come to know you, because Lord, that is the most important thing of all."

I finished my prayer, saying, "You know what we want, but thy will be done. If Dad's time on earth is up, then thank you so much for the time you've given us with him. Thank you that I've had this wonderful father." I had complete peace as I drove home, the peace that transcends all understanding, the peace that you can only get from God when you completely trust Him. Of course, my desire was that my father continue to live, but I trust God, and if God had a different plan, so be it.

The good news is that Dad had a triple bypass. He's doing well, and we're very grateful for that. The game isn't over for him, and that's good news because we are still praying for him to become a believer in Jesus Christ, he and my mother both. During this incident, I know my mother wondered what she would do if my father wasn't around. At that time, they had been together more than 55 years and had witnessed the death of a few of their friends and the effect it had on the surviving spouse.

Some people put their confidence for their own lives in their spouse. "He's my everything. He's my life. And if he dies, I have nothing." That might seem true for some; but if you are a Christian, then your spouse is not your everything. God is your everything. That spouse will die one day, and then what are you going to do? Will you give up on life? Or will you choose to finish strong?

This made me think about how easily we put our confidence in things that can fail us. In what do you put your confidence?

Some people put their confidence in the U.S. government. Now, I love this country, but I seriously doubt that my kids will ever benefit from Social Security or Medicare. It won't be there for them by the time they get old, so they can't put their confidence in our government to support them. They can put their confidence in the government for many things, but not to support them.

How about the bank? Sure, put your money and your confidence in the bank; but now in 2011, you don't keep more than $250,000 in the bank because that next dollar is uninsured. The banks will only insure you some of the way.

What about real estate? Some people put their confidence in real estate. They say you can't lose, yet real estate markets have crashed many times, and as of this writing in 2011, that market is currently down for the count.

How about doctors? People put confidence in doctors to save their lives, but they don't save everybody. They miss some. They're human, and they make mistakes.

And lawyers, can they save us? We can't always rely on them, either.

Sometimes, we rely on a person spiritually smarter than us to protect us, but it won't work. Every person, somewhere down the line, will fail us and let us down. The only thing that will not fail us, ever, is Jesus Christ's love.

Jesus said, "And surely I am with you always, to the very end of the age" (Matthew 28:20b). God will never leave you or forsake you (Genesis 28:15, Deuteronomy 31:6, 8; Joshua 1:5, Hebrews 13:5). Jesus Christ will never fail you. If that sounds like a bold statement, so be it; but I speak from a life that has tried everything: drugs, sex, money, power, possessions, relationships, anything you can think of, and I can promise you from my heart that none of them has satisfied me, none of them. Only Jesus Christ has satisfied me and stayed with me through thick and thin.

That got me thinking about my favorite Bible guy, Peter (also known as Simon). Why is he my favorite? Because he was prideful and stubborn and he failed so often, and he was human, but most of all, because he loved Jesus so much. As I struggle, fail, and am prideful, I can tell you today that I do not deserve to be sharing with you the Word of God. I am not worthy, but I do so only by the grace of God, a privilege for which I am grateful. When I think of where I've been and what I have become, it's just a miracle, and I am truly thankful.

When I struggle and fail, I always turn back to Jesus and find comfort in this story. It starts in Luke 22:31 with a warning from Jesus to Peter: "Simon, Simon, Satan has asked to sift you like wheat." And you know what? Satan desires to sift us like wheat too. You and me, your pastor and mine, all of us, Satan is out there trying to sift us like wheat.

Sometimes, I think I'm just stupid because Jesus has given me very clear instructions on how to fight Satan and how to avoid his fiery darts, and I just don't follow the instructions. Those instructions begin in Ephesians 6:11: "Put on the full armor of God..." When I put on God's full armor, Satan can't get me. Invariably, if I'm being attacked, it's because I've left an area of my life open by not putting on that full armor of faith, truth, righteousness, prayer, and the Holy Spirit. If all that armor is in place, then Satan just can't defeat me, and I can finish strong.

In Luke 22:32a, after warning Peter about Satan, Jesus goes on to say, "But I have prayed for you, Simon, that your faith may not fail." I just have to cry with joy in my heart that Jesus Christ is there praying for you and me. As our intercessor, our defender, our Savior, and our Lord, He is with God, interceding on our behalf. We're so lucky because not only did Jesus pray for Peter, but He also prays for us every day. It's beyond me that when I'm weak, when my body fails, when I don't do what I'm supposed to do, there are brothers and sisters in the Lord and the Lord himself praying for me. I'm overwhelmed with joy. Christ himself said, "But I have prayed for you, Simon, that your faith may not fail." Now, reread that verse, but substitute your name for Simon's name. Peter's faith is his weapon. Hey, Peter, if your faith fails, you're in big trouble, but Jesus is praying that your faith may not fail. And faith is our weapon too.

Jesus goes on to say, in Luke verse 32b, "And when you have turned back, strengthen your brothers." There is no doubt in Jesus Christ's mind what this battle's outcome will be. "Hey, Peter, Satan is trying to sift you like wheat. There will be a fight. I've prayed for you, prayed that your faith is strong. It will end, and you will overcome, and when this is over, and you've turned back, strengthen your brothers." It doesn't matter if you stumble. What matters is that you finish strong and help your brothers do so.

God says the same to us. There's a spiritual war going on. Satan will attack us, but God has promised us victory over Satan. Satan can't defeat us. God's Word applies to us as well as Peter: in our own lives, we will fight the battles with Satan, and when we have turned back, when we are strong again, when we have fought our fight and come up from the bottom and been lifted up, we are to strengthen our brothers.

What a great life battle cry. Hey, what's your purpose? Oh, me? I strengthen my brothers. I'm out there edifying the body of believers. I'm out there accomplishing the Great Commission. I'm making believers for Jesus Christ. I'm fulfilling my purpose... and yet, when it comes down to it, I'm often just like Peter, boasting that he'll stick with Jesus even if everyone else abandons Him (Matt. 26:33) and then failing Him within hours of making such a claim. Jesus had responded to Peter's boast with a sad prediction: "...before the rooster crows today, you will deny three times that you know me."

That's exactly what Peter did. Like Peter, I fail Christ when I don't live up to the commitments I make in His name. Do I promise to minister in an area of the church or to a person and then back out? Do I proclaim the importance of forgiveness while harboring a grudge against someone? Those are just a couple of examples of quitting rather than finishing strong in Christ's name.

Well, you know how the story turns out. Peter, indeed, denies Jesus Christ three times that very same day. Now, this amazes me—the second and third times, Peter actually says, "I don't know the man" (Luke 26:72, 74). And the third time, just as he finished denying he knew Christ, the rooster crowed. The Lord turned and looked straight at him, and then Peter remembered the words the Lord spoke to him, "Before the rooster crows today, you will deny me three times."

What did Peter do? God's Word tells us, "And he went outside and wept bitterly" (Luke 26:75).

I often think about how Peter must have felt not long after that, looking at Jesus hanging on the cross, knowing that he let down his Lord. He failed his Savior. He blew it. And the Bible tells us he wept bitterly. I can't help but think of the times in my own life when I failed Jesus, and I have to tell you I also wept bitterly because I knew that God deserved so much better from me. I knew that I was told what to do, and I just fell short and didn't do it.

Many of us know that feeling. We also know that we have a choice. We can allow such an experience to enslave us because we have lost confidence, or we can use such an experience to inspire us to a greater confidence in Jesus. If I put my confidence in myself, I will be disappointed, discouraged, and diminished. However, if I turn to Christ and seek His forgiveness and restoration, I will be enabled and empowered, like Peter, to finish strong.

If you can imagine how Peter felt at that moment, then you'll see that Satan uses that against every Christian. Satan wants to make you believe you're a loser. Do you ever have this kind of conversation in your head? "You have no right to tell others about the Word of God. How dare you? If these people only knew the real you, they'd laugh at you." Satan uses that trick to get us to quit the game before it's finished.

God, however, despite our failures and even in the midst of them, wants to lift us with His grace and use us for His glory because the game isn't close to being over. When we are weakest, God's power shows through all the more clearly to a watching world (2 Corinthians 12:9), a watching community, a watching group of coworkers or family members. How does that happen? Call it a transfer of power if you want, but when we have that sense of failure and understand our own human limitations, we stop putting confidence in ourselves and put it all in God. We know we can't do anything about the situation or circumstance, and we allow God's power and purposes to flow through us... and God handles it... His way.

If Peter could do it, so can we. Why? Because of the grace of Jesus Christ, which is how Peter did it; ultimately, he completely submitted to that grace. In spite of how deeply disappointed Christ must have been in Peter on that forlorn morning, He washed all the hurt away and replaced it with His unconditional love. Jesus never uttered those four discouraging words, "I told you so." Instead, He repeatedly demonstrated four of the most powerful words to the human soul: "I love you, anyway." As a result, Peter went on to save thousands and thousands of people and to live a life glorifying Christ. And we can too.

It made me think of some great comebacks in sports, like the Buffalo Bills in a playoff game against Houston in 1999. They were down by 32 points at the half, and they came back to win the game, which I believe has to be the greatest comeback I ever saw in sports history. You can think about some great comebacks in your own life. How did any of these people get the opportunity to come back? They came back because the game, the task, or the job wasn't over.

Whether it's halftime in the stadium, the halfway flag on the racetrack, intermission at the school play, or your midlife moment, it's not over until the appointed end. The ending matters because the ending ties the story together; it's where we make sense of all that happened before. It's when the final score is reported.

The end is also the point at which there are no more comebacks. Here's what I mean. I don't want to be sitting at the end of my life, knowing the final chapter is here, and have regrets. I challenge each of you today to think that same thought. Is there any regret? Is there something we want to do or still have to do for the Lord? If the final chapter were written today, would you have regrets?

Author, marketing guru, and motivational speaker Tony Robbins has a theory, and he's built an incredibly successful business on it. His premise is that you need to go for the things you want to do in life. Take action; the sooner, the better. People from around the world travel for miles and pay thousands of dollars to attend his seminars to learn how to "go for it." How does he make them go for it? His message is something like this: Imagine the things you want and imagine if you try to get them and you fail. That would stink, right? And that's what's holding you back from going for them, you think you might fail. Could anything be worse? Well, imagine sitting there when you're 75 years old, rocking on your porch, and knowing you didn't go for those things, and it's too late. You can't go for those things anymore because your body won't let you. Your health won't let you. Think of the regret, guilt, and shame you will feel. Now, my friend, which is worse?

Obviously, Tony gets them focused on the end of their lives, the wasted opportunities, and how stupid they would feel then for not trying. Forget if they can get a hit; they are too scared to even *swing* the bat. Robbins leads them to turn their thinking around; so instead of thinking, "What if I fail?" they think, "What if I succeed? I'll be way ahead of the game." Exactly! And people get out of their chairs, motivated to go on to live these great lives, and so, they swing the bat and "go for it."

We don't have to pay thousands of dollars to travel to a seminar to hear that message. All we have to do is be in a saving relationship with God through Jesus Christ, and we'll hear that message right out of God's Word. Paul says, "I pray also that the eyes of your heart may be enlightened in order that you may know the hope to which He has called you, the riches of His glorious inheritance in the saints, and His incomparably great power for us who believe" (Ephesians 1:18–19).

Why should the eyes of my heart be opened? So that I will live a blessed, full life on this earth, so that I will experience the full measure of Jesus Christ in my life, so that I will know the rich reward of an inheritance in heaven, and so that I will experience His great power at work in my life.

Paul reminds us here, as believers, that we have access to God's great, incomparable power, and that if we aren't accessing it, we're really blowing it. Remember Jesus' words in John 15:5, "...apart from me you can do nothing"? Unless we stay connected to God, we act in our own strength, in our own confidence, and when we do that, we can be confident that we will fail ourselves, others, and God. Here's a simple illustration, but I think it works: We can say we will vacuum the rugs in our house, but if we don't plug our vacuum cleaner into the electrical outlet, we will not be very effective at vacuuming. We can focus on the right task; we can be observant of what we do; and we can put forth much time, energy, and commitment, but do we think it will be effective without the electrical power? We can finish the job, but it won't be very well done, will it?

Many of us go about our Christian lives the same way, focused on tasks and activities and expending time, energy, and commitment until we wear out and burn out. The tasks are done, but not done well; we might have been working at the wrong task altogether?

Why? Because we're not plugging in. We don't spend time with God, and that means we cannot access His power and strength to complete the job He wants us to do and do it well. Here's what Paul said in Acts 20:24, "...I consider my life worth nothing to me, if only I may finish the race and complete the task the Lord Jesus has given me—the task of testifying to the gospel of God's grace."

Paul knew his purpose in life. Because he loved God so much, the only thing he wanted to do was to finish the task God gave him, testifying to the Gospel of God's grace. What's your task?

I asked God that question, and His answer was John 15:16. The task of every believer is this: "You did not choose me, but I chose you and appointed you to go and bear fruit—fruit that will last. Then the Father will give you whatever you ask in my name." Your mission in life is to bear fruit that will last. How do you do that? Simple. Wherever God has put you in your life, glorify Him and give Him credit for everything. You live a life that reflects Jesus Christ. When people see you, they know you believe in Jesus Christ. You're available to witness, and your life is a witness. The way you live attracts people to Him.

That's how you go and bear fruit. Your career doesn't matter, whether you're a teacher, a rocket scientist, pastor, president of a big company, or a bus driver. It's irrelevant. That's just an occupation. What matters is what your heart reflects. God says we know a good tree by its good fruit and a bad tree by its bad fruit.

Healthy fruit trees don't quit producing halfway through the season, do they? They are in a continual cycle of production, which includes a time of rest, so to speak, but regardless, such a tree will produce until the end of its life. And likewise, we keep bearing fruit until the end, so we can finish strong and say the same thing as Paul, "I have fought the good fight, I have finished the race, I have kept the faith" (2 Timothy 4:7). Can you say the same thing today? Could you stand in front of Jesus and say that? If not, then you need to change some things right away.

You have to examine your life in the light of God's Word. If you're doing something wrong, if there's some sin separating you from living a godly life, deal with it today in repentance and confession. Change it now!

Don't wait. Life is fleeting. You never know if you'll be like my Dad, waking one day and having a heart attack. Psalms 39:4 says,

"Show me, O Lord, my life's end and the number of my days; let me know how fleeting is my life." We have 60, 70, maybe 80 years, maybe less on this earth, and then we're through with these bodies, which are like disposable diapers (use them once and throw them away). We get to use them for a very brief time, and then, they are thrown away. You could even think of the body as just a rental property, because the Christian's true home is heaven. We know that someday, our bodies will die, and this earthly life will be over.

My goal is to finish strong so that when my day comes, I'll hear that famous verse, "Well done, good and faithful servant! You have been faithful with a few things; I will put you in charge of many things. Come and share your Master's happiness!" (Matthew 25:23).

What about you? On Judgment Day, you will stand in front of God, and He will ask, "Were you faithful with what I gave you? Forget what I gave Jack or the guy down the street. Forget that. This is about what I gave you. Did you multiply what you were given?"

If you made God a priority in your life, then in all likelihood, you multiplied what God gave you. If that's the case, God will bless you. If you didn't make God a priority, you will still have your spot in heaven, but you will miss some rewards God had for you.

Do we really live out the priorities we claim? As a teenager, my son Ricky used to say that playing the saxophone was his top priority, but he didn't want to practice enough and rarely did. He didn't see the disconnect, but it was evident to the rest of the family. Ricky had a blind spot... and we all do. Sometimes, we need to stop listening to what we say is important and look at what we're doing to know for certain what's important in our lives. The bottom line is not what we say, but what we do. Do we live a life reflecting Jesus Christ? Yes, you can go to a comedy club. Yes, you can play baseball and do many things you enjoy... as long as God is truly your first priority. Does worshipping Him on Sunday have first priority over the NFL kick-off time, golf tee time, or fishing boat departure time? Does studying His Word come before studying the mall directory or the movie schedule? When you truly put God first, He will bless those things you do and enable you to enjoy them.

However, if God is not the first priority, you won't have peace in your life. You won't have the peace that transcends all understanding. You might call yourself a Christian. You might come to church, and you might even love God, but you'd be missing the blessings God wants you to have on earth and rewards in eternity.

In the book of Matthew, God tells us, "I have come that you may have life abundant and life eternal." God wants you to have an abundant life now, meaning a fulfilling, satisfying, joyful life now, and later, an eternal life in heaven. God has a purpose for every person's life. Psalms 138:8, "The Lord will fulfill His purpose for me; your love, O Lord, endures forever--do not abandon the work of your hands."

God has a perfect plan for your life, but you can interrupt that plan by saying no to God. How is that possible? Let's use an earthly example. Let's say you own a television production business, and you want your son to take it over.

"Son," you say, "I will groom you for the business. I want you to start in the mailroom. From there, I'll move you into a writing job. From there, I'll move you into a cameraman's job. After that you'll be an actor, a director, an editor, and then a management executive. You'll learn every part of this TV company, and then, you'll be president of it."

"Dad," your son says, "I don't want to do that. I want to be president today."

You know he's not equipped to be president today. You know that in order to be a good president and run the company well, he needs training in all these areas. And your intent is to train him in all these areas. Why? Because you're mad at him, and you don't like him? No. Because he's your son, and you want to bless him exceedingly and abundantly, more than he can ask or imagine.

But if that son says, "Dad, I'm not doing that. I want to be president right now. I won't start in the mailroom," then he can't be president. He's interrupted the blessing you had for him. Will you still love him? Yes, absolutely. If he goes and robs a bank, you'll still love him because he's your son and always will be. And when he gets out of prison, you'll try to help him live a good life. You'll try to bless him in some other way, but he missed the blessing you had for him. He missed it. He blew it.

I pray today that we do not miss the blessing God has for us because His blessing is the one we should desire the most. If you live for God, and you are obedient to Him, He can fulfill His perfect plan for your life. Simply be obedient to God wherever He puts you. And how long do you have to do that? Until the end.

"Well, Jack," you say, "that sounds good in theory, but how do I do it?"

There's only one way, and that's to stay close to God. He tells us so in John 15:5, "I am the vine; you are the branches. If a man remains in me and I in Him, he will bear much fruit; apart from me you can do nothing." Could God be any clearer? Do you want to finish strong and get His blessing? Stay close to God. Put your confidence in Him alone. God has harsh words for the person who puts his trust in anyone else. "This is what the Lord says: 'Cursed is the one who trusts in man, who depends on flesh for his strength and whose heart turns away from the Lord. He will be like a bush in the wastelands; he will not see prosperity when it comes. He will dwell in the parched places of the desert, in a salt land where no one lives" (Jeremiah 17:5–6).

I sure don't want to hang out in a spiritual wasteland like that. The verse continues with encouragement for those who place their trust in the Lord. "But blessed is the man who trusts in the Lord, whose confidence is in Him. He will be like a tree planted by the water that sends out its roots by the stream. It does not fear when heat comes; its leaves are always green. It has no worries in a year of drought and never fails to bear fruit."

When my dad clung to life, I did not worry. Instead, I had peace because my confidence is in Jesus Christ. And if you want God's full blessing, that's where your confidence needs to be. God goes on to say in Jeremiah 17:10, "I the Lord search the heart and examine the mind, to reward a man according to his conduct, according to what his deeds deserve."

We're not talking about salvation, a one-time action. We're talking about your reward as a Christian. God says, "I search the heart and I examine the mind to reward you." It's a test. Your faith is tested. Jeremiah 25:5 tells us what to do. "... Turn now, each of you, from your evil ways and your evil practices, and you can stay in the land the Lord gave to you and your fathers for ever and ever."

We turn from our evil ways by turning to the Lord for forgiveness: 1 John 1:9 says, "If we confess our sins, He is faithful and just and will forgive us our sins and purify us from all unrighteousness." What a great deal. If we turn from our evil ways and confess our sins, God will still use us, and He will still bless us.

These Scripture promises are for everyone who trusts in Jesus Christ as God's son and as their personal Savior. Does that include you?

Think about it. Jesus Christ said that He is Lord and Savior. He didn't say, "I'm a nice guy." He didn't say, "I'm a prophet," as other religions have described Him. Historians across the world and across the cultures acknowledge that Jesus Christ lived. That's not the question. The question each person has to answer in front of God on Judgment Day is what did we believe about Jesus Christ?

Do we believe what He said about himself? "I am the living Son of God" (John 9:37). Either He is the living Son of God... or He's the biggest liar that ever walked this earth. There is no in between.

In spite of His brutal death on the cross, Christ finished strong. He arose from the grave and now sits at the right hand of God our Father, interceding for us, interceding for you, because He wants us to finish strong too. Regardless of your starting point, Jesus wants you to make an amazing spiritual comeback. But remember, to do that, you've got to stay in the game and keep playing. That, my friend, is where the rubber meets the road with God.

3

Three Strikes, You're Out!

Three strikes and you're out! Does that sum up how you feel about your life sometimes? Things didn't turn out how you expected, even after you poured yourself into your job, your family, and your education. You keep swinging, but it's one, two, three strikes, and you're back to the dugout. You failed. How does that happen to a believer?

It's not too hard to figure out. I heard it said once that the problem is that we think we know God's plan, and when we don't accomplish it, we get down on ourselves. We measure what we think are our small results against our high expectations. If we don't like the results, we think we've failed, or sometimes, we think *God* failed because He didn't do what we expected, we hoped, or we thought was right.

Take Jonah, for example. The guy is famous for many reasons, but I've learned something very specific and important from him recently that I share later in the chapter—something I hope you'll have the wisdom to learn from me rather than having to experience for yourself. You see Jonah *knew* God's plan because God had spoken directly to him and told him what his task was, but Jonah *disagreed* with God's plan because his heart was not aligned with God's heart. His heart was set on seeing God destroy his enemies because he, Jonah, had already decided they didn't deserve saving. You (and I) would never have such a thought, would we? Or is there already someone in your life you think of that way? The way Jonah thought of the Ninevites? If so, strike one.

On the other hand, maybe you're one of those people who can let go of their expectations and their definition of successful results and keep on going no matter what others say are the results or "score" of their particular work. These people never strike out because of how they relate to God. I'll give you one example I love to share.

Billy Regan, a friend of my parents, died in 2005 at the age of 77. He was a Christian, and when he heard that I was one as well, he told my Jewish father that he wanted to meet me. Billy was a firefighter, and after he retired, he counseled other firefighters with addiction issues and other problems. After the 9/11 terror tragedy in New York City, he was down at the World Trade Center counseling firefighters and police officers, something he continued to do until he died.

When I finally met Billy, I could almost see God oozing out of this guy. He was just a wonderful, wonderful man of God. We talked; we exchanged letters, tapes, and inspirational stuff. I found out later that Billy had cancer and was dying, so I called him in the hospital in New Jersey.

I asked, "Billy, how are you doing, brother?"

He said, "Jake (a nickname my father has called me since I was a little kid because his father's name was Jacob), I'm doing great. I know where I'm going. I'm going to be with the Lord soon. I'm not worried at all. I'm not fearful. As a matter of fact, I feel really bad for everyone else around me because they're kind of taking this pretty hard." Then, he said something I'll never forget, "Do me a favor."

"What's that, Billy?" I asked.

"Tell your mom and dad that I wasn't scared; tell them that I knew where I was going; that I'm going to be with the Lord. So, Jake, if you can use this as a witnessing opportunity, please use my life, use my knowledge that I know I am going to heaven to be with God forever and ever. When you talk to your parents, use it as a testimony to them."

"I will. You can count on me, Billy. Thanks."

When Billy died, I got the opportunity to share that very testimony with Mom and Dad. And I thought how amazing it was that in life and in death, Billy Regan was a testimony for Jesus Christ. Billy's concern was not for himself; his concern was for lost souls. No doubt, when he got to heaven, he heard, "Well done, good and faithful servant."

Billy Regan (unlike Jonah) stayed focused on the work he felt God had given him to do, witnessing for Jesus Christ and counseling others in need without judging them. Billy Regan did not stay focused on his own expectations or definition of success. He did not keep score of how many conversions he'd made or how many counselees he'd healed. He knew those things were up to God, not him.

As adults, we understand that not every person who hears about Jesus will know Him as their personal Lord and savior. Does that mean the person giving the testimony failed? No. We also know that not every counseling session will be successful. Does that mean the counselor failed? No.

Hearing no to Jesus or seeing a counselee walk away didn't stop Billy. He didn't base his efforts on a *self-imposed scorecard* of how he thought God defines success or failure. He simply kept at the work he was given to do and left the results and evaluating up to God, an approach that carried him through a terminal illness and into the arms of his Lord. For Billy, that *was* success and that matches my definition of success also. What about yours?

Here's another story I want to share because this one hits so close to my situation. It's about my friend Zicky. Isn't Zicky a cool name? He's in his thirties, and married with three kids. Zicky has a bad case of Crohn's Disease, a digestive system disorder, and he will likely have surgery. We spoke not long after his diagnosis.

He said, "Jack, I'm an athletic guy. I have a family. I'm so scared about the future and what's going to be. I doubt I'm going to be able to play sports anymore. There was so much I wanted to accomplish for God. There was so much I wanted to do, and I feel like I failed."

All I could do was listen. Then, he said, "But you know what? I've been thinking and praying, and I've come to realize it's all in God's hands. That's my New Year's resolution. I'm giving it all to God."

All I could think was that, finally, God had Zicky exactly where He wanted him to be, and that was trusting in Him. And that's exactly where God wants you and me. He wants us to reach the point in our lives where we say, "God, I don't control it. I can't do it. It's all in your hands."

I think a lot about Zicky, about how he had felt like he was a failure, as if he hadn't accomplished what God wanted him to. I think about him because I've felt the same way, as if I'd struck out and failed God. In 2002, I sold my business to focus full time on a charity I started in 1993 and I must tell you it didn't go the way I expected it to.

One day, I got so frustrated that I actually said out loud to God, "You called me into this, remember? Then, I sarcastically added, "I sure hope it's going the way you want." Then, the Holy Spirit reminded me that it's not about what I want or expect; it's about God's plan. It's always about His plan, not mine; and when I finally yielded it all to Him and agreed with His plan, His timing, and His method, the frustration stopped. Why? Because I shifted my focus back to the God of the plan and away from what I thought God should do and what I thought God's plan should be.

Maybe you can relate to that feeling of failure and maybe you have even said to yourself, "I thought I would accomplish this for you, Lord, and I'm not accomplishing it. Why?" As I've grown in my faith, I've come to believe that the one bottom-line answer to that question is that our focus is on ourselves rather than God. It's a very subtle difference, but hang with me. Repeat the above quotation out loud: "I thought I would accomplish this for you, Lord, and I'm not accomplishing it." Now, circle every "I" in the sentence. Can you see the focus on self—my thought, my action, my accomplishment, my failure. If we back up to when our plans began, it was probably, "This is what I am thinking about, Lord, here's what I am going to do for you. Now, please bless my efforts. (And, by implication, don't bless others who might keep me from accomplishing it.)" We try to get God to line up with our judgment of things or people and what should or shouldn't happen, and then we wonder why we strike out and burn out.

My friends Billy and Zicky were great examples for me of how I needed to change my plans to agree with God's plans. Do you have a testimony in your life about how you did that?

What is a testimony? Legally, it's a declaration of fact. Spiritually, it's your story of how you came to believe in Christ or how God moved you, inspired you, and spoke to you (and you listened), causing you to take a new, closer, and better path in your walk with God. For me, combining the two reminds me that how I live my life should prove I have become a Christian. Here's what I mean. It would not be enough for me to love my wife just on my wedding day. No, the vows of love I made and the love I profess for her that day should be demonstrated throughout the life of our marriage. True love is living out the promise, not just declaring it. Do I live as if I've been changed by God, as if I believe there is hope for something beyond the here and now?

When people watch us at home, at work, and everywhere in between, and they see us holding on to our faith, going back up to bat, swinging again and again and again; not giving up or quitting.

When they see us behave like that, they see *hope*. They can look at us in our hour of crisis, watch our response of faith, and believe that there is hope because they see someone still standing and persevering, who hasn't lost faith in God—someone still fighting the good fight, like my friends Zicky, Billy Regan, and I hope, you and me.

I can't say the same about Jonah, who had his own plans and his own life, until God spoke directly to him about what He wanted Jonah to do. Notice that God didn't tap Jonah on the shoulder and ask him what he'd like to do for God's sake. Nowhere in the Bible will you find God asking a person for his or her plans. God's plan always prevails. That is evident throughout the entire Bible.

Jonah made some truly boneheaded moves. After spending so much time with him in this chapter, I think of him as "Jonah the Boner". Let's learn from his mistakes, so we don't act like boneheads in our walk with God.

In chapter 1 of Jonah, the NIV subtitle reads, "Jonah Flees from the Lord." Strike one Jonah. Running away from the Lord is always a strike against you. It's amazing how stupid Jonah was. What about you and me?Now, let's start reading the verses. "The word of the Lord came to Jonah, son of Ammitai, go to the great city of Nineveh and preach against it because its wickedness has come up before me" (Jonah 1:1–2).

Did you catch that? *"The word of the Lord came to Jonah."*

Has God's Word reached you? Or do you wonder why you haven't heard from the Lord? Do you think that maybe the Word of the Lord came to Jonah and told him to go to Nineveh, but the Word of the Lord hasn't reached you yet?

Really? Do you have a Bible? Then, you have God's Word. And if you look for a clear instruction, here are a few that should keep us all busy for a little while, a lifetime even: "Go and bear fruit that will last." "Go and make disciples." "Be a light in a world of darkness." "Love your neighbor as yourself." You don't have to go to Nineveh to do that, but you might have to go across the hall or the street.

What did Jonah do with the clear instructions God gave him? Verse 3 says, "But Jonah ran away from the Lord and headed for Tarshish. He went down to Joppa, where he found a ship bound for port. After paying the fare, he went aboard and sailed for Tarshish to flee from the Lord."

Of course it's strike one, Jonah. God speaks to you and you run away? What were you thinking Jonah? But you know what? I'll bet God asks you and I today, "What are you thinking? My Word has reached you. Why do you run away from me?" Is there really any acceptable answer for that?

Jonah paid a price to get on a ship, thinking it would save him from having to do what God wanted him to do. When instead, it cost him. And trust me, there is always a price to pay when you try to flee from the Lord. I say, "try to flee," because we can't run away from God. If you want proof, spend some time reading Psalm 139, verses 7 and 8: "Where can I go from your Spirit? Where can I flee from your presence? If I go up to the heavens, you are there; if I make my bed in the depths, you are there."

Jonah ran away, so what did the Lord, our loving God, do? The same thing He does with you and me. He comes after his wayward son. And since He is God, He is not chasing him down on foot like a scene from a movie. No, God does it his way. Verse 4 says, "...the Lord sent a great wind on the sea, and such a violent storm arose that the ship threatened to break up." Never forget that God controls everything, the wind included. He can do anything He wants. God can put any obstacle, place, person, group, circumstance, or thing into your life or remove them, anytime He wants.

The violent storm threatened to break up the ship. "All the sailors were afraid and each cried out to his own god, and they threw the cargo into the sea to lighten the ship." That makes sense; this is a big storm, we might drown, let's lighten the load, get rid of the cargo. Seems like a reasonable idea. And what was Jonah doing? Sleeping soundly below deck. Verse 5 of Chapter 1 goes on to say, "...The captain went to him and said, 'How can you sleep? Get up and call on your god. Maybe He will take notice of us and we will not perish.'" The captain tried anything and everything to save his skin. He cried out to his gods, but that didn't seem to work, so he thought maybe they should try Jonah's God. What did they have to lose?

Don't people do that a lot when they're desperate and threatened, facing fear, anxiety, or the end of their life? Don't they then take a shot at Jonah's God, which is our God, Jesus Christ? And, of course, our God responds even at that late stage of the game, but oh, what they have missed!

Next, the sailors cast lots to find out who was responsible for all this trouble, and of course, the lot fell on Jonah. Can you picture the sailors glaring at him? They peppered him with questions, "'What do you do? Where do you come from? What is your country? From what people are you?' He answered, 'I am Hebrew and I worship the Lord, the God of heaven, who made the sea and the land.' This terrified them, and they asked, 'What have you done?'" They knew he was running away from the Lord, because he had already told them so (Jonah 1:8–10).

At that point, the sea became violent, and the men panicked. They asked Jonah for advice on what they could do to make the waves settle down, so they wouldn't die. So, Jonah told them, in verse 12, "'Pick me up and throw me into the sea,' he replied, 'and it will become calm. I know that it is my fault that this great storm has come upon you.'"

I give Jonah some credit here. At least he acknowledged that it was his fault. At least he was smart enough to connect the dots: I (Jonah) ran away from God; I ignored the Word of God; now, He's coming after me. And he stepped up to the plate with the only possible solution to how these men could save their lives, lives he had put at risk. He admitted it was his fault and asked them to throw him out of what he originally thought of as his lifeboat. Well, that apparently didn't seem right to the sailors. So instead, they tried hard to row the boat back to land but couldn't because the waves had become worse. These guys had the right heart; they didn't want to see Jonah drown, but it didn't matter. They had to throw Jonah over, or they would all die, so they begged God for mercy in advance. "They cried to the Lord, 'O Lord, please do not let us die for taking this man's life. Do not hold us accountable for killing an innocent man, for you, O Lord, have done as you pleased.' Then they took Jonah and they threw him overboard, and the raging sea grew calm" (Jonah 1:15).

Instantly, the sea grew calm. God doesn't always work that fast, but in my life, I've found that when I finally stop fighting his plan, even if it means I think I will sink, the turmoil in or around me seems to subside very quickly.

And the men who survived? Scripture says they "greatly feared the Lord, and they offered a sacrifice to the Lord and made vows to Him." These guys responded properly. They saw what Jonah's God was capable of; their lives were spared; and they immediately believed in God's power and miracles. What about you? Do you believe in God's power and miracles? Do you offer your life as a sacrifice to Him?

You probably think, "That's just great, Jack. That worked out swell for the sailors, but Jonah drops to the bottom of the ocean." Well, not exactly. "...the Lord provided a great fish to swallow Jonah, and Jonah was inside the fish three days and three nights" (Jonah 1:17). Jonah was drowning; he was doomed; and you and I we're no different. We were drowning; we were going down; we would spend all eternity in hell, and yet, the Lord saved us.

Let's think about what our response would be, and let's see what Jonah's was. Remember, at that point, Jonah was a dead man. He was stuck inside a large fish's belly with no exit signs, no scuba gear, nothing. Without God's intervention and grace, he was a dead man. You and I were dead men walking until the Lord provided us with a way out of that death.

Jonah's first reaction was to pray. Is that your reaction in a crisis? "From inside the fish, Jonah prayed to the Lord his God. He said, 'In my distress I called to the Lord, and He answered me. From the depths of the grave I called for help, and you listened to my cry" (Jonah 2:1–2).

I want you to listen carefully. No matter how bad things are, no matter how deep your despair, God hears his children's cries and prayers. He hears your prayers and your cries today, just as He heard Jonah's prayers and cries. So, I ask you, are you in a fish's belly today? Is there a financial storm, a spiritual battle, a health battle? Is it a relationship, a family member, business partner, a spouse? Is it forgiveness, anger, sin, addiction, malice, rage, envy? Is it pornography? Is it any other sin separating you from God? Is that thing swallowing you alive? God hears your voice and your prayers.

God heard Jonah's prayers... what happened next? Jonah continued praying. "You hurled me into the deep, into the very heart of the seas, and the currents swirled about me; all your waves and breakers swept over me. I said, "'I have been banished from your sight; yet I will look again toward your holy temple." Jonah turned back to God, sought God, trusted God, and searched for God, even while he was in the pit. Having faith in God is always the answer to any circumstance, any situation, and any trouble you'll ever have.

Jonah's prayer continued, "The engulfing waters threatened me, the deep surrounded me; seaweed was wrapped around my head." It's not fun when God has to do things to get our attention, is it? We keep trying to fix the circumstances of our lives instead of getting closer to God and listening to Him; or we go to Him with all our problems and say "fix this, fix that," instead of seeing if He wants to replace our problems and our brokenness with something better.

We need to pause here and appreciate what Jonah did with his prayer. He saw things getting worse and acknowledged his responsibility. Because of his disobedience, because he fled from what

God wanted him to do, he brought major trouble into his life. This trouble also put others at risk, and it meant that he, Jonah, could not receive any blessings from God. The point? God has something for us to do; He has something He wants to tell each of us, something He wants to accomplish with each believer's life. He has all these blessings He wants to give because He loves us so much; but how do we react? If we turn and run away from the Lord there is always a price to pay. Did Jonah pay the price? He was banished from God's sight; the waters engulfed him; and then he was stuck inside a fish with seaweed wrapped around his head. Nice day at the beach, huh?

Did he realize how bad things were? Yes. In Jonah 2:6, he said, "To the roots of the mountain I sank down." In our day, we call that hitting bottom. "The earth beneath barred me in forever." There was no way out for Jonah, and he knew it; and yet, he could still muster enough faith to cry out to God, "But you brought my life up from the pit, O Lord my God." Tell me, who else can bring your life up from the pit of death? Show me. Show me another god. Show me your money, your looks, your house, your job. Show me who can bring you up from the pit when your circumstances bury you. Jonah reminds us today, and I pray that God reminds you today that God alone can do that.

I just want to tell you that I know how Jonah feels here. I know God pulled me from the pit of drug addiction many years ago when I first got saved, and I know I need to make the most of the time I have left in my life by obeying God. Here's what Jonah says in Chapter 2 verses 7 and 8, "'When my life was ebbing away, I remembered you, Lord, and my prayer rose to you, to your holy temple. Those who cling to worthless idols forfeit the grace that could be theirs.'" Forfeit God's grace? How scary is that? And what's a worthless idol? It's anything in your life that you put before Jesus Christ, whether it's a job, a relationship, a possession, or money. It's worthless compared to God's grace. Scripture says, "What does it profit a man to gain the whole world if he forfeits his soul?" (Matthew 16:26). God spoke to my heart recently and said, "Jack, if you're not satisfied with what you have now, you wouldn't be satisfied if you had two hundred times more, or two thousand times more or two million times more." We each need to be satisfied with the gift of life God has given us.

Jonah continued praying, his attitude corrected, "'But I, with a song of thanksgiving, will sacrifice to you. What I have vowed I will make good. Salvation comes from the Lord.'" Jonah was as good as dead, and he knew it. He finally said, "I surrender Lord. I'm yours. I'm praying to you. I get it now. Salvation comes from you and I'm making this promise, Lord. I'm singing your praises, I'm sacrificing to you, thanking you and I've made a vow and I'll make it good."

God must have shaken his head the way parents do when their kids finally yield to their authority after having suffered for their stubbornness. Jonah was finally a life sold out to God, at least in theory.

What does a sold-out life look like? Paul said, "It's not I who live but Christ who lives in me" (Galatians 2:20) The Bible says, "He must increase," meaning Christ, "and I must decrease." So, what happens in a sold-out life? You forget your wants and preferences and do what God has revealed for you to do. Jonah said all the right things, "Oh, God, save me. I promise I'll be good. I'll be your boy from now on, Lord."

And what did God do? In His wonderful mercy, He rescued Jonah again. What does God do for you and me? In his wonderful mercy, He reaches out and rescues us again. "And the Lord commanded the fish, and it vomited Jonah onto dry land" (Jonah 2:10). God commanded the fish. God still controlled the situation, despite how hopeless it looked from Jonah's viewpoint. God, who is, was, and always will be in control of every situation in our lives, rescued Jonah again. And He does the same for us today.

Think you don't need rescuing? Think you don't need "saving"? Think again. There is "salvation," the one-time transaction that guarantees your place in heaven, but there is also "sanctification," the lifelong process of becoming more and more like Christ. When we run away from God and his Word, as Jonah did, we interrupt that sanctification, and God says there will be a price to pay for that. The longer and harder we resist, the higher the price, until in Jonah's case, it was literally a life-and-death issue. Death to you, Jonah. Your going over the boat, your going to drown. Jonah finally cried out, "No, no, no, Lord. I'm sorry. I'm sorry." And God said, "Okay, Jonah, I think you get it now. Come on out. I'll give you another chance."

How many times has God said that to you in your life? "Okay, buddy, I'll give you another chance." You know what? There comes a time we run out of chances. We have to pay attention, and we have to make the most of this time we have.

Here's what happens in chapter 3. God still wanted to use Jonah. After all, He didn't just rescue Jonah to let him sit there. The original assignment still waited to be done. Here's what God said in Jonah 3:1: "Then the word of the Lord came to Jonah a second time." A second time—if he'd listened the first time, think of all the misery he could have avoided for himself and all the stress, trouble, and disruption he would have saved the captain and his crew. God's Word to Jonah is still the same: "Go to the great city of Nineveh and proclaim to it the message I give you."

This time Jonah was a little wiser for his experience, as most of us are right when we hit bottom. We're humble at that point, but you know what? It's not enough to hit bottom. You must stay there, and by that I mean that you must stay humble. The Bible says that Jonah obeyed the Word of the Lord and went to Nineveh. Well, great. Jonah got it right this time. He obeyed the Lord. Do you obey the Word of the Lord? Are you obeying the Word of the Lord at this time in your life when God is speaking to you? What Is God talking to you about today? What has God spoken to your heart that He wants you to do? What is it that He wants you to give up? What is it that He wants you to change? What is it that He wants you to embrace?

Let's look at what happened and see how it applies to us, starting with Jonah 3:3. "Now Nineveh was a very important city—a visit required three days. On the first day, Jonah started into the city. He proclaimed, 'Forty more days and Nineveh will be overturned.' The Ninevites believed God. They declared a fast, and all of them, from the greatest to the least, put on sackcloth." The Ninevites believed God. They responded. They did the right thing when convicted by the Word of God. Amazing! Israel's greatest enemy acknowledged and responded to her God! Isn't that what God had in mind all along? What a blessing for Jonah to be the messenger who saved an entire city of people!

What about you? Have you been convicted of your sins? Do you do the right thing when God speaks to you and tells you to repent and turn from your sin? All Nineveh, her leaders included, responded. Jonah 3:6–9 says, "When the news reached the king of Nineveh, he rose from his throne, took off his royal robes, covered himself with sackcloth and sat down in the dust. Then he issued a proclamation to Nineveh: 'By the decree of the king and his nobles: Do not let any man or beast, herd or flock, taste anything; do not let them eat or drink. But let man and beast be covered with sackcloth. Let everyone call urgently on God. Let them give up their evil ways and their violence. Who knows? God may yet relent, and with compassion turn from his fierce anger so that we will not perish.'"

Unbelievable! The king of Nineveh was actually betting-- on God's mercy-- and he got it right the first time. Verse 10 concludes Chapter 3 on an encouraging note: "When God saw what they did and how they turned from their evil ways, He had compassion and did not bring upon them the destruction He had threatened." God was merciful, which all along was his plan.

God is always merciful when we show true repentance. When you and I act like Jonah and become wayward sons or daughters, God in his mercy warns us that our destruction will come. If we continue to disobey, He will throw us out of whatever lifeboat we think will save us, and He will let us sink if we don't turn back. Why? Because God loves us that much. For Him to accomplish the perfect plan He has in mind for each of us, our lives must be fully surrendered to Him. So, why do we keep fighting God's plan? It's our sinful nature of course! God's Word says that He is able to bless us abundantly and exceedingly more than we can ask or imagine. God wants to say, "Well done, good and faithful servant" when we show up in heaven. He is pleased to share his happiness with us now so we will know the peace that transcends all understanding. But to have those blessings, we need to surrender to Him.

God's plan is fulfilled. Nineveh is saved. Is Jonah now a hero? Or is he still a bonehead?

Let's look at how he responds to saving Nineveh in chapter 4. "But Jonah was greatly displeased and became angry." Strike two Jonah!

Displeased and angry? Why Jonah? God was probably thinking, "I just saved you from the whale's belly. I just turned your life around. You promised you'd serve me and love me. You understood salvation came from me, and now, I've forgiven the Ninevites because they prayed too, because they repented too, and Jonah, you're all upset and pouting?" Is that how you react when God doesn't come through the way you wanted Him to when you obeyed Him? Maybe you, like Jonah, are obeying, but you are disagreeing with God's plan, and thus have a serious grudge against God.

Jonah was upset because God showed mercy to the Ninevites. Jonah didn't think they deserved to be forgiven. Jonah didn't think they deserved to be spared. Jonah didn't think they deserved God's love. Do you ever look at someone that way? "That person doesn't deserve forgiveness. That person doesn't deserve heaven." You say that person is a murderer, a rapist, a robber, a thief, a two-timer, an adulterer, a homosexual, a whore, a drug addict, alcoholic or a what? *He's just like you and me.* He's a sinner. We all are sinners, and none of us deserves God's forgiveness. Jonah's foolishness had followed him out of the fish and onto dry land. He had the nerve to question God's love, forgiveness, and compassion for others. Jonah was upset that the Ninevites got off scot-free and didn't pay the penalty for their sins.

Many Christians have that same hardness of heart like the prodigal son's brother. Do you remember the story about the prodigal son coming home? (Luke 15:11–32). The father killed the fattened calf, put the robe and the ring on the son, and said, "My son was dead, and now, he's alive, let's party!" And all the while, the brother complained. "This isn't fair. My brother squandered all my father gave him. I've worked here and busted my butt for my father. I never get any parties. How come he gets a party?" The father said to him, "You've been with me always. Everything I have is yours. But your brother, who was lost, is now found. Your brother who was dead is now alive. Come, let's rejoice." The older brother was too selfish to celebrate. He already had access to everything of the father, and so do you. If you do not receive it and enjoy it, then it's your fault, just like that brother. Then, you're the idiot, because God has it, and it's available for every child, believer, son and daughter of God today, from the beginning of the world and until the end of time. It's there. God offers it to all, and for Jonah, that was the problem.

Jonah was "greatly displeased and became angry" and in Chapter 4 verses 2 and 3, he vented at God: "He prayed to the Lord, 'O Lord, is this not what I said when I was still at home? That is why I was so quick to flee Tarshish. I knew that you are a gracious and compassionate God, slow to anger and abounding in love, a God who relents from sending calamity. Now, O Lord, take away my life, for it is better for me to die than to live." Talk about a whiner. Jonah ran because he didn't like God's plan; yet God tried to bless despite his behaving like a rebellious brat. He finally did what God told him to do, and he still struck out because he resented God's plan. Jonah tried to justify his own sin and in so doing, looked even more foolish by saying he'd rather die than see God's mercy given to others.

Hmm, this sounds familiar to me, and it probably does to you, too, if you've ever spent any time around people. In the office, in the sales world, on the sports field, even at the family dinner table, in whatever arena you pick, you can hear this same complaint: it's not fair, they got the good stuff, and they didn't deserve it. If you're up to bat in the game of life and that kind of thought is being lobbed around in your head, get over it, because if you don't, you will indeed strike out.

God replies with a simple question to Jonah, in what I always assume is a rather strained tone at this point: "Have you any right to be angry?" It's not hard to read into the message, did you create the world? Did you create the mountains, the trees, the clouds or the rivers? None of us did those things; only God because only God could! Have you any right to question my actions or any right to be angry? Scripture reminds us that God's ways are higher than ours.

Are you angry with God right now? Read on, because Jonah was, and it cost him.

Jonah didn't answer; he just pouted and sat down at a place east of the city, made himself a shelter, and sat in the shade, waiting to see what would happen to Nineveh. "Then the Lord God provided a vine and made it grow up over Jonah to give shade for his head to ease his discomfort, and Jonah was very happy about the vine." Even in the midst of Jonah's temper tantrum, God, still loving his disobedient son, provided a vine to ease his discomfort. And even in your rebellion, God loves you so much, He will provide something to ease your discomfort, but don't miss this next point. "Jonah was very happy about the vine." The point: All the blessings God wanted to give Jonah were now reduced to a little vine for shade. How sad is that? God had all these great plans for Jonah.

"Jonah, I will use you. I called you, go speak to Nineveh."

"No, Lord, I'm running away." (Strike one.)

"Jonah, come back. I'll save you."

"Okay." Jonah came back onto dry land.

"Jonah, I will use you again. Go speak to the people of Nineveh."

Jonah spoke. They respond and they are blessed. So now, he was ticked off, and he didn't trust God's judgment. He was bummed out, and he pouted. (Strike two.)

Jonah kept whittling away at the blessings God wanted to give him until all that was left for God to bless him with was a little vine to give him a little shade. How pathetic.

Are you willing to settle for a small shady spot rather than the abundant blessings God wants to pour out on you? Have you run away like Jonah? Are you mad about something you think is unfair? Are you upset at God's timing? God says, "Look, I still love you, Jonah (or fill in your own name), but now, all I can do to bless you is give you this little piece of shade. So, I'll do that for you because I love you, son. But I had these great big plans to bless you, and I can't do that now."

Maybe it's like that in your life today, but God wants to change it. God doesn't want you to settle for that little vine and a crappy spot of shade. God doesn't want to see you in circumstances of despair and defeat. God wants to see you standing in victory, in the victory of Jesus Christ. There is victory for every child of Jesus, and that victory, joy, and trust in God should be evident by the joy and peace in every believer's life regardless of the circumstances and trials going on in his life. The Lord always loves us no matter how disobedient we are, but we miss the blessings of God when we are disobedient.

I know a little bit about this thing with Jonah, this wayward son trading great blessings for a small slice of shade in a desert. My son Ricky, whom I love so much, was 21 at the time, and I had many blessings I wanted to give him. But guess what? He wound up in jail for a couple of days from drugs and alcohol. He did something stupid. We had to bail him out of jail, and we had to bring him to a halfway house for the second time. Sounds a little like Jonah, doesn't it? My son didn't listen the first time; oh, he heard. He went through rehab, and he went through the halfway house. Then he came out and chose to do the wrong thing again. Now, he pays the price. Do you know what blessing he asks me to give him now? In the halfway house this time, he needs a bicycle because the police have impounded the brand new car we bought him two months ago for his 21st birthday. It's gone, forfeited. They're not giving it back. My son wants a bicycle, a used one, so he can get to a job interview—and he needs the job because he lost the last one—a tremendous management position and opportunity that my friend offered him, a job he worked at for a year and blew because he fell back into drugs and alcohol.

Now, to be clear, I, too, have a problem with drugs, so I understand addiction. The point I make is that the only thing I can bless him with now is some food and maybe a used bicycle, rather than all the great blessings his mother and I had in store for him, *and I can't give him those things because of his disobedience.* He suffers the consequence of that disobedience. I pray, and ask you to join me praying that would not be my son's lifelong circumstance, that instead he would learn from it and turn to God, as Jonah did.

So, back to Jonah—he was happy about the vine, but verse 7 says, "But at dawn the next day God provided a worm, which chewed the vine so that it withered." The Lord gives, and the Lord takes away. God still controlled every circumstance, every second of Jonah's life. Verse 8 continues, "When the sun rose, God provided a scorching east wind, and the sun blazed on Jonah's head so that he grew faint. He wanted to die, and said, 'It would be better for me to die than to live.'"

Jonah whined a lot, didn't he? His shade was gone, and his first reaction was melodrama: I have nothing, so I want to die. Do you ever do that? "My money is gone; I have nothing, so I want to die... my wife is gone; my husband is gone; I have nothing, so I want to die... my child is gone; I have nothing, so I want to die." You can say that about your job, car, health, home, looks, prized collections, whatever, but is that what it's about? Is your life about possessions and people? God says if that's it, you don't get it. God says I'll just take it all away until you realize that the only thing you have, the thing that makes you wealthy and rich, is your relationship with me.

Once again, God answers Jonah with a question. "'...Do you have a right to be angry about the vine?' 'I do,' Jonah said. 'I am angry enough to die.'"

The guy is willing to cut off his nose to spite his face, so to speak. Strike three, Jonah!

Jonah wasn't so angry about the vine. He was angry that the Ninevites received free repentance he didn't think they deserved. Jonah's heart didn't align with God. Jonah looked at the Ninevites as needing to be judged for what they'd done, but God looked at them as children whom He loved and wanted to save. Personally, I am truly thankful that God looks at us as children He loves and wants to save and forgive.

Here is the great news. God wouldn't let Jonah waste his life, and He won't let you and I do that, either. Jonah was mad at the things of the world he couldn't control, blessings God bestowed on others and things of the world he deemed necessary, coveted, or thought he was entitled to. So that, when they were taken away or lost, he vented his anger at God, claiming he'd rather die than not have those things. We're sad at the loss of money, a loved one, health, relationship, or a job. Suddenly, people are depressed; they want to die, as if that possession or thing was what their worth as an individual was based on. Only in the world's eyes. Never in God's eyes are we judged by the things of the world or the things we possess, for God's reward to us is based on our faith. God has already passed judgment on every person, and the verdict—guilty of sin. The penalty for sin is death. But the good news of the Gospel and the great news of Jesus Christ is that Jesus Christ has paid our penalty for us so that we would live. We will live forever with Jesus and God in heaven, and right now, we have God's Holy Spirit living in us as a deposit of our guaranteed place in heaven. Our sin debt is paid. We are free in Christ. Hallelujah! We are free in Christ.

As for Jonah, admit it. If you were God right then, wouldn't you just want to smack Jonah in the head? I definitely would've screamed "Strike three Jonah, you're out!"

Thankfully, God doesn't do that to us (not very often, anyway), or else I wouldn't be here today with all my life's strikeouts. Listen to what God says to Jonah (and to you and me) in verse 10, "But the Lord said, 'You have been concerned about this vine, though you did not tend it or make it grow. It sprang up overnight and died overnight. But Nineveh has more than a hundred twenty thousand people who cannot tell their right hand from their left, and many cattle as well. Should I not be concerned about that great city?'"

God doesn't want Jonah concerned about temporary things such as a vine for shade. He wants Jonah to be concerned about other people's eternal fate, regardless of how badly they've behaved, in the same way that God is concerned about our eternal fate. Can you hear God's point of view: "Wasn't I concerned about you, Jonah? Wasn't I concerned about you, Jack? Wasn't I concerned about you, reader? Wasn't I concerned about you, church? Wasn't I concerned about every single person when I sacrificed my son, the thing that I love the most? Jack, you say how much you love your little daughter and your two sons. I took my son, the thing that I love the most; I put Him on the cross; and I let Him be killed. I ordained that He pay the price for your penalty, for your sin. I ordained that He be sacrificed for you because I love you so much. You're not in charge, Jonah, Jack, reader. You didn't create things—vines, cars, jobs, or anything else."

I find it interesting that the book of Jonah ends with this remark from God ("should I not pity Nineveh"), no summary about Jonah getting his act together or asking for forgiveness. So, I do think it was "Strike three, you're out" for Jonah. He was not dead, but just out of the place where God could bless him.

I don't ever want to get to strike three with God, and I hope you don't, either. So, here's one of the most important things I've learned from Jonah's story—I don't want to limit God's ability to bless me by choosing to be disobedient. And as God works in my heart, and I grow closer to Him, I'm constantly reminded of who I am, much like Jonah , and who I am not—namely, God. Now I focus on spending my life trying to be more like God and growing closer to Him, which, amazingly, brings me so much joy, peace, love, and happiness.

So, when those "strike one" times inevitably come into my day, and they will because I am still a sinner, I know that I don't have to strike out. What I have to do is check my focus. Is it on me or on God? I have two great examples, Billy and Zicky, as well, to remind me of that lesson.

While I'm alive down here on earth, I know that I can still end up out of the game, riding the bench back in the dugout, deep in the stormy sea, or even sinking into it, but I also know that I don't have to stay there. And neither do you.

If you're stuck in the dugout, if a circumstance in your life is swallowing you alive, cry out to God. He can deliver anyone from anything at anytime in any way He chooses. Just ask Jonah; but my prayer is that you (and I) wouldn't be such boneheads in the first place.

4

Pass the Salt

Sometimes, you just have to add salt. You taste something, and it's just a little off, it misses the mark, but you shake a bit of seasoning over it and boom! The flavor pops out.

I enjoy cooking, especially the barbeque and grilling out and, over the course of several years, I've created my own secret recipe for steak seasoning, which I package and market as "Jake's." (Jake is my old nickname from my New York childhood.) Even though the recipe is a secret, if you read the ingredient label, you'll see that the first one is salt. Why? Because salt really does draw out the best flavors. (You can order some for yourself at www. jakessteakseasoning.com and let me know what you think.)

Adding salt is especially important for a Christian because a low-salt diet has no place in the Christian's life—the spiritual life, that is. I learned that the hard way a few years ago when I started to lose my spiritual direction because I mixed up my priorities. I'll tell you more about that in a minute, not because I want to, but because God prompts me to share it in case you face something similar. You can think of this chapter as a taste test for why you shouldn't give up the spiritual salt in your life and, if you do, how to get it back.

Hindsight can be a helpful thing. As I look back at what happened to me in 2006, one thing I realize is that my steadfastness failed or, at the very least, it was diverted to other pursuits. I could only see that for myself after I read a *Guidepost Magazine* article about a gospel singing group called The Blind Boys of Alabama. They are a great singing group, *and* they really are blind.

The article said they met in 1939 in an Alabama boarding school for the blind. They shared a love for the Lord and a love for singing, and about five years after they began meeting, they decided they were good enough to go out and sing gospel songs for the Lord, good enough that maybe they could make enough money to get out of what they called "this treacherous place." They said the boarding school was horrendous; it was like a jail. They called themselves The Blind Boys of Alabama and promised the Lord, "If you will stay with us and stick by us and sustain us, we will serve you faithfully until the end."

Another gospel singer's star was rising at the same time. You might have heard of Sam Cooke, but not for gospel; he wrote several popular songs, including "You Send Me" and "Oh, What a Wonderful World." A record company discovered Sam Cooke and encouraged him to go into rock-and-roll music because, as they put it, "The world is changing." Of course, they saw profit potential in his talent, so they offered him a huge record contract, and he took it.

The record company offered the same contract to The Blind Boys of Alabama. "There's money," the record company said. "There's fame and fortune. Look at Little Richard. Look at Elvis. This is the way to go. You guys have to make the plunge."

As the story goes, The Blind Boys said, "No thanks. We promised the Lord that we would serve Him faithfully until the end." They turned down the offer for fame and fortune in the world because, as they put it in the article, "We had to be steadfast, and we were, all of us."

When I read that, I thought, wow, what great faith. I want that kind of faith in my life. I want to have that kind of response in my life in every situation. I want to stand on God's promises, and I want to keep the promises I've made to God and not be lured off the path God has set before me by the offer of worldly pursuits.

As God would have it, The Blind Boys of Alabama went on to fame in gospel. They never went to rock and roll, and today, they are very grateful for deciding to be steadfast for the Lord. Today, they know millions of people have been influenced over the years for the glory of God through their gospel music.

As God would have it, Jack went on to falter in his steadfastness, to lose his saltiness, not to imitate The Blind Boys, and to lose some influence he could have had for the Lord in others' lives. Yet today, I am very grateful for that valley in my Christian life because of how it has shaped me. If you are going through something similar, my hope is that God will inspire you to turn back to Him. Turning back is important because otherwise, we are like salt that has lost its flavor.

Jesus warns us specifically about this in Matthew 5:13: "You are the salt of the earth. But if the salt loses its saltiness, how can it be made salty again? It is no longer good for anything, except to be thrown out and trampled by men."

How scary is that? We know we're the salt of the earth. God tells us we're to be salt; we're to live out the Word of God; and we're to have God living through us so that others will thirst for what we have. But if we lose our godly flavor, then we're worthless to God because others cannot "taste" Him. God says that unsalty salt isn't good for anything; it's ineffective, and it has lost its purpose. So, what do we do with something like that? We throw it out, the same way we would with one of those plug-in air fresheners when it stops smelling good. It goes into the trash.

So, here's where it gets personal. I lost my flavor. I blew it. My peace disappeared. I was aggravated, angry, and antsy about life, and I had an attitude. Do you see all that bad stuff building up, and I'm still in the first letter of the alphabet? I had to apologize to my wonderful wife because for those couple of months I'd been a bit of a bear and rather belligerent (not doing any better with the letter B, am I?). Proverbs 31:10 says, "A wife of noble character who can find? She is worth far more than rubies." I found a brilliant, valuable one, and I forgot to polish my treasure, my gift from God. Sorry, honey.

Looking back, I can see that I focused on the world, on ministry, business, commitments, obligations, all things that seemed justifiable. In my mind, it was all very necessary, but Proverbs 14:12 warns, "There is a way that seems right to a man, but in the end it leads to death." The way I was going seemed right and justifiable because I worked on ministry stuff (well, some ministry stuff, but not all ministry stuff), but I was also very busy, maybe too busy, with charities and some business deals and real estate. I rationalized it by telling myself that most of my efforts were given to ministry but, in all honesty, I wasn't winning souls.

In one case, a friend of my wife Beth specifically said she was searching for answers to God. That's normally a big clue that I (and you) should talk to somebody about Jesus. I told Beth to set up a meeting, but I didn't pursue it, didn't follow up, didn't make it my heart's passion, and guess what? The friend moved several states away. We never met, and I lost the chance to influence her for Jesus.

Then, I met two guys through some real estate investing I had done. I knew they weren't believers, so I did what many of us do in the name of sharing our faith. I dropped a few hints about church and Jesus, but that's it... after all, we were in the midst of negotiating another real estate deal. Then, one day, I woke up and realized I was truly more interested in their wallets than their souls. I was disgusted with myself and even said out loud, "I am off the path." But even though I said that, even though I sensed it, I also said, "Well, we've still got to do this deal, so when I finish that task and cross a few others off the list, I'll focus on Jesus because then I won't be so distracted."

I had a to do list and a deal to close. I didn't know if it would take me another week or another month, but when I got there, I figured, "then I'll focus on Jesus." What a huge mistake. Where was my faith? My faithfulness had faltered; my priorities were shuffled. What I claimed was most important and what I knew was most important did not line up with how I spent my time. I was lost in the world. Oh, you could see me. You could track me with a GPS. You could take a picture of me with a camera phone, but I was spiritually missing in action.

On top of that, my marriage had a few tense spots, and it was my fault. I was losing money and feeling the financial strain, and I continually worried about the future. I ignored Luke 12:22–30 where God says not to worry. The Holy Spirit brought those verses to mind, and I told him to be quiet because I was too busy worrying. I did not trust God; I could tell (in hindsight) because I tried to carve out and secure my own future.

I couldn't see my hypocrisy at the time. In the midst of all this hand wringing, growling, and complaining, I asked the Lord, "Where do you want me? What do you want me to do in ministry?" but I didn't stay still long enough to hear Him answer. As only God can do, this little valley in my life was actually a blessing. It made me realize how close I came to drowning in the sea of the world. At first, I thought it wasn't such a big deal, that I was only "a little bit" off the path, but God showed me that how far I was off the path wasn't the issue. What's the difference if you're a little off or a lot off? You still missed. If you missed that putt by 1 foot or 50 feet, you missed. If you missed that runway by 10 feet or a mile, you missed; you crashed. God's path is there to help us stay safe and to enable us to receive all the blessings He wants to give us.

The problem is that it's so easy to step off the path. Lots of worldly temptations just wait for us, if we'll just step down this side street or walk through that open door. It makes me picture myself walking down a narrow street with a carnival of temptations off to either side—kiosks, vendors, great smelling food, and comfy places to just kick back and prop up the feet. You know, I'll just step off the path here for a moment and take a break. (By the way, what's the current carnival act of temptation in your life today?) But God's path always bypasses those things, so understand this: the path that God has marked out for each of His children is designed to protect us from the things that will derail and even destroy us. What is excluded from my path might not be from yours, but it's God's decision.

You see, we have God, but we also have an enemy, Satan, who likes to tempt us to leave the path. Satan is subtle, and he's deadly. John 10:10 tells us that the thief (Satan) comes to steal, kill, and destroy. If I let my guard down, he can steal some of my joy and my focus and kill my faith, which will destroy me personally and likely my family. How? All that had to happen was for me to be just a little off God's path. I didn't make God my first priority. I got distracted by the world. I didn't get alone with God daily; I didn't study His Word; I even pushed it aside when the Holy Spirit brought verses to mind; and gradually, I lost my saltiness. I was shaken by circumstances and events, stopped focusing on God's narrow path, and lost my way. I made myself an easy target. My life and my faith turned bland and dull, and it spilled over onto those around me—my wife, family, friends, and business associates—not to mention those with whom I should have shared the Gospel.

It scared me because I think if we don't live our life in such a way that people can see God through us, which is what's supposed to happen, then Satan just shrugs us off. It's like we're playing on his team. Now, that's a scary thought.

God had to shake up my world to get my attention.

Is God shaking your world? Check your location—are you off the path He has marked out for your life? It's common. Jesus warns us of this in Matthew 7:13–14, "Enter through the narrow gate. For wide is the gate and broad is the road that leads to destruction, and many enter through it. But small is the gate and narrow the road that leads to life, and only a few find it."

As believers, we have entered that narrow gate of salvation, which we can never lose; however, we can easily wander off "the narrow road that leads to life" if we do not stay close to God and His Word. If we just plop down on the other side of the gate and hang out there, if we bring all our habits and attitudes with us through that narrow gate, if our lives aren't any different, then what could possibly make someone want to follow us through that gate? If there is nothing different about us to make others thirst for what "going through the gate" gave us, what's the point?

We are supposed to be salty and full of the flavor of God so that others will be influenced to have Jesus as their Lord and Savior. Let me give you an example from what I call a living parable, which God showed me in 2010. It happened in Orlando, Florida, at a Southside Johnny concert. The band's full name is Southside Johnny and the Asbury Jukes. They are a rock-and-roll band from New Jersey. They play Jersey Shore, Bruce Springsteen-type music. I've loved Southside's music for more than 20 years. I've been to many of their concerts at a lot of different places.

One thing you can be sure of at a Southside concert is that you will be up dancing, singing, and happy. The music is alive; it's uplifting; and it's great; so, I was really looking forward to that. I went up with a buddy of mine, and maybe 400 people were at the show. The first thing I noticed was that everybody in the audience was sitting down. I thought, hey, why are they sitting? Southside has come out. He started to play. I was in the back row. One other guy, maybe about twenty feet away, and I were standing up, dancing, moving, and singing, but everybody else was sitting down. I thought, hey, wait a minute, something is wrong here. Don't they know who he is? It's Southside Johnny! You're supposed to be up and dancing.

Right at that very moment, Jesus put on my heart—Jack, it's the same as salvation. There are people who see and hear the Word of Jesus Christ, and they just sit and don't respond. You think, wait a minute, don't they know who He is? He's Jesus Christ, the Creator of the world, Master of the universe, King of all kings, your God, your Father who loves you so much, and you don't respond? God's Holy Spirit, at that very moment, reminded me of John 14:11, it says, "Believe me when I say that I am in the Father, and the Father is in me; or at least believe on the evidence of the miracles themselves."

So, Southside Johnny played, and he was five, six, maybe seven songs into the show. That one guy and I were still the only ones up dancing. I looked around, wanting to scream at the rest of the crowd. "What's the matter with you people? If you don't know who Southside Johnny is, then okay, fine, but come on, listen to him play! Now that you've heard him, why aren't you up dancing? Can't you hear the music and see his talent? Isn't that enough to get you up and moving and excited?" I danced and wondered how stupid could these people be. If you don't believe based on who Southside is, then how about believing based on what you see and hear? They heard and saw Southside Johnny right in front of them, but they still didn't want to get up and respond. How could they not respond?

It was the same thing when people heard Jesus speak, when they heard the Word of God preached. How could they not respond right then? If that didn't do it, if you sat there, and you saw it was Southside Johnny, you saw it was Jesus Christ, and you heard the music play, and you heard the Word preached, and then you saw the people around you jumping and dancing with joy, and their lives were filled with peace and happiness, then wouldn't you at least want to join in and participate in that? Why would you want to miss it? When people see Jesus Christ reflected through our lives, they should want a piece of it immediately. It should be contagious and infectious—it should make others *thirsty* for what we have that they don't.

About halfway through the show, after Southside Johnny said "By the way, you know it's legal to stand up and dance, don't you?" About 30 people responded and stood up and started clapping and dancing. At the show's end, by the last encore, about two and a half hours later, more people had gotten the vibe and responded, based on what they saw. Granted, many of them figured it out late and missed much of the show's joy, but at least they finally figured it out and didn't miss the whole purpose and **all** of the show's joy.

When the last song started, almost everybody was up dancing, clapping, and singing. Yet I couldn't help looking at the people who didn't respond because it was sad. They missed the whole show. I wanted to shake each by the shoulders and say, "You just sat there through the whole concert. You saw it, and you didn't respond, and you didn't get up. Are you dead?"

Jesus says the same thing to us, that we are spiritually dead, dead if we do not see and respond to the message of Jesus Christ, if we do not see and believe in the miracles themselves. Some will never get it, no matter what, no matter how evident it is, even if it's right in front of their face singing and dancing. Remember, Jesus said if they didn't believe Moses, the prophets, or the disciples, they wouldn't even believe someone raised from the dead because their hearts were so hardened (Luke 16:31). I thought, Lord, this is amazing. You've given me this live parable tonight, and I thought I was just going to see Southside Johnny play some music. I now want to affect the people around me for Jesus with the way I live my life, like the way Southside Johnny does for Rock and Roll with the way he plays his music. The Blind Boys of Alabama could see that staying on God's path would bring them joy and satisfaction, and they chose that. God blessed them mightily. Isn't it interesting that even after salvation, we have choices to make about which path to follow? It's our responsibility, and we are held accountable (often on this earth but certainly once we die and face God). Do we live up to the flavorful potential we are given? It doesn't matter whether we affected millions of people with our music, like the Blind Boys did, or 400 at a concert, or one friend. Were we salt to the people God placed in our lives?

Does my saltiness make others thirsty for Jesus Christ? Is there anything I can do to improve the flavor of my life enough to have that effect on others?

I believe the answer is found in Matthew 7:13-14 "Enter through the narrow gate. For wide is the gate and broad is the road that leads to destruction, and many enter through it. But small is the gate and narrow the road that leads to life, and only a few find it" Now look closely at the end of Matthew 7:14, a piece of the verse we often overlook. It says, *"but small is the gate and narrow the road that leads to life,* (emphasis mine) and only a few find it." We know the small gate is our entry into heaven through Jesus. What is the life that the narrow road leads to? God promises abundant life on earth (spiritual abundance, not necessarily material) and eternal life in heaven with rewards based on what we did on earth. When we live our lives rightly related to God and focus on living according to God's ways (than we are staying on his narrow road as we live), that abundant life we experience becomes salt to the world, which then draws others to Christ. That abundant life might look like peace in the midst of economic turmoil, hope in the face of a crisis, or joy in the midst of crushing circumstances.

Remember once you pass through the gate, the road leading to life is narrow. I picture a small gate with an even skinnier path on its other side. It's easy to miss the narrow path. You must look for it, but some people don't want to. They are content just to get through the gate, and maybe they just sit on the other side, like the people sitting in the audience at the concert. Sitting is easier than finding and walking the narrow path and besides, with a narrow path, you can't see very far ahead, and you don't know what might happen, so why not just hang out here where it's comfortable and safe?

I'll tell you why I won't settle for a dull, sit-in-the-seats-and-let-the-concert-pass-you-by place. I want the life that leads to God! The gate is small, but there is so much more to God's blessings for us than just coming through the gate. If you want more blessings from God, then walk the narrow road leading to the abundant life he promises. I believe that many Christians miss that. Oh, they get the gate; they get that they're in heaven; but they miss the narrow road leading to life, the abundant life God intended for every believer, every child of his, to have.

I look back and realize when I allowed my saltiness to become bland by wandering off God's path, it had a negative impact on others which I am not happy about. Today, I'm so grateful because I can see the Father's hand. I can see the blessing. I can see the molding and the shaping God did in my life so he could use me more because I had to learn these things before I could go forward. It is important because I don't want to make that mistake again. I am so grateful to God that even though I'd gotten off the path a little bit, the Holy Spirit told me where to go. I knew how to get back to God.

So what do you do if you find yourself off the path and life and Satan have figuratively kicked the crap out of you and you're hopeless and full of desperation? You cry out to the Lord. And he hears you, even when you don't know what to say.

Psalm 40:11–12 says, "Do not withhold your mercy from me, O Lord; may your love and your truth always protect me. For troubles without number surround me; my sins have overtaken me, and I cannot see. They are more than the hairs of my head, and my heart fails within me." Have you ever felt like that, like you were hammered by life's circumstances? Like Satan had you by the throat?

David, a man after God's own heart and a great king, wrote Psalm 40. Yet, just like you and me, he went through, what he must have felt were crappy and aggravating trials and tribulations. Are you crying out as David did (Psalm 40:13) "Be pleased, O Lord, to save me; O Lord, come quickly to help me"?

Are you sometimes so overwhelmed by circumstances and situations of life, by Satan's attacks on you, that all you can pray is, "Lord, I'm clueless. I don't even know what to pray or what to say to you."

Sometimes we just need to stand still and know the Lord is our deliverer (Psalm 46:10–11). There are and will be times in our lives when all we can do is just "be," just sit there. We can't control the circumstance. We can't control the actions or behaviors of others, medical outcomes, or Wall Street's roller coasters. All we can do is sit still and know God is our deliverer.

Now, you might ask me, "Hey, Jack, how did you do it? You told us that you had these problems, and you came back to the Lord, but how did you do it?" I'll tell you. With the world collapsing around me, and I was the only one who knew, I went away for three days to pray and meditate, something I should have done six weeks sooner.

I went into a hotel room and literally didn't step outside the door for three days. There are tremendous benefits to shutting yourself off from the world and getting alone with God. In the Gospels, it seems Jesus did it daily. He was the Son of God, so why would He do that? He knew God's plan, yet so important was His daily affirmation of communication with God that even though He knew God's plan, He made time to be alone with Him and prayed to God every day to keep His saltshaker full.

It was truly a privilege to be alone with God. If you go through a similar circumstance in your life, I urge you to do the same thing. It doesn't have to be three days. Try one day. Get out of your rat race, stop going from one thing to another, and get alone—shut yourself in a room—with God. Can you be sure God will show up? Here's His promise, from Jeremiah 29:13, "You will seek me and find me when you seek me with all your heart."

Getting alone with God means I have to seek Him with all my heart. And when I did, here's how He spoke to me. He gave me verses 8 and 13 from the 12th chapter of Daniel. To set the stage, Daniel had visions and dreams, and he sought interpretation from the Lord. He wasn't quite clear what some stuff meant, and in verse 8, Daniel said, "I heard, but I did not understand. So I asked, 'My lord, what will the outcome of all this be?'" Daniel's confusion was about the visions he'd been given for the future. Isn't our confusion often rooted in our inability to understand what happens and how it will affect our futures? Listen to what the Lord told Daniel, and He tells us, "As for you, go your way till the end. You will rest, and then at the end of the days you will rise to receive your allotted inheritance" (Daniel 12:13).

How beautiful and reassuring is that Word from God. "You don't have to understand everything, just trust me to handle it. Go your way until the end. Go do what I called you to do. Go live your life. Go make disciples and let me work through you."

God said the same thing to me. "You found the road home, Jack. I'm still with you. Go your way; stay on the path I've marked out for you until the end. Go do what my word calls you to do; go live your life by my word; go make disciples; and let me work through you... go, believing the promises that you already know."

What are those promises? Here are a few that should keep me

busy for the rest of my life: God will never leave me or forsake me (Deuteronomy 31:6, 8, and Joshua 1:5); God is with me always (Matthew 28:20); God gave me the Holy Spirit as a deposit and a guarantee of my place in heaven (2 Corinthians 1:22 and 5:5); no weapon formed against me can prosper (Isaiah54:17); the prayer of a righteous man is effective (James 5:16); I'm made in the image of God (Genesus1:26); and God has a perfect plan for my life and a perfect plan for your life (Jeremiah29:11).

I know these promises, but will I go my way down the path He has marked out for me, living as if I truly believe these promises? It matters. Why? Because my belief affects God's work in me and through me, and that affects my ability to flavor the world around me.

In Matthew 8:13, the Centurion comes to Jesus, asking Him to heal His servant. Jesus says to the Centurion, "Go. It will be done just as you believed it would." And his servant was healed at that very hour. Did you see it? That little word *go*. Go your way, trusting God to handle it.

Go, Jack (go, Reader); go forward on the path that God has marked out for you and don't be distracted by the attractions on the side streets and carnival kiosks of this worldly life. Ignore their shouts, their advice, and their instructions about how to live your life. Trust God to handle the marriage, the finances, the ministry, the rat race; trust God to handle them according to His Word and His promises. Go forward on the road to life, toward God, and make disciples. God is in control. Don't sit and worry about it anymore. Go do what you're supposed to do. Your place in Heaven is assured. You have your reward. Go do what you're supposed to do.

Ecclesiastes 9:12 reminds us even more why we need to have

that attitude. It says, "Moreover, no man knows when his hour will come: As fish are caught in a cruel net, or birds are taken in a snare, so men are trapped by evil times that fall unexpectedly upon them." We don't know when the end will be, and we control nothing. Bob Dylan wrote, "Time is an ocean, but it ends at the shore." Time is vast, but it does come to an end , just like your life. So what can you do? What can you do if this snare can come upon you at any minute, and if you can be trapped by evil times at any minute? You can't control those things, so you go. You go and live your life, and you trust God. You rejoice in the Lord. You live the abundant life, and you fight the good fight. In today's slang, we'd say, you keep on keeping on.

At a Promise Keepers event, a speaker talked about how important it is not to worry about how God gets things done. Just leave the "how" to God. That can be hard because our human nature wants to know how things will get done. It's probably a control issue for us. We spend so much time questioning how God will work out His promises to us, it's as if we don't believe He'll succeed. God, how will you deliver me from this mess? Since I can't see any way out, how can you possibly find one? It sounds silly when I put it that way, doesn't it?

We spend time worrying about the "how" that's none of our business and neglect the "what" that *is* our responsibility—trusting Him completely. What if you called an ambulance because you were having a heart attack? Your first question wouldn't be how the paramedics are going to save you, would it? No, you would just say, "Save me!" They are the experts; you trust them to do their thing right and save your life, and that's all you care about.

For me, the best example of letting go of the "how" issue is my car.

I put my key in the ignition, and it goes. It gets me from here to there. I have no clue how it works. I have no clue how the pistons work or how gas gets to the engine. All I know is that I do my part—I put the key in, and it does its part and moves. And that's good enough for me.

So, why isn't that good enough for me when it comes to how God does things? Why don't we trust God completely? We should, and we need to, starting now, if we want to be blessed abundantly.

When we trust God completely, we have no regrets, no coulda, woulda, shoulda haunting us in our later years. I'll close this chapter with a story I hope speaks to every one of you reading this book. It's about my friend, Sam, who just was fired after more than 30 years of working for a major auto company. They said they were cutting back because of the economy and sorry, pal, you didn't make the list.

Sam and I talked, and he said, "I'm not worried about my future. I know God will provide." He's fortunate enough to have a pension, so he has bucks to fall back on. But he said, "I have one regret."

"What's that?"

"I wish I had taken my vacation time." He didn't mean it from a standpoint of money. He meant that he'd wasted time working and striving for the world's definition of success. Instead he could have and should have, spent that time with his family. He missed things like watching his kids grow up. He worked so hard. He devoted so much to the company that he missed his children growing up, and now he regrets it. He can't get that time back.

I hope and pray that you and I will never have that regret when it comes to our Christian life, that we'll never look back and say we didn't take the time to be the salt of the world by living our lives for Jesus to draw others to Him.

I can tell you that the blessings I got when I turned back to God were so awesome and better than any I've known before. I believe that God will do that same thing in your life today if you will turn back to Him and focus on adding back the salt flavor of God to your own life. Then, He can accomplish His purpose for your life, no matter where you are, what your age, or what you've done in the past.

Take a look at your life and ask yourself... does it need a little seasoning? If the answer to that is yes, then the next words out of your mouth should be, "Lord, please pass the salt!"

I pray the following words of Psalm 34 would pierce your heart and that God would use them to speak directly to your spirit right now.

> I sought the Lord, and He answered me; He delivered me from all my fears.
>
> Those who look to Him are radiant; their faces are never covered with shame.
>
> This poor man called, and the Lord heard him; He saved him out of all his troubles.
>
> The angel of the Lord encamps around those who fear Him, and He delivers them.
>
> Turn from evil and do good; seek peace and pursue it.
>
> The eyes of the Lord are on the righteous and his ears are attentive to their cry;
>
> The Lord is close to the brokenhearted and saves those who are crushed in spirit.

A righteous man may have many troubles, but the Lord delivers
him from them all;

Psalm 34 (verses 4–7, 14–15, 18–19)

It doesn't get any better than this! We should all be rejoicing at how much God loves us! Are you? Answer honestly...it's another moment of truth where the rubber meets the road with God in your life.

5

The Devil's Credit Card

What's in your wallet? No better yet, who's in your wallet? More specifically, who have you allowed into your spiritual wallet? Have you granted the devil access to your spiritual treasure?

We hear a lot these days about our credit scores (or ratings): what they are, how they are calculated, why they matter, and how they can help or harm us as we go through life. It's a surprise to learn that, sometimes, these scores can even affect a hiring decision. Who knew? Many of us do now. Now that we know, we need to pay attention. Credit ratings affect many parts of life, and a poor rating can make simple things such as getting a car or home loan difficult, more expensive, or impossible altogether.

Except for the case of identity theft, these scores are within our control. If we're careless about allowing others to use our credit card, other people's actions can damage our rating.

And no, this chapter won't nag you about how you spend money. This chapter is about how we can take a perfectly good rating—and I mean that in the literal sense, as God's children—and give someone permission to ruin it.

As Christians, we are God's children, and we are heirs to His heavenly riches. We didn't always have that status. Before we believed in Jesus Christ, before we were saved, we had no "credit standing" with God. There was absolutely nothing we could do to earn a good enough score to have access to heaven. Ah, but because God loved the world, He sent His only son, Jesus Christ, to make a way for us to be reconciled to God, so we could have a relationship with Him (John 3:16).

Once we became Christians, we received a perfect credit rating in God's sight because of what Jesus did for us. What is the credit limit, or boundary? Living our lives to please God (stay with me on my credit card analogy; it will be worth it). If we read all the small print that comes with the Visa or MasterCard, we'll find lots and lots of rules, and lots and lots of ways for them to whack us for high interest rates and big bucks when we screw up. If we read God's material, which we can even get in a large print, plain English edition, nothing is hidden. It's all spelled out for us. The bottom line: because we're saved, we can never lose our heavenly inheritance. Visa might cancel our platinum card, but God never cancels our adoption as His child, so our identity can never be stolen. We, however, can do things that will limit the blessings (and credit line) God gives us.

Credit cards require payments within certain windows; the grace period for late payments narrows as the economy huffs and puffs its way through a serious recession. Miss the grace period, and penalties kick in. In other words, the rule of law, with hefty penalties attached, replaces grace.

In God's spiritual economy, grace replaces the rule of law. It's in Romans 6:14: "For sin shall not have dominion over you, because you are not under law, but under grace." Next to the message of salvation and the joy accompanying it, this had to be the greatest thing I have ever heard as a believer. We don't fully grasp this element of faith, maybe because of its simplicity. Let's take this verse apart and make sure we really get each piece of it and why it's so important for us to understand.

Sin: This verse doesn't talk about a specific sin, but about the sin nature we all inherited from Adam, meaning the fallen state of mankind. In that fallen state, the sin nature controlled us. Our choices, thoughts, desires, attitudes, priorities, everything in our lives was subject to that fallen, sinful, imperfect nature that kept us separated from God.

Shall not have: Sin no longer has the tyrannical control over us it once had. It can hang around; it can try to make inroads; it can try to manipulate and distract, but it cannot reclaim authority over us.

Dominion: control, rule, authority, lordship, kingship... you get the picture.

You are not under law: The Old Testament law was given to expose sin. Without rules, so to speak, we'd never know if we did something wrong. Think of the interstate with no rules. Us Floridians think of I-95 along the East Coast. As difficult as that road sometimes is, just imagine if there were no traffic laws. However, when we see the sign "Speed Limit 65 MPH" and realize, oops, we're doing 80, we now know we are breaking the law because the law has been posted. In the Old Testament, man did whatever he wanted to, and believe me, there's stuff in there that wouldn't be allowed on late night TV even today—things that shock many people reading it for the first time. Then God gave man the Old Testament law, so the people would know what was right and what was wrong. And, of course, no one could keep every law perfectly because of man's sin nature. God put the law in place to show us our need for grace.

You are under grace: In the New Testament, the requirements for perfect obedience to God's law are done away with because Jesus fulfilled God's law perfectly, and we can have the perfection of His life credited to our account. Sometimes, GRACE is used as an acronym such as this—God's Riches At Christ's Expense. If you are a believer, you are granted access to God's riches—His mercy, comfort, forgiveness, strength, power, and more—because Christ bought it for you with His life.

"For sin shall not have dominion over you, because you are not under law, but under grace" (Romans 6:14). Maybe another way to word that is, "Your sinful human nature (your natural tendencies to want to be your own god and to do things that are contrary to God's desires) no longer controls you, no longer rules over you, no longer has authority over you, is no longer the king over your life. As a Christian, you are now under God's authority thanks to what Jesus Christ did for you when He died on the cross (in God's view, Christ traded His perfect life for your imperfect one, so you could have access to heaven)." Sounds awesome.

Then, why do you and I still struggle with our sinful nature? We each would picture a different type of sin: alcoholism, adultery, lying, greed, gossip.... If you need help with your list, just check out Colossians, chapter 3. We still have these struggles because of the devil, who is real, even though some folks deny His existence. On the other hand, there are people and churches who blame everything on the devil, giving him credit for all the sins that happen.

I want to lay the groundwork here that the devil is real because God says he is real, but we will not give the devil any credit. We are going to take back the credit card that we have lent him.

A survey from an evangelical Christian company reported that 64% of evangelical Christians do not believe there is a devil. How that could be, I don't know! That just calls God a liar. You don't have to believe the devil exists, but it does not change that he is real. You do not have to believe the Holocaust happened, the 9/11 tragedy happened or that Babe Ruth hit 714 home runs, but it does not change the fact that those things happened.

The devil might be alive, but he is not well. Let's look specifically at "the devil" (alias Lucifer, Prince of Darkness).

There were three named angels in the Bible, and you probably know them: Michael, the warrior angel, also known as the archangel; Gabriel, the messenger angel, the one who gave Mary the message that she would be the mother of Jesus; and Lucifer (now known as Satan, the devil), an angel of God. As a matter of fact, he was the anointed cherub. He was supposedly the most beautiful of all angels.

In Ezekiel 28:14–15, God says, "You were anointed as a guardian cherub, for so I ordained you. You were on the holy mount of God; you walked among the fiery stones. You were blameless in your ways

from the day you were created till wickedness was found in you."
Most theologians agree that this refers directly to Lucifer.

Of course, Lucifer was blameless (perfect). Like Gabriel and
Michael, God created him for God's purposes. We know that he was
beautiful, and he walked back and forth in the midst of fiery stones.
He was perfect in His ways from the day he was created, but note the
end of that description and the verse that follows, Ezekiel 28:16, "...
till wickedness was found in you... and you sinned. So I drove you in
disgrace from the mount of God, and I expelled you."

Lucifer sinned. Did you know that a created angel could do that?
It's right there in Scripture. God created Lucifer and gave him beauty
and a specific role and authority, but that wasn't enough. Lucifer
wanted more, and he tried to take it, which was a sin. God will not
have anything impure, anything sinful, in heaven, and so He cast
Lucifer out. Lucifer lost his heavenly position, and he was stripped
of the authority he once had.

Some years ago, I had a big television production company
with 200 employees. I paid my chief financial officer $100,000 a
year and gave him lots of authority in that role. Then, my partner
and I found out he stole from us. We stripped him of his authority.
Before we threw him out the door, we told him he could pay back
the money or go to jail. He was smart enough to pay it back, and
if he were ever foolish enough to try to walk back in the company
door, he'd be arrested. He was stripped of his authority, and he
couldn't even enter the building. It's the same thing for Lucifer and
his "exit" from heaven.

That's an example we can easily relate to on a physical level. But on a spiritual level, do you believe that Satan has no authority in heaven? That is the first question. Let's see what the answer is.

Isaiah 14:12–15 talks about Lucifer's fall. "How you have fallen from heaven, O morning star, son of the dawn! You have been cast down to the earth, you who once laid low the nations! You said in your heart, 'I will ascend to heaven; I will raise my throne above the stars of God; I will sit enthroned on the mount of assembly, on the utmost heights of the sacred mountain. I will ascend above the tops of the clouds; I will make myself like the Most High.' But you are brought down to the grave, to the depths of the pit."

Did you notice the first identified sin? Lucifer desired to be like God, even to be above Him. Bad idea, trust me, and that's the sin nature we have as well, wanting to be our own gods and ignore the real one.

God cast Satan out of heaven, and whatever heavenly authority Satan used to have was gone. Can you imagine how outraged he was? His goal of making himself like the Most High was crushed and eternally destroyed. So, be became God's enemy... and ours.

Now, let's step back to Genesis, to the beginning, to set the stage, starting in 1:26:

Then God said, "Let us make man in our image, in our likeness, and let them (man) rule (have dominion) over the fish of the sea and the birds of the air, over the livestock, over all the earth, and over all the creatures that move along the ground." So God created man in His own image, male and female He created them. God blessed them and said to them, "Be fruitful and increase in number; fill the earth and subdue it. Rule over the fish of the sea and the birds of the air and over every living creature that moves on the ground."

God created man to have dominion over all the earth and gave man, through Adam and Eve, authority to exercise dominion over creation, over the fish, the birds, and every living creature that moves on the ground.

Next question: Do you believe that God blessed Adam and Eve? Adam and Eve were blessed with God's presence, His fellowship, His love, and the peace that came from that perfect relationship with God. They were blessed by being under His authority, and they had great freedom in that position. Adam understood that he had God's authority to do what he did, such as naming the animals, because God had given it to him (sort of a Power of Attorney thing). "Okay, Adam, as long as I've given it to you, you can use this power. It is not your power; it is my power. I give it to you to use in ways in keeping with my desires." And God gives you and me the same power. How is that? When we are rightly connected to God through Jesus Christ, we can speak on behalf of God because our speech (verbal and nonverbal) will represent God's love, mercy, forgiveness, and so on.

And what happened next? The Bible says Adam and Eve sinned. Why? Why would they go from being content and blessed and having great freedoms in the Garden to sinning? What happened? They allowed themselves to be tricked.

In the entire Garden, they were not supposed to touch just one tree... and so far, so good... until Satan, who had become God's enemy, came into the picture. He was royally ticked off at God, but there was no possible way for him to go after God or harm Him. So, what did he do?

He did the next best thing. If he couldn't be above God and if he couldn't harm God, then he would go after God's image, God's children who He loved so much—Adam and Eve. He had no authority to do anything to them, *but they could permit him to enter, thus giving him the authority to impact their lives.* Remember, Adam and Eve had been in the Garden with that forbidden tree since they were created, and it was never an issue. Once they allowed Satan to trick them, though, they sinned. That sinful nature has been passed down through every generation since.

Adam and Eve forfeited their God-given authority to Satan, and sadly, we do the same thing. Satan can't steal it or borrow it, but we can give it to him. As Christians with a perfect credit rating in God's sight, we still get to choose our actions, and if we're not careful, we can be deceived as easily as Adam and Eve. Deceived into handing over our spiritual credit card and suffering for it. When that happens, we can "damage" God's credit rating in the eyes of a watching, skeptical world.

We forfeit our authority by stepping out from under God's hand. God blessed everything in the Garden, and He blessed Adam and Eve, but the moment they sinned by doing the one thing God had told them not to, the Word of God says that their eyes were opened, not to God's power, as Satan had promised, but to their own nakedness.

Let me emphasize this sharp contrast. In Genesis 3, Adam and Eve had this great relationship with God. They walked with Him in the coolness of the morning; they talked, hung out, and everything was great, but the moment they ate of the tree, their eyes were opened, and they saw that they were naked. They hid themselves from God. Can you imagine God coming into the Garden, calling and calling for Adam? He didn't have to do that. He's all knowing. He knew where Adam was all the time, but He gave Adam the choice to come out of hiding on his own.

Finally, Adam told God he was hiding (as if anyone could hide from God) because he was naked and afraid. And God asked a simple question in Genesis Chapter 3 verse 11: "Who told you that you were naked?"

I want to pause here to make sure we see two opposites unfolding. In the beginning of creation, Adam was with God. He was a kingdom man; he only understood kingdom principles of purity, perfection, oneness with God, and peace. When he stepped out from under God's authority, his eyes were opened to a nature with which he was unfamiliar. Adam was naked before he ever realized he was naked. He just did not know it; he did not see it because there was nothing impure or sinful about it. Then, however, he saw it from different eyes; he saw it through the eyes of Satan, who had dominion over him—because he had given it to him. As a result of believing Satan's lies Adam and Eve were kicked out of the Garden of Eden.

First Satan, then Adam and Eve, and then all humanity were excluded from heaven because of sin. Satan wanted to be god, but when God kicked him out, he figured, hey, if I can't have heaven for myself, then I'll just destroy as many of "God's images," men and women, as I can.

Every one of us is born into the world with that devilish credit rating that will destroy our life and our eternal hope. Here's the good news, though. We have a free offer from God that's amazing—He'll wipe away every stain on our spiritual credit score, and He'll put Jesus' perfect rating on our account. This one-time transaction doesn't transfer your balance, but rather, it completely obliterates your balance. The fee to join—faith in Jesus Christ and then by living a life that pleases God, you are empowered to tell Satan to take a hike. Though it doesn't mean Satan won't try to undermine our desire to live a godly life. There will be battles to fight, but God will fight those for us and with us because we are part of His kingdom. Kings get really offended when an enemy starts messing with their people!

As believers in Jesus Christ, Satan has no authority over us to lead us astray except that which we give him, and that's what the rest of this chapter is about.

So, let's see, we left off with Satan tricking Adam and Eve, and everybody got kicked out of the Garden, out of heaven, and out of God's presence. People didn't know right from wrong at that point because there were no "rules" or laws to live by, until God instituted the Old Testament law. Then, the people saw their sins, as they could now define perfection (follow perfectly the 10 commandments and 632 laws of Leviticus). They realized there was no way they could live a perfect life. How could they? They had inherited a sinful nature from Adam.

Fast forward through several thousand years to Christ and the New Testament, where the exact opposite happened when you and I were born again. In our beginning, at our birth, we had the old sinful eyes, the sinful nature, because it had been passed down through Adam. That nature had dominion over us. It drove our choices, our thoughts, feelings, passions, attitudes, everything—we were outside heaven with no way in, and we had no fellowship, no connection to God. We were only familiar with the sinful kingdom nature, not

God's holy kingdom nature. Then, Christ came to earth. Why? God explains It clearly "The reason the Son of God appeared was to destroy the devil's work" (1 John 3:8). He came to break the authority of the devil over our lives, and once we were saved, our eyes were opened to the spiritual nature, and we could see again as Adam saw in the Garden of Eden, and we could again have fellowship with God.

Now, back to the question of why we still struggle with sin. Why? It's because we still have this mind and these memories filled with our old nature. It's still there, even though it can't reclaim its authority over us. We still have it; we did not get rid of it. But with Jesus' power, we can destroy its influence over us.

"But, Jack," you say, "if Jesus destroyed the devil, shouldn't that mean that he's gone? Did Jesus destroy the devil?"

Let's look at what Scripture says. In fact, always go back to Scripture to see if things line up. One of the many names for the devil is the prince of this world—he cannot rule in heaven, but he rules over the earth. How? Remember, when Adam and Eve sinned in the Garden, at that very moment they transferred their authority to rule over the earth to Satan. We've just said God's word showed us that "the reason the Son of God appeared was to destroy the devil's work" (1 John 3:8). The devil's work is to keep people from God, but Jesus, while speaking to a crowd, announced, "Now is the time for judgment on this world; now the prince of this world will be driven out" (John 12:31).

Remember, the devil was cast out of heaven and lost his authority in the heavenly realm. God owned the earth and gave authority over it—dominion, the right to rule—to Adam and Eve. Satan still had no authority to do anything, until, catch this, until Adam and Eve forfeited their authority to him.

They had no right to do that. They were the property managers for God's Garden, if you will, and nowhere in their contract did it state they could "sublet" that authority, transfer or assign that authority to anyone else. It's not so hard to picture—have you ever lent something to someone , only to find out that that person passed the right to that item to someone else you did not authorize?

So, Jesus came to drive out the prince of this world, to make a way for us to get out from under that unauthorized authority and get back into a relationship with God. Up to the time of Christ, the only way for people to deal with their sin, guilt, and shame was to obey God's laws perfectly, which no one could do. You could either perfectly obey every law from birth (impossible), or you had to make animal sacrifices at prescribed times to atone for your sins.

When the time was right, Jesus came to earth to make the perfect, ultimate sacrifice that would destroy Satan's plans. Jesus was fully God, yet fully man, and He lived a completely sinless life on earth. His death paid the price for all our sins and satisfied the laws of God that we broke. Three days after He was crucified, the tomb was empty—Jesus had risen from the dead. He now sits at God's right hand. His perfect, sinless life gave Him the perfect, untarnished "credit rating" He still offers to anyone who believes in Him. This spiritually perfect rating gives us forgiveness for our debts (sin debts, not financial), entry into God's family, an eternal home in heaven, and blessings on earth and in the life to come. Even death cannot have authority over us because we will rise, as well, to be with Christ in heaven as Romans 6:7 So wonderfully tells us "anyone who has died has been freed from sin."

Dominion, rulership, authority. Because Christ died for our sins, our sin nature no longer has the right to tell us what to do. In fact we are given a new nature. "Therefore, if anyone is in Christ, he is a new creation; the old has gone, the new has come!" (2 Corinthians 5:17). Before Christ entered my life, my sin nature covered me, like an old jacket I wear (and believe me, my wife wishes this jacket would pass away). But, when I became a Christian, I became a new creation. God took away my sin nature just as I would take off this jacket, and He tossed it away. Psalm 103:12 puts it this way, and I love it: "...as far as the east is from the west, so far has He removed our transgressions from us." Wouldn't it be nice if those credit-rating bureaus would do the same thing for us, financially speaking?

God takes all that history about our past actions and sins reported on those ratings, and He wipes it away, where it can never be found again, and in its place, He puts a perfect, pristine rating. That old rating, that old nature, no longer has dominion over me. Who wouldn't want that?

That perfect rating is already yours for the taking. God makes that offer to everyone, but He won't force it on anyone. It's our choice. Back in the Garden, Adam and Eve, who lived in perfection, chose to sin and lost everything. Today, because of Jesus Christ, we, who live in a sinful world, can choose God's perfection and gain everything. And just in case your mind wanders off to material things, let me assure you I am talking about gaining everything spiritually: a sinless record before God; a guaranteed place in heaven; peace, joy, and hope in the midst of earthly turmoil and challenges; and freedom from a sin nature that, if given free reign, will cause you pain, angst, regret, anger, and death.

Sounds like an easy choice to me. Today, I hope that God will show you how to walk victoriously in Jesus Christ. In Colossians 1, starting in verse 9, Paul prayed for believers in his day, and I would like you to think of it as a prayer about you as well:

For this reason, since the day we heard about you, we have not stopped praying for you and asking God to fill you with the knowledge of His will through all spiritual wisdom and understanding. And we pray this in order that you may live a life worthy of the Lord and may please Him in every way: bearing fruit in every good work, growing in the knowledge of God, being strengthened with all power according to His glorious might so that you may have great endurance and patience, and joyfully giving thanks to the Father, who has qualified you to share in the inheritance of the saints in the kingdom of light. For He has rescued us from the dominion of darkness and brought us into the kingdom of the Son He loves, in whom we have redemption, the forgiveness of sins.

Knowledge of His will, spiritual wisdom, and understanding—these things will transform our minds and strengthen us for the spiritual battles we face. And no matter how hard the battle seems, we must remember that Christ has already delivered us from death and from sin. The cross, gruesome as it is, was the greatest moment in the history of the world because it was on the cross that all your sins and mine were nailed for eternity. Christ said, "It is finished" (John 19:30). The power—the dominion—of sin over us is broken. At the moment of His death, the Bible says the veil in the temple separating the Most Holy Place from the Holy Place was torn from top to bottom. The veil kept a holy God separated from a sinful people, but when Christ died for our sins, there was no longer any need for that separation because Christ's death made a way for us to be in God's presence without that veil. It was done once and for all time. (And for the record, some scholars estimate that this veil, this curtain, was nearly sixty feet high and four inches thick—impossible for even two horses pulling at either side to tear apart, and yet, it was torn from top to bottom the instant when Christ died.)

But for now, we still have this problem—Satan still bugs us. It's like the kid in school who keeps poking at you but not quite touching you—trying to start a fight and get you in trouble. What's up with that? Spiritual warfare, that's what.

Back to our credit card analogy: You get a fresh, clean card with a perfect score and guess what happens? Your mailbox, your answering machine, your cell phone, your computer are all inundated with offers trying to tempt you to get back into debt, back into the behaviors that put you at financial risk and into stress and trouble. Those new offers for other cards can tempt you, but they have no authority over you, unless you give it to them by accepting their offer (taking Satan's sin bait) and thereby allowing them to affect your behavior in ways that will lower your credit rating. Staying out of debt means breaking old patterns and habits that got you into that situation in the first place.

So, even with a perfect spiritual rating, we still struggle with sin. Our old sin nature, those thought patterns and memories and habits, sometimes with help from Satan, will fight against the changes we have made to live a life that pleases God. We have to fight back... but this is not a physical battle, it's a spiritual one, right? We see this in movies and TV all the time, the battle between good and evil spirits, but is it real? Here's what the Bible has to say in Ephesians 6:12: "For our struggle is not against flesh and blood, but against the rulers, against the authorities, against the powers of this dark world and against the spiritual forces of evil in the heavenly realms."

We must fight this battle. The leader of the spiritual forces is Satan, the prince of this world. He has already lost the war, but that doesn't mean he will go happily into that good night or, in his case, the lake of fire for eternity, not without taking as many of God's images (people) with him as he can. So, we have to fight, but how? Back to Ephesians 6:13–18a, we find instructions:

Therefore put on the full armor of God, so that when the day of evil comes, you may be able to stand your ground, and after you have done everything, to stand. Stand firm then, with the belt of truth buckled around your waist, with the breastplate of righteousness in place, and with your feet fitted with the readiness that comes from the gospel of peace. In addition to all this, take up the shield of faith, with which you can extinguish all the flaming arrows of the evil one. Take the helmet of salvation and the sword of the Spirit, which is the word of God. And pray in the Spirit on all occasions with all kinds of prayers and requests.

If you put on the full armor of God, the devil can't get you. If you leave a piece of the armor off, absolutely he is going to get you.

Since you have been saved, have you found yourself still struggling with sin in your life? If you are like me, you would say yes, and I think

I know why. I didn't get saved until my thirties, and by then, there were things in my life that had made such a pattern in my mind that I am susceptible to *allowing* them into my life, even though I am already changed. It's a habit or a way of thinking so ingrained in me that often I'm not even aware of how it affects me. Let me use tennis to explain it.

I used to play tennis in high school, and I was pretty good for a while, except for this one problem. I did not hit a backhand well, so instead of working at overcoming that weakness, I'd run around the backhand, which took much more effort, and I'd hit it forehand. Occasionally, I hit a backhand, but I had no confidence in it. That became the pattern for how I'd respond when the ball crossed the net on my left side. I certainly had the desire to become a better tennis player, but I wasn't willing to pay the price. I wasn't willing to practice and put in the discipline necessary to get to the top of the game and to develop an instinctive backhand. So, my game stayed never got any better, I never became a great player, and now I don't even play tennis anymore.

It is the same with our Christian life. God's desire is that we would be champions, that we would be the best we can be. It's not His desire for us to be scared to get over something, scared to give something to him, scared of the devil. No, no, no! We must be willing to change, but we must work at it. When God reveals to us an area of weakness, where we need to build up our strength to respond according to His Word, we should do it. We work at it so that we can respond instinctively to the incoming challenge—Satan's fiery darts—in a way that will please God. Otherwise, the old patterns of our sin nature creep back into our lives.

"Respond instinctively?" you ask. "That's a lot of work, Jack. How am I supposed to do that?"

Don't ask me; ask God. Look at Romans 12:2: "Do not conform any longer to the pattern of this world, but be transformed by the renewing of your mind. Then you will be able to test and approve what God's will is—His good, pleasing and perfect will." In the spiritual sense, we still have some muscle memory that conforms to the pattern of our old nature (sin), and because of that muscle memory, it seems it is easy to live in that halfway life, with this old sin nature still attached to us. And we create a doctrine in our minds that expresses why it is still alive. We justify it in our minds rather than realizing that it has no authority over us, except the authority we give it. The devil still tries to take your authority from you, so he can rule over you and wreak havoc in your life; but remember, as a believer in Jesus Christ, you have authority in the kingdom of God and you stand underneath the mighty hand of God.

Did you notice the verb *transform* in the Romans 12:2 verse? Transforming your mind is how you break away from the old patterns. The battlefield is in the mind, in how we think. So how can we fight this battle?

God tells us how: "For though we live in the world, we do not wage war as the world does. The weapons we fight with are not the weapons of the world. On the contrary, they have divine power to demolish strongholds. We demolish arguments and every pretension that sets itself up against the knowledge of God, and we take captive every thought to make it obedient to Christ" (2 Corinthians 10:3–5).

Our weapons in warfare are not carnal; they are not silver bullets and machine guns. The enemy we deal with is spiritual, and our weapons must be spiritual. Because we belong to God, we have His divine power to demolish strongholds. What is a stronghold? It is something that has gotten you, something that you can't get out of, something that keeps you tangled up and unable to break free. God has given us mighty weapons to pull these down.

If you're dealing with addiction, greed, lust, anger, dishonesty, whatever it is, you know the power it has over you, and you know that mere human words or mantras cannot break that power. You need divine power to break down that stronghold in your mind before you can physically break free of that problem in your life. Let's look at 2 Corinthians 10:5 again. Paul assures us, as believers, that through our relationship with Jesus Christ, we have divine power that will enable us to demolish arguments (some translations use the word *imaginations*) and pretensions that would try to go against God. Arguments and pretensions are in the mind, and they often sound like this: "I don't have a (drinking/gambling) problem," or "I can quit (lying/stealing) whenever I want." I put parentheses around those words to emphasize that everyone of us has to fill in that space with our individual issue.

Is there anything in your mind exalting itself against God's knowledge? An example of this would be wrestling with something you don't want to hear from God on and finding yourself thinking, "Who needs God, anyway? The Bible can't tell me what to do!" Or maybe Satan throws some familiar fiery darts at you: "You'll never amount to anything... you're just a drunk... what makes you think you can stop using cocaine, abusing your wife, stealing, or lying?"

When those things show up in our minds, remember that God's weapon has the power to overcome those strongholds. We have a responsibility to battle along with Him by bringing every thought into captivity and making it obedient to Christ (look at the end of 2 Corinthians 10:5). Another way to say it is that our responsibility is to take those fiery darts that come at our minds and specifically put them under Christ's authority. The next time you face that temptation to indulge in the spending habit or the drug of choice and you hear that tired old thought, "go ahead, I told you you'd never change," stop right there and tell that thought to hit the road (or got to hell where it belongs) because you are under Jesus Christ's authority and power. Let Satan know that his message belongs in the junk mail file.

This is spiritual warfare, and it will not go away; but then again, neither will God. I want us to have a reality check. That war has already been won. Satan was never going to win against God. He tried, and he lost everything the second he was thrown out of heaven. Satan even knows he's lost the war, which is why he is so bent on keeping people away from God. There are still battles raging, however, but the battlefield that needs you is the battlefield of your own mind. You need to concentrate on that fight.

The enemy is out there in full force, but if you're saved by the blood of Jesus Christ, then Satan can't defeat you. You can defeat him quickly by reminding him of what happened at the cross. Remind him of what Jesus did there; remind him of the resurrection; and remind him that he will spend eternity in the lake of fire while we will spend it enjoying heaven.

Then, bring your thoughts back under the authority of Jesus, who finished the battle for us once and for all, and who holds in His hand your eternal credit rating—perfected by and paid for by **HIS** blood. Now, when we look at how you lived your life, then we, along with Jesus, can see if you were a good credit risk or not! Keep your credit rating right with God. It's another moment of truth for you, *where the rubber meets the road with God.*

6

Because You Said So

I have a friend who has been a very caring and effective pastor for the last 18 years. Yet now, he quietly expressed concerns and doubts about his weaknesses and shortcomings as a pastor. We all have them, whether we're businessmen or pastors, husbands or fathers; we all have concerns about our shortcomings, and we all have times of doubt. Then, he smiled.

"What happened?" I asked.

"My son went to the skate park." He laughed at my bewildered expression. "He's 11 and just couldn't wait to do the half-pipe (a u-shaped structure used as a field in extreme sports such as skateboarding and snowboarding), but he kept hesitating. Four or five times, he'd start then back off. You ever stand on the edge of a diving board and have second thoughts about jumping into the pool?"

I nodded.

"Same thing. All the older kids kept brushing past him and dropping over the edge, having a blast. But he was scared. Finally, I put my hand on his shoulder and said, 'Son, you have what it takes.'" His eyes sparkled and misted at the same time. "And he did it. Not perfectly, but he made the leap of faith and did it. As I watched him, I heard God speaking to me that exact same phrase, 'Son, you have what it takes.' That was so liberating because I realized that I'd focused on how my human weaknesses limited me rather than focusing on what I could do with God's power working in me. Later that night, I asked my son what made him finally believe he could do it."

"What did he say?"

"He looked at me and said, 'Because you said so, Dad.'"

Because his earthly father said, "You have what it takes," the son overcame fear and experienced the joy of the half-pipe. Because my friend's heavenly Father said, "You have what it takes," my friend no longer focuses on his doubts and limitations but on God's power to work through him and to enable him, and he can again experience the joy of ministering in God's name.

My friend wasn't the only one who needed to hear those words of encouragement, "You have what it takes." The promise from God is clear, and yet at times, we doubt our... what? Our worthiness? Our abilities?

I doubted, too, and I bet you could say the same thing. Focusing on God's strength and His promises is a message we all need to hear because Satan loves to get every one of us focused on our weaknesses, shortcomings, and failures, rather than on God's power.

If you have put your faith and trust in Jesus Christ, you are God's child, and you have what it takes to handle life. And what exactly do you have? You have God. "So do not fear, for I am with you; do not be dismayed, for I am your God. I will strengthen you and help you; I will uphold you with my righteous right hand" (Isaiah 41:10). God is with us, even at the skate park, even at the edge of the half-pipe, and He promises to strengthen us and help us. God won't give up on us either. Just look at Philippians 1:6 "... being confident of this, that He who began a good work in you will carry it on to completion until the day of Christ Jesus." Do you still wonder about His power working in you and whether you have what it takes to handle life? Look at what God says: "His divine power has given us everything we need for life and godliness through our knowledge of Him who called us by His own glory and goodness" (2 Peter 1:3). "I can do everything through Him who gives me strength" (Philippians 4:13). For added reassurance, remember this: "For God did not give us a spirit of timidity, but a spirit of power, of love and of self-discipline" (2 Timothy 1:7).

With all those verses and many others, we can be confident, steadfast, and sure that God is with us, enabling us to live our lives for Him. We can be obedient, even when it means dropping over the edge of the half-pipe that suddenly appears in our life-road, because we know we have what it takes; we know because God said so, because we have Him.

We should be able to do that, but sometimes, we get off track. The wheels fall off the skateboard, or the curb is higher than we thought, and we tumble over. We hesitate. We stand at the edge of the diving board and have second and third thoughts.

Recently, I was a little discouraged with my—I don't know what you want to call it—my position, my place, my future, my life. I don't know. I don't even know how to describe it. Then, God put this on my heart—it really doesn't matter how things are; it matters how I think about them. It matters what my view of them is.

What do I mean? Picture this—if I handed you a pair of glasses with red lenses, and you wore those glasses, everything would look red to you. But everything is not red. Everything just looks red because you put on red glasses. Then, of course, if we put on blue lenses, everything would look blue.

If I look at everything through the lenses of my imperfect, limited human ability, I will falter, hesitate, and doubt; I will not move far beyond my starting point because "I" said I can't—if I focus on myself, not God. But if I exchange my imperfect glasses for God's perfect ones, the lenses I look through will tell me I have what it takes because I have God and His promises, and if He tells me to do something, I can do it.

So, how do we look at the world? Do we look at it through a lens of concern, where everything is an issue; everything is a cause to be worried about? I recently thought I had a hernia from a sports injury. I worried about it for a while, and before I even found out the diagnosis, I said, "Wait a minute. I should jump up and down thanking God that it's something that can be fixed." Instead of worrying about it, I can thank God that there's a solution.

How about a lens of fear? Of what are you scared? Are you scared of dying? Are you scared of living? Are you scared of your body failing or of not having enough money? Go back to Scripture and God's word when fear strikes, "So do not fear, for I am with you; do not be dismayed, for I am your God. I will strengthen you and help you; I will uphold you with my righteous right hand" (Isaiah 41:10).

When we look at life through faulty lenses, it prevents us from fully obeying God, and it limits the blessings we can receive. If my "lenses" are fearful, then my reaction to God's command will be to hesitate. For example, if I'm fearful about having enough money, I will hesitate or simply refuse to obey God's command to tithe and to be generous, and I will miss the joy such actions bring. However, if I wear God's lenses, then I believe His promise to provide always for my needs, and I can freely obey (2 Corinthians 9:6–11).

We should look at things through God's eyes. What lens does God put on? Of course, you know what the Bible says. We're to put on a lens of love, and we're to reflect God in all things. Because our salvation is assured, we should put on a lens of gratitude, gratefulness, and joy, and we should rejoice because God says so. If we look at everything through that lens, how would our lives change? Try to think of one specific way your family or career might be impacted if you were to express gratitude, gratefulness, and joy.

How would Jesus look at the world? We know that Jesus looks at the world with mercy, grace, and compassion, which are unending. Ephesians 3:17–18 puts it this way: "...And I pray that you, rooted and established in love, may have power, together with all the saints, to grasp how wide and long and high and deep is the love of Christ..."

This side of heaven, I doubt we can truly grasp just how vast the love of Christ is. It's like trying to explain to my younger two kids, when they were three and five, that their mother and I were planning for their future. To kids that age, the future means the next snack time; but at our ages, it means so much more. They have no idea that we contribute to the Florida prepaid college program and that we've set up a savings account for them. They have no idea how much we bless them and put aside for them so that they'll have the benefit of it later. God laid on my heart that He does the exact same thing for you and me. It even says so in 1 Corinthians 2:9: "No eye has seen, no ear has heard, no mind has conceived what God has prepared for those who love Him."

We can't fully grasp the extent of God's love for us, but we can trust that it's real, and it's big. We can trust that when we become one of His kids, we have access to all that plus His power for living our lives, which includes the power to obey His instructions for how we should live.

I spent the first 33 years of my life on a downhill run ending in the gutter. God can show up there too. That's when I finally said, "OK, God, your way has to be better than mine, no matter what your way includes." I made that choice, and 20 years later I've never looked back. I believe we all have two choices every morning when we wake up, I mean it. It's a choice I am free to make, a choice either to complain about the circumstances that are or to appreciate what I have, even when that is just the clothes I wear. It applies to you as well. It's just that simple. You can choose to complain about the circumstances that are, or you can choose to appreciate what you have. God lets you choose. "Then choose for yourselves this day whom you will serve..." (Joshua 224:15).

I've chosen every morning to appreciate the gifts and blessings God gives me. They are not necessarily possessions or worldly wealth. Often, it is knowing that I have God himself. Listen to what Psalm 46 says, "God is our refuge and strength, an ever-present help in trouble. Therefore we will not fear, though the earth give way and the mountains fall into the heart of the sea...'Be still, and know that I am God; I will be exalted among the nations, I will be exalted in the earth.' The Lord Almighty is with us; the God of Jacob is our fortress."

Do you hear? God tells you, "I'm your refuge. I'm your strength. You don't have to fear. Be still; calm down; quit worrying." Life's short, and God is in control. Either we can complain about our lives, or we can be blessed by living our lives in obeying God's Word.

That sounds good, but I also understand that there are two ways to look at everything. If you've ever coached a football or baseball team or played on one, you certainly know that the coach and the players have two different views. Or how about an employee or employer? I've been on both sides of that one, and I can tell you that you definitely view the same thing differently, depending on which camp you're in.

As an employee, the person doing the work, I have certain expectations of my employer. I expect my employer to pay me on Friday when he said he would pay me. I expect him to provide a workplace in which to accomplish my work. I expect that if I needed any specific training or skills, he would train me in those areas. I expect that I'd have at least semi-competent management in place to direct me as I go. I expect that if I needed certain tools to do the job, they would provide me those tools. I think those are reasonable expectations for an employee to have of an employer.

And what should the employer expect from the employee? As the guy signing your paycheck, I expect you to show up on time. I expect you to do the job we paid you to do. If I pay you to fill water glasses, you shouldn't be making copies of your football pool picks or favorite recipes on the copy machine. I expect to get an honest day's effort from you, and you should focus on the task and not be on your cell phone half the day with your girlfriend or boyfriend. I expect that if you needed to learn some additional skills while doing your job, you would do that. That sounds reasonable to me.

What happens if you're the employee, and you choose not to do what the employer wants? What happens if instead of filling the glasses of water, you decide to make personal copies? What happens if you don't feel like doing your assignment today? Yeah, I'm a Delta Airlines pilot, but I don't want to fly those jets today. Yeah, I'm a bank teller, but I don't feel like doing transactions today. You want me at work at 8:30? No, I think 10:30 is better. And I'll make as many personal calls as I want.

If that's what you expect as an employee, you should also expect that you wouldn't be working there very long. You would expect that quite soon the employer would tell you that you're off the team because you're not doing what the boss said to do. You are certainly free to make that choice, but your choice also includes the consequence. Choose this day whom you will serve, remember?

You can say, "Coach, I'm not going to practice when you want me to practice" and "Boss I'm not coming when you want me to work," and that means that you choose not to be part of that team or company anymore. And when that team celebrates the Super Bowl trophy or that company hands out bonuses, you're not part of it. You don't get to share in the glory or in the profit of it. Everybody else is happy and celebrating because they did what they should, and they get the reward and the blessing they deserve because they functioned as a unit. They were willing to do what the boss said to do because the boss said so, and it ultimately proved to be in their best interest.

God looks at us and says the same thing. "The body is a unit, though it is made up of many parts; and though all its parts are many, they form one body. So it is with Christ." (1 Corinthians 12:12). Yet we live our lives here on earth like selfish, spoiled employees or players who have no concern for our coworkers or teammates, but only for our own well-being, not realizing that individually, we cannot win.

Only by sacrificing ourselves for the team, by obeying our coach or boss, by taking action "because the boss says so," do we become winners. The same is true in our spiritual life. When we obey the Lord, we will experience the joy and victory of the Lord. How do we get there? Most of us need directions, and Psalm 51 will help point the way: "Restore to me the joy of your salvation and grant me a willing spirit, to sustain me...You do not delight in sacrifice, or I would bring it; you do not take pleasure in burnt offerings. The sacrifices of God are a broken spirit; a broken and contrite heart, These, O God, you will not despise" (Psalm 51:12, 16, 17).

"Sacrifices" implies a continual offering to God of a broken and contrite heart. Let's be clear about two things: having a broken and contrite heart does not mean existing in a state of despair and depression; it means being humble and repenting of our sins before God. The other thing is that we must stay humble and broken before the Lord because we continually sin. It's not about outward actions, bringing animal sacrifices and burnt offerings as they did in the Old Testament. Those were outward actions that did nothing to deal with matters of the heart. It's so easy for us to send flowers, candy, or jewelry that "says" we're sorry to someone while our heart is really screaming "It's still your fault, and I will rub your face in it as often as possible." It's about our attitude before God, and that's what this psalm gets at. Our attitude is visible, and it reveals the spiritual condition of our heart: obedient or not?

Nowhere is our attitude more evident than when God asks us to do something that seems, well, use any adjective you like: weird, illogical, improbable, stupid, silly, a waste of time, pointless. A great example of this is the fishing passage in Luke 5, starting with verse 1:

One day as Jesus was standing by the lake of Gennesaret, with the people crowding around Him and listening to the word of God, He saw at the water's edge two boats, left there by the fishermen, who were washing their nets. He got into one of the boats, the one belonging to Simon, and asked him to put out a little from shore. Then He sat down and taught the people from the boat. When He had finished speaking, He said to Simon, "Put out into the deep water, and let down the nets for a catch." Simon answered, "Master, we've worked hard all night and haven't caught anything. But because you say so, I will let down the nets."

Peter and the boys had been out fishing all night, and they caught nothing. They wasted the night, came up empty-handed, and they were heading home, ready for some rest. But there was Jesus, telling them to put the nets down again. Was He nuts? They were the professional fishermen, not Jesus. They probably thought, "What do you mean 'put the nets down again'? We were just out there, and there were no fish. Nada. Nothing. We tried everything." But they hadn't tried God's way.

Peter had a decision to make. Would he obey God? Peter made the right choice. He said, "Master, we've worked hard all night and haven't caught anything. But because you say so, I will let down the nets." Here's the passage according to Jack: "OK, we've busted our tails all day, used every sales pitch, every parenting trick, every counseling tool, and every (fill in the blank), and nothing has worked, but because I trust you, because you are the boss, I will do what you say." I will do it again, *your way*.

Sure enough, the story continues in Luke 5:6 where the Bible tells us, "When they had done so, they caught such a large number of fish that their nets began to break. So they signaled their partners in the other boat to come and help them, and they came and filled both boats so full that they began to sink. When Simon Peter saw this, he fell at Jesus' knees and said, 'Go away from me, Lord; I am a sinful man!' For he and all his companions were astonished at the catch of fish they had taken…"

They were astonished. Why? Because they were the experts, the supervisors, the business owners, the ones with the training and the experience that told them not to bother putting the nets out again because all their prior efforts had been in vain. Yet, when they chose to listen to Jesus and obey His instruction, God blessed them abundantly beyond belief. So, here's something for each of us to think about: What is happening in my life right now? Have I tried everything I know to do and nothing has worked? Is all my expertise, advice I've gotten from others, and the knowledge I've bought in self-help books and seminars useless? What does God's Word say about what's happening in my life right now? Have I obeyed His instruction, even if it seems illogical, pointless, or silly? What have we said to God?

Our answer to God, no matter what, needs to be, "But because you say so, I will obey." What have others said? We can look at some others in history who have said, "But because you say so" to the Lord. How about Noah? Imagine Noah getting instruction from God: "Go build an ark." Yeah, as in, "Hey, Noah, go be a laughing stock; let everybody think you are totally out of your mind." Put that into the twenty-first century... can you picture someone saying, "I quit everything. I will build a spaceship to go to the planet Pluto." Noah said to God, "Because you say so, Lord. I've heard you, and I don't care what the world thinks. I do what you say."

How about Joseph, sold into slavery by his brothers? He could have been the most bummed out, bitter man in history. He could have responded to his situation as the world does when a tragedy strikes, a baby dies, somebody gets sick or loses a job, or a relationship explodes—"Lord, you must not love me if you let this happen to me," or "There can't be a God. Who would allow this to happen?" That's what the world says, and sadly, it's what some Christians sometimes say. But God says, "No, I love you so much. I ask you to trust me in faith and obedience. I ask you to say, 'Because you say so, Lord,' and do as I say, so I can bless you." Despite injustice after injustice, Joseph followed God's way, and God blessed him beyond his wildest dreams. God used all the tragedy and trouble Joseph experienced, not just for Joseph's good, but also for the good of nations (did you catch the plural?). Thousands and thousands of lives were affected, including ours.

How about Job? He lost his health, friends, kids, livestock, and employees, and yet, he stayed faithful to God. Job didn't understand it, didn't like it, and it all upset him, but he said, "After my skin is destroyed this I know that in my flesh I shall see God. I know that You can do everything. No purpose of yours can be withheld" (Job 19:25–27). The Bible says, "The Lord blessed the latter part of Job's life more than the first" (Job 42:12) because no matter what happened, no matter how much worse things got, Job's response was to trust God.

What about the ultimate "Because you say so?"

Jesus is about to be crucified. He knows this is His purpose, His mission, the reason He left heaven and came to earth. He is to be crucified to pay the price for the sin of mankind, and yet, even He says His soul is overwhelmed with sorrow to the point of death (Matthew 26:38). Three times, He prays to His father, asking if it's possible for the cup to be taken from Him, but if not, "yet not as I will but as you will" (Matthew 26:39, 42, 44). He wanted any other way, but if no other way existed, then He wanted God's way and nothing less, and it cost Him dearly.

The ultimate "Because you say so" was done for your benefit and mine, not Jesus' benefit. "Not what I want, but what you want, Lord." Even death. It's not always about my benefit. The world benefited from Jesus' response, millions benefited from Joseph's response, and maybe someone you know, maybe even you, benefited from a similar response from a person you will never meet.

When God gives you a "Because I say so" moment in your life, what do you say? "Yet not my will, but yours be done?" Or do we make excuses like the people invited to the feast who then made excuses for not showing up in Luke 14:15–24, "I'm busy. I have to feed my animals." Another said, "I have to go look at this field I invested in." Others said, "My father died." "I recently got married." Of course, the parable tells us that those who made excuses were shut out of the feast because the doors were closed. They'd said they would be there (yes, I believe there is a God... yes, I believe Jesus was real) but they didn't take the step of claiming their seat at the banquet (I'll get around to the Christianity thing some day... what's the hurry?), and they lost out.

Don't get shut out of the blessings God has in store for you. Obey, because God says so. Accept responsibility for what you do and for what God says. Live according to God's Word. Look at what Romans 13:11 says "And do this, understanding the present time. The hour has come for you to wake up from your slumber, because our salvation is nearer now than when we first believed".

God is saying, "Wake up. It's getting closer and closer to the end, and you need to pay attention to what you do." Why? Because God says so. Because "Just as man is destined to die once, and after that to face judgment, so Christ was sacrificed once to take away the sins of many people; and He will appear a second time, not to bear sin, but to bring salvation to those who are waiting for Him" (Hebrews 9:27–28). You die once, and that's it. There is no second chance. If you're still alive when Jesus returns, note that verse we just looked at. He does not offer salvation the second time around; He's coming back to gather up those who have already said yes to Him. If that doesn't include you, say hello to hell.

God is saying, "Wake up. Judgment is coming. Make your decision for Christ, and live for Him." It's not such a difficult choice. If there were a fire in your house, you'd want me to wake you up. You'd want me to make sure you didn't go back to sleep, but that you got up and took action that would save your life. You'd be happy, and you'd thank me for waking you up.

God nudges you right now as you read this. He says, "Wake up, take action, because I said so, because I know what's coming, and I know what's in your best interest. If you are part of my family, you have what you need to do what I say. Son, daughter, you have what it takes."

God made an incredible sacrifice on our behalf. He gave His son's life on the cross so that you and I could become His sons and daughters. Why? Because He loves us that much. And when someone loves you that much, doesn't it make you want to do your best for that person? Doesn't it inspire you to make a sacrifice in return?

Making sacrifices reminds me of a specific incident in 2007 with my oldest son, Ricky. We were driving to a concert, and I asked, "Son, how's it going at college?"

"Good, but I'm going to drop one of my classes."

"No problem," I said. "You have to replace it with another one."

"No, I'll just take some classes over the summer. Lots of people do that. Nobody graduates in four years anymore."

I looked at him in disbelief. Honestly, I had to let this go for a couple of days so I could cool off, but here's the bottom line—he had no clue of what it costs us to send him to college, no clue of the sacrifice his mother and I have made and how much more it would cost us to pay for his housing and food for another summer and extra year. We didn't plan for that. We planned for four years. And if he really knew the value of what it cost, he would never talk like that. In fact, he would work harder to finish on time or sooner because he would appreciate the sacrifice his parents made for him. He would finish on time or sooner "because Dad said so," because that's what Dad said the finances had figured on.

God laid on my heart that we sometimes do that same thing with Jesus. We take for granted the value of Jesus' sacrifice on the cross. He paid a price for us that we could not pay ourselves. He paid the "tuition," so we could be admitted to heaven. And what do we do? We live as if what He did had no value; we do what we want; we act as if there's plenty of time; and we act just like everybody else in the world.

God says, "No, I paid a price for you so that you would glorify me by how you live." Do you live that way right now? Or do you live your own way at the skate park, at home, at school, or at work? It really doesn't matter where you are. You'll have what it takes to handle the half-pipes and any other surprises or challenges that come your way in life... because you have God.

How do I know? How can you be sure? Because God said so.

7

Pain, Pain, Go Away

My sciatica was killing me. And I was grateful. It was early in 2001, my family and I were being attacked spiritually in several areas, and physically, I was in serious, life-altering pain. All of those challenges combined almost succeeded at taking our focus off what we believe God called us to do. It took a little while to realize that this was Satan trying to discourage us and get us off track any way he could, but once we realized that, my wife and I came together stronger than ever. We turned everything over to God and laid our problems at his feet. Yet this pain had dragged on nearly three months and wasn't getting better. What got better was my attitude. For the most part, I can usually say, "Lord, I'm yours, do with me what you like. Of course, I would like not to be in pain, but I'm yours regardless, and we are going forward."

Years ago—many years ago, fortunately—when I went through drug rehab, the counselor looked me in the eye and said, "Jack, your problem is that you have a lack of gratitude. That's a major problem with all drug addicts and alcoholics. They're just not grateful for what they have in life." He was right. I was raised in a loving, committed family. I had a great childhood, received a college education, and yet, I didn't truly appreciate or value the life I was given.

God says the same thing to you and me. Are you grateful for all God has done for you? You have a loving God who is completely committed to your best interests. He has adopted you into His family and made you an heir with Jesus. Yet, do you realize what He has done for you? If you don't, you can never get to the level of gratitude that will change your attitude and your life.

Recovering from drug addiction or alcoholism is easier when you are grateful for the life you were given. God tells us to be grateful and thankful always. In Colossians 2:6–7, it says, "So then, just as you received Christ Jesus as Lord, continue to live in Him, rooted and built up in Him, strengthened in the faith as you were taught, and overflowing with thankfulness." Do you get up every morning and overflow with thankfulness? It's not a natural inclination. The natural inclination is to grumble, huff, and complain about things because that is our habit. What would happen if instead of stumbling, mumbling, and grumbling into our day, we chose to develop a new habit of thankfulness? It's not that hard to do, really. Give thanks for a bed to sleep in, a roof, indoor plumbing, hot water and soap, electricity for air conditioning or heat, for coffee or tea or breakfast. The list is endless if we choose consciously to see everything we have and express gratitude for it all.

Gratitude will change your attitude, and attitude will change your actions. Instead of road rage and horn honking, maybe you're the one who yields to another driver or buys a cup of coffee for the guy in the car behind you at the drive-through window.

What else does Scripture say about gratitude and thankfulness? In 1 Thessalonians 5:16–18, we are instructed to "Be joyful always; pray continually; give thanks in all circumstances, for this is God's will for you in Christ Jesus." Not some circumstances, not a few, not when you feel like it, but in *all* circumstances, we are to be thankful and joyful—even when I'm flat on my back in agony.

The normal reaction anyone would expect me to have is to become aggravated and irritable, which then makes me aggravating and irritating to other people. But why shouldn't I be that way? I was in severe and constant pain.

Here's what I was thinking back then.

I already had one back surgery in 1987 and now it was 14 years later and I was getting slammed again with back pain. So severe, it was to the point where I could see how people who live with chronic pain would think about committing suicide. I understand that if there were no way out, if you believed that you would have to live this way every day for the rest of your life, there might be a day when you might say it just hurts too much, take me out. I can see someone reaching that point. By God's grace, I have never had that thought. By God's grace, I had gratitude for whatever life dealt me. Obviously, I wanted the sciatica pain to pass, but I was at peace with whatever happened because God laid on my heart that I need to follow his instructions clearly. The instruction I learned about the most is giving thanks in all circumstances.

The first thing I learned is that it's all about focus. Focusing on what we don't have brings misery. Focusing on what we do have, on the blessings we've received, brings joy. Since I used to have a television production company, I tend to think in terms of filming. It's your life; it's your film; and it's your camera. What will you focus it on? What will you take pictures of in your life—the things that stink or the joy and the blessings?

Jesus speaks to that question of focus in Luke 21:34. He says, "Be careful, [when God tells you to be careful, that's a good way to know He wants your attention] or your hearts will be weighed down with dissipation, drunkenness and the anxieties of life, and that day will close on you unexpectedly like a trap." Some translations use the word *surfeiting* instead of *dissipation*. I looked them both up, and they both carry the meaning of excessive indulgence of meat and especially drink. In this passage, the Greek word includes the idea of having a hangover headache along with the mental confusion that accompanies too much alcohol and the consequences of actions taken while under the influence. In our day, we can include drugs in the mix as well.

I can speak to that, given my lifestyle of dissipation before I became a Christian, and even, for a time, after becoming a believer, but not committing my total heart to God. Maybe booze or drugs don't apply to you, but everyone has had to deal with the anxieties of life, and I've seen those do much more damage to many more people than alcohol or drugs.

The obvious "life" anxiety I dealt with then is chronic pain. I really believe that God used this as a lesson to teach me about focus.

It's hard not to focus on the pain, but I think God showed me that doing so is like focusing on my past, which I am so tempted to do when the going gets tough. I thought about the pain and how it limits me, and I get into a thought cycle that occupies every waking moment—the pain limits my activity, so I think about all that I can't do, which gets me upset or angry, and those feelings feed the thoughts about the pain. That cycle of thinking, of focusing, keeps me from doing anything else.

I believe that God shows me how I've done the same with other areas of my life by dwelling on my past. If I focus on the past, I get caught up in regret or a sense of what I've lost, wasted or failed at, and it keeps me from moving forward in His power. If I stay in that thought cycle, I miss what God has for me in the present, which affects my future. Concentrating on the pain makes it impossible to give thanks or cultivate a grateful attitude for what I still have. I end up looking at what I don't have, which is the freedom to get out of bed and do something as simple as get dressed or toss the ball with my young son, instead of looking at what I do have, which includes many blessings and hope.

Jesus even warned against focusing on the past. In Luke 9:62, He says, "No one who puts his hand to the plow and looks back is fit for service in the kingdom of God." If you look back, you can't move forward toward the kingdom of God, can you?

God did not say I will have pain the rest of my life as punishment. What He teaches me is that focusing on what I think I lack prevents me from being grateful, prevents me from enjoying and appreciating what I do have, and prevents me from being useful to Him. Not fulfilling God's calling in your life is like that. It is no fun; it stinks; and I don't want to live my life that way. So, if my sciatica is a tool in God's hand to kill that part of me that holds me back from His best, then thank you, Lord.

I'm learning. I'm saying, "Thank you, Lord, for teaching me in order for you to use me the way I have asked you to use me and the way I know you want to use me." I'm learning that I have to focus 100 percent on the task I'm given, and for now, each morning, the first task is to be thankful. It's one day, one morning at a time, waking up and thanking God again so that I'm ready for the next thing He has for me to do, so that I'm ready for Judgment Day because I don't know when it will come. I'm grateful that God has taken me to this spot, so I can learn not to allow my heart to be weighed down with anything that would hinder my being close to Him, as Jesus warned in Luke 21:34.

I urge you to do likewise. Begin by giving thanks for what you do have and by being aware of what you focus on. If we don't pay attention, if we focus on the wrong things because we're in a wrong state of mind (whether from overindulgence or from the anxieties of life), Jesus says our hearts will be in the wrong place, and we will miss the opportunity we have to be ready when the Day of Judgment comes. I want my time and life spent living for God to celebrate and reflect the gratitude and love I have for God. I hope others can see how I showed it on earth and how it influenced others, as opposed to living my time on earth replaying a pity party for myself and seeing how it drove others away from Christ.

Then, finally, I started to get some relief from the pain. I felt much better; the severe pain was gone; and I was so grateful. I kept thanking and praising God. Sometimes, you have to lose what you have before you realize how much you have and how much you take for granted (like that Jimmy Stewart movie *It's a Wonderful Life*). When I was in pain, laying in that bed for weeks, basically crippled, only one thing mattered to me; and it really aggravated me. I wanted to get out of bed and have a baseball catch with my son, Jackson, who was two and a half years old at the time. The thought of not being able to do that was the worst. I remember thinking, man, if I can just get out of bed and play baseball with Jackson, I'll never complain about anything. I felt so stupid for being caught up in the world previously, and I prayed that God would change my heart and let me love people unconditionally, as he does. Of course, I got a little better, got out of bed, played some ball with Jackson, and then my mind and my heart made a beeline for the usual concerns of life. I caught myself complaining about something like the weather or the interruption of the cable TV show.

You know what? When you lie in bed in pain, and you are unsure if or when it will end, you realize that one day, life will be over, and you would be smart to enjoy what you have. So, here is what happened to me. I called out to God when I had this crippling pain because I needed Him, and God responded to my spirit, "Jack, why have you strayed so far from me?"

I thought, wait a minute. I didn't stray far from you, God. How far can I go, Lord, when I'm stuck in bed? At least I still go to church, and I read my Bible.

God said it again. "Why did you stray so far from me?"

He made me realize that I needed to repent, not for any specific deed, but just for looking again at the world and not focusing 100 percent on Him. God treats us all individually, but when He tells you to do something, you have to do it. Pastors often preach about meeting God at the place you left Him or last disobeyed Him; for me, I have a specific call that I have to follow, just as you have a specific thing in your life which you have to respond to God about.

That night, I sat there in bed, thought about the example in Luke 18 of the Pharisee who prayed at the temple, and bragged, "Hey, God, I'm great! I give 10 percent of everything, and I am not like these other bad guys." There was a tax collector nearby, also praying, who beat himself on the chest and couldn't even speak. Jesus said that the tax collector had repented, and the Pharisee hadn't. This might sound strange, but I just sat there and started pounding on my chest that night, not enough to hurt myself, but that was all I could do. There were no words to say to God except "I'm sorry, help me."

How does God respond to that? Well, I'm a father. When I hear my young son Jackson calling "Daddy, Daddy," I know he wants me to come and get him. That night, after I beat myself on my chest, I thought, "Daddy, Daddy"... It wasn't for my earthly father; it was for God, the God who I know loves me as I love my son and more. And just as I hear my son's voice calling out to me, and I can't wait to get there and pick him up because I love him so much, I want my heavenly father, my God, to pick me up and hold me, and He did. When I'm in pain, when I suffer, I know I can call to Him, and He will be there. I don't ever have to doubt that.

In Luke 24:38, Jesus asks, "Why are you troubled, and why do doubts rise in your minds?" We should have no doubt and no trouble in our minds about anything. How many signs do we need from God? How many times has He shown up in your life? How many times have you prayed and felt His Spirit? I understand that the flesh, our human nature, wins once in a while, but as we grow in our relationship to God, those times of doubt should become fewer and fewer, and we should find ourselves not doubting God.

What can trip us up, though, is not just our own human nature, but also the doubts other people sprinkle into our lives, people who won't understand or flat out reject our efforts to focus on God. They might do things that will undermine our faith. It's nothing new, according to 2 Peter 3:4, "They will say, 'Where is this "coming" He promised? Ever since our fathers died, everything goes on as it has since the beginning of creation.'"

Satan started it in the Garden of Eden and carried on his tradition of distorting the Word of God as he tried to tempt Jesus in the desert and distract Him from focusing on His mission. Jesus stood fast because He knew the Word of God and could catch Satan in his tricks. If we are serious about our faith, we should also know the Word and be able to tell when someone distorts it. If we don't, we will easily be swayed and distracted.

Another way we lose our focus is that we forget to live in the present. Why do you think it's called **the present**? I like to think of living in the present as a gift to open and enjoy. I can't do a thing about what's past, and I'm not in charge of the future. In Luke 12:22–34, it teaches us, "Don't worry. We have nothing to worry about. God will take care of us, He has prepared a place for us and He is with us every step of the way."

So, think about it. The future is in God's hands. We know, as believers, that God has a perfect plan for our life, and He had it before the beginning of the earth. We know that our names are written in the Book of Life, and indeed, a place is prepared for us in heaven. That's the future, so we shouldn't worry about it.

How about the past? Gone. I can't un-spill that puddle of milk on the floor no matter how much I want to. I could spend my whole life crying that I spilled the milk and praying that I didn't spill it, but I did, and there is nothing in the world I can do to change what happened. (Bruce Springsteen says it well in one of his songs, "We cannot undo these things we've done.") Now, substitute something from your past, something you regret and wish you could change. Divorce? Drunk-driving accident? Financial failure, be it from stupidity, lack of knowledge, or greed? What about all our past sins, all that guilt we carry around in our emotional baggage? What about those things other people have said about us that still drive our choices or beliefs about ourselves? What about all our failures and the times we let down the people we love or the times we did the wrong thing? If you believe in Jesus Christ, God says all that is forgiven, forgotten, and cast aside "As far as the east is from the west, so far has He removed our transgressions from us" (Psalm 103:12).

The past is gone. Will I be so stupid as to carry something around with me that God has already forgiven? Why? God does not want that—but our enemy, Satan, does. If Satan can distract you from focusing on God, he'll condemn you with what you have done wrong and keep you in the hand-wringing, self-pitying mode. God, on the other hand, tells us that, as believers, if we do something wrong today, He will still love us. How is that? "If we confess our sins, He is faithful and just and will forgive us our sins and purify us from all unrighteousness" (1 John 1:9).

We can't control the future because God does. The past is gone, and we can't relive it, even if we want to. All we have is this present, this gift from God, to enjoy one day at a time. Life is a gift from God. Don't start wondering about how much time you have left or else you'll miss the show! I love to go to Bruce Springsteen concerts, but I don't go into the show and think, "I wonder how long he'll play..." or "oh crap, he's playing my favorite song now, but it will end soon and then there won't be any more music." What would be the point of focusing on such thoughts? I can't control how long he plays. I am at the concert simply to enjoy each song he plays for as long as he plays it. And that's it!

If I take an airplane flight, I can sit there and worry about what the pilot does or when I will get there. But if I do that, I steal the joy of the moment worrying over something I can't control. I don't fly the plane; the pilot does. It is his job to worry about it. My job is to sit back and relax.

Well, God is our pilot (not our co-pilot, by the way). He's in command. We have our own work to do, whatever He's called us to do, but God is in charge of the flight. He's the pilot. It's the same with our lives. God created us to worship Him and to bear fruit that would last. He has already ordained and predestined what we are to do. It is our job just to be obedient and enjoy the ride. Did you know that you are allowed to enjoy the ride? Even when the ride gets bumpy, scary, and hard, even when the ride puts me flat on my back in pain, I can choose to shift my focus off what I think I don't have and develop the gratitude attitude by staying focused on God. I can give thanks *in* (not *for*) all circumstances because I know God has planned my future. When I rest in that, I can enjoy the present more than I ever believed possible.

Paul said in Ephesians 3:20 that God is "...able to do immeasurably more than all we ask or imagine, according to His power that is at work within us." Every Christian believer should be able to rest in complete confidence and assurance in the Lord. His rest is where you find joy and peace, peace that surpasses all understanding (Philippians 4:7). If you don't have that, then your life is nothing but a series of diversions you create to try to pass time, to occupy our mind, so you don't have to think about why you aren't happy. Many people live that way because they are captive to pain that is not easily escaped. The pain might be emotional, psychological, spiritual, or physical.

The only true escape from any kind of pain is with God. In 2 Peter 2:19–20, Paul describes the human condition without God as being captive, or enslaved, to whatever has mastered you. What has mastered you or enslaved you? What is in your life that you feel you can never escape, that has you trapped? The list is familiar: drugs, sex, food, money, alcohol, status, anger, power... whatever yours is, it's a private issue between you and God, whether you acknowledge it to Him or not. He already knows about it, and He promises you freedom from those things; but to experience that promise, God needs to be the first priority in your life.

It doesn't mean you will be called into ministry. Trust me, you'll know when that call comes, and you'll know if it comes, but that doesn't mean you should be idle. No, wherever God has put you, do what God has you do right there. Start by worshiping God and bearing fruit that will last.

How do we bear fruit that will last? We spread the Word; we plant seeds; we harvest; we tell people why we're so happy and joyful in the midst of, and especially in spite, of our circumstances. How can we do any of that if we are miserable and aggravated like so much of the rest of the world? If that describes us, why would anyone want to be like us? Our grateful attitude should cause others to stop us and say, "Excuse me, but why are you so happy? How come you weren't offended by that, how come you're not upset, or why are you so calm when everybody else is screaming his head off?" Then, we can tell them it's because we have the peace our Lord and Savior Jesus Christ promised.

An interesting side effect of behaving that way, of bearing fruit and living in the peace that comes from Christ, is that it changes how we look at others. And that's a good thing. Romans 2:1 says, "You, therefore, have no excuse, you who pass judgment on someone else, for at whatever point you judge the other, you are condemning yourself, because you who pass judgment do the same things." I've had to ask God to forgive me for looking at the speck in my brother's eye while ignoring the plank in my own (Matthew 7:5). Why do I bother with such confessions when maybe no one else even knows what I thought? Because I want to know God better, which comes from obedience. In 1 John 2:3–6, we are told, "We know that we have come to know Him if we obey His commands. The man who says, 'I know Him,' but does not do what He commands is a liar and the truth is not in him. But if anybody obeys His Word, God's love is truly made complete in Him. This is how we know we are in Him: whoever claims to live in Him must walk as Jesus did."

So, if we want to really know God, obedience is not a negotiable issue, it's a prerequisite to being a disciple. Furthermore, God says that if we don't obey Him, then His love won't be made complete in us. Sciatica or not, I am at the stage in my life where the only thing I want is for God's love to be made complete in me. That is the only thing that makes me happy. That is what lets me enjoy my family so much. That is what lets me enjoy life so much and appreciate my friends and the ability to get up in the morning and be alive, especially since the sciatica flared up. If I used the pain as an excuse to stop obeying, I would be ashamed to face Him when my time comes. 1 John 2:28 says, "And now, dear children, continue in Him, so that when He appears we may be confident and unashamed before Him at His coming."

I don't want to be ashamed when God comes; do you? We can't take the attitude of "I'll get to it later, I still have time," or "When I reach this goal, I'll do that." We don't know when He is coming back, when we will be taken out, and we have to stand before Him. When that day comes, I want to experience the feeling Jude had (Jude 24–25). It says, *"To Him who is able to keep you from falling and to present you before His glorious presence without fault and with great joy*—to the only God our Savior be glory, majesty, power and authority, through Jesus Christ our Lord, before all ages, now and forevermore! Amen."

Notice Jude's first reference to God is that without God, we would all fall. With God, we don't have to fall, which is a good reason to live a life with gratitude.

Do you also see how Jesus presents us to God without fault? There's another reason to shift your focus to gratitude. I can barely imagine Jesus presenting me to His father as faultless because I know myself. I know that in this earthly existence, I have to fight against faults, sins, and weaknesses every day, so when the Bible says I'll be presented as faultless, hey, I am grateful.

Is that the only place the Bible promises that? No. In Ephesians 1:3–5, God says He holds us holy, blameless, and above reproach. Another version says "holy in His Spirit, without blemish and above reproach." If God, our heavenly father, Daddy, creator looks at us that way, we should put all our focus on that and live a life of gratitude! Why would we not excitedly live up to that description given to us by God himself?

Do it wherever God calls you, whether you are parking cars for a living, you are the president of Coca Cola, or you are flat on your back, wondering when the pain will lighten up enough to let you go play catch with your kid.

As for me, I give thanks to God out of a grateful heart, because through this pain, He teaches me to keep my focus on Him and all that He has done and will do in my life. My sciatica was killing me, but it made me focus on the sin in my life which needed to be dealt with, right then and there, and for that I'm grateful. Are you experiencing any pain today (physical or emotional), if so could God be showing you there is something He wants you to deal with in your life today? Are you grateful? Will you deal with it?

Photo Section

PICTURES FROM THE PAST

George and Alana Hamilton: The tannest couple in Hollywood, if not the entire world. Here we are discussing possible TV opportunities for both of them. I only wanted to work with him to get his tanning secrets.

Suzanne Somers: A truly great person, very sweet and professional. She went from a career in comedy to becoming queen of the infomercials in the 90's. She was one of the first celebrities to "cross over" to infomercials with great success. I'm smiling because I've got my arm around her and she's smiling because she always smiles!

Pamela Anderson: At one time, the hottest woman in America. Known for her wild rock and roll boyfriends, it was for me the modern day equivalent of meeting Raquel Welch in her prime. Pam was wonderfully kind. We never dated, only because she never did ask me out. I assume because, I didn't have the rock and roll bad boy look she was attracted to.

Barbara Walters: Literally the queen of broadcast news reporting. Perhaps one of the most respected TV reporters of our time, known for her great interview scoops. Here I am with my wife Beth and Barbara. I know she was trying to get Beth to "spill her guts" about me, so I got us away from there as quickly as possible!

Brandy Ledford: Blonde at that time and a star on the TV series "Baywatch." In this picture, she was just days away from being named Playboy Playmate of the year. Hey what can I say, I had an eye for talent. Like most young woman who start out in the business, she was genuinely sweet and seemed very naïve (That's probably how most of them get there in the first place). However years later, Brandy's infamous sex tape with Rocker Vince Neil had become an internet classic. Just for the record, I have never seen it.

Marshall Faulk: One of the greatest NFL running backs of all time. Always smiling and happy, but a fierce warrior on the field. I asked him for some tips on how to be a great running back so I could pursue a flag football career. He gave me great advice... "Stay away from the tacklers!" Upon second thought, maybe I'll just sponsor a flag football team!

Louie Anderson: Great comic who has a heart as big as his body. Understated and overshadowed by some of the great comics of the time, Richard Pryor, Robin Williams, Billy Crystal, John Belushi, John Candy, but nonetheless a GIANT among his peers. Hilariously funny, made me laugh so hard I thought my insides were going to burst out. Here we are in Vegas together where I gave him some of my best jokes and told him he could use them whenever he wanted...I never saw him laugh so hard.

Montel Williams: Here I am with Montel before he became famous, this was when he was looking for his break to get national TV exposure. We talked about him hosting an infomercial for us, but before we could get it going his career really took off. I was very happy for him, he worked hard and earned everything he got. 17 years and 3000 talk shows later Montel finally saw the infomercial light and did one in 2009. I was right, I knew talent when I saw it!

Jerry Springer: I told Jerry, "You are way to average looking, there is nothing unique about you. You need a point of difference if you want to be a success." I didn't realize he would go crazy with his guests and start a talk show circus, but it worked. He was different and successful!

Kevin Nealon: Just in from taping Saturday Night Live, Kevin is a comic genius, a TV and movie star. He's just plain funny and very likeable. I tried to make fun of him and make him laugh, but I just kept cracking myself up. He told me there is definitely a difference between "comic genius" and being an idiot...but he encouraged me to keep practicing.

Oscar De La Hoya: A true boxing champion and a great marquee figure. He has reigned on top of boxing for over 20 years. Every one loves him and he is a great guy. There was golfing by day and gambling and partying by night. At the end of the night he went the distance and I was out for the count by midnight! That's why he's champ.

Mario Lemieux: Could easily be the greatest hockey player of all time. A true champion in sports and for charity causes. His Mario Lemieux Foundation supports cancer and neonatal research. Nobody has a bad word to say about him. Here I am telling him I respected him, but I was better on the "ice" than he was...he just looked at me quizzically. So I pulled out a bottle of bourbon and started to pour it over ice...Hey, back then I thought those things were important. Thank God my values and my life have changed. Mario...true gentleman that he was didn't punch my lights out.

Daniel Baldwin: Probably the least famous of the Baldwin brothers (Alec, William and Stephen), but a very sweet guy. Major drug issues in his life, but a talented TV and movie actor. Hopefully after his many bouts with drug abuse and addiction he is on the right path. As always, I suggested to him that path is Jesus.

Emmitt Smith: NFL Pro Football Hall of Fame running back, possibly the greatest ever. A sweetheart of a man, we enjoyed some time with him in Lake Tahoe. We were playing blackjack at the casino, but he was playing for $10,000 a hand and I was playing for $25.00 a hand. It made me wonder if I chose the wrong career or was just a bad gambler.

Carlton Fisk: I remember when I was a kid hanging out at Yankee Stadium and "Pudge" was a rookie with the Red Sox. He was such a great guy signing autographs and taking time to talk to and encourage us young kids, even though we were Yankee fans. Now that's a true American Hero for you. By the way, notice my T-shirt in this picture, hey, what can I say...it's true!!

Aaron Spelling: A television genius and legend, even at this old age he had a kind word and advice for a rising young hot shot like me. Aaron has since passed away but his advice to "think out of the box" and to "create new stuff and be different"... has stuck with me until this day. You need to be original...in television and in life. No one likes an imitator (at least not for more then one night).

Mike Schmidt: Hall of Fame baseball player, hit over 500 home runs, a true talent on the field. Mike and I were never that close, maybe he thought he was better then me with all those home runs! Anyway, my home runs now come for Jesus and I couldn't be happier.

Danny Ainge: I remember this animated conversation with Danny. I questioned his sanity for quitting pro baseball to play pro basketball, and he questioned mine for claiming Jesus Christ was God's only Son and the only way to heaven. At the end of our conversation Danny was

still a Mormon and I was still a born again Christian. I'm still praying for Danny...I hope he's returning the favor (he seemed pretty mad).

Bruce Jenner: The original Olympic Hero of my generation. 1976 Olympic Gold Medal Decathlon champion. Even more amazing was that Bruce got his picture on a box of Wheaties cereal. So he accomplished two things I really wanted to do. So, what happened to me? I eat Wheaties with my own picture pasted to the box. Hey, who says dreams can't come true. Bruce went on to do some successful TV acting and motivational speaking. As for me, well you know the story.

Ted Danson: TV Star of one of the most popular sitcoms ever, "Cheers." Ted also did many other sitcoms and movies. A great guy; even though he appeared in many comedies he was a serious man. Well known in my day for his romance with black actress Whoopi Goldberg, and the famous incident at her Friar's Club roast (look it up if you dare or care).

Judge Judy Sheindlin: Here are my wife Beth and I with TV's famous Judge Judy. She invited me on to her show as a guest judge, but I told her I thought all criminals were guilty and deserved to die. She knew I was just kidding so she just looked at me and laughed. I wasn't even going to get into the Bible issue "judge not lest you be judged." Somehow I think she would have stopped laughing then. Anyway, a good time was had by all.

Spencer Christian: Long time ABC weatherman and wine connoisseur, Spencer was one of the hosts for a series of holiday specials I wrote and produced in 1992. Now those were some fun times. We had Rip Taylor, Dr. Joyce Brothers, Peabo Bryson, Chakka Khan. Also part of the cast was Eva Larue and John O'Hurley (JPeterman on Seinfeld) who met on our show and would later marry each other. Who knew I was also a matchmaker. Other celebrities were on our shows, but it was the cast dinners every night for a week straight that I remember the most...Spencer really knew his wine!!

Robin Williams: Here are my wife Beth and I with the funniest man alive, Robin Williams. I have long been trying to convince my wife that I am the funniest man alive, and I constantly tell her jokes and make clever comments and observations to prove it. Only, she doesn't yet quite grasp the full value of my comic genius, but she loves me anyway. Well, I got Robin to admit I was funnier then him, and Beth heard it loud and clear. (Ask her, she will tell you it's true!) Except, I think Robin was just being funny!

Darryl "D.M.C" McDaniels: One of the originators of Hip Hop music. His group, Run- D.M.C. are hip hop legends. Darryl told me his wealth and fame from his success in music were never enough to make him truly happy. He grew depressed and contemplated suicide. He has since come to love and appreciate life. He wrote his life story as a way to motivate and encourage others who were suffering from the same feelings, so they wouldn't give in, wouldn't quit, and would come back and find meaning in a life of helping others. His story is a true inspiration to me and I love to watch him work with charitable youth organizations to give young underprivileged kids a chance at a better life.

Walter Case: A compelling "case" if there ever was one. Perhaps the greatest harness racing driver of all time, but overcome by personal issues and a battle with drugs and alcohol that got him divorced and in jail. You can see by his bloodshot eyes he was not in great shape that particular night. How about my shirt? Those were the days of sex, drugs, gambling and rock and roll, but I didn't have to advertise it so well! Anyway the shirt is long gone and I am still hoping Walter gets another chance at life and his driving career...he was the greatest!

John McEnroe: "Mac" still playing great tennis on the senior tour. Here I'd just told him he how great I thought Jimmy Connors was, and I think he lost his match that day and the food stunk at dinner... Lets just say he wasn't thrilled!

William Shatner: TV and Movie Star "Captain Kirk" is alive and well and negotiating deals on Priceline. I asked him if I could get a better deal on hotel rooms and he said something about beaming me up. Nonetheless, a pleasure to be around. Bill is still going strong at 79. Must be all that space travel.

Steve Garvey: Baseball great and hall of famer. Here he was in my office at my TV production company. We were using him to host a segment on one of our sports shows. At that time, he had gotten into a little trouble for "playing the field" on his wife. But nothing can take away from his accomplishments on the baseball field. Satan wants us to think our errors in life make us worthless, but we believers are to remember nothing can take away our accomplishments when we live a worthy life for the Lord. We are all in God's Hall of Fame, based on our  faith. Our names are written in the Lambs book of life and can never be blotted out. Unlike Pete Rose, Mark McGuire and Roger Maris, there are no asterisks in heaven next to our accomplishments...only the loving arms of God our Father, for all eternity!! Now look, you've got me preaching in the picture captions...how'd that happen?

Stephen J. Cannell: One of television's great creative minds, a man way ahead of his time. Created and produced some of the greatest police/crime television series ever (including The A-team, 21 Jump Street, The Rockford Files, Wiseguy, Adam 12, The Commish, and Renegade). Also, an accomplished author. He gave me great advice, "Just keep churning stuff out, something is bound to hit." Well, I did that and it worked!

Ivan Lendl: One of the greatest tennis champions ever and a fierce competitor. I think he was asking my advice on which racquet to buy at the Pro Shop we were in, but then again, maybe my hearing wasn't so good. He could've been telling me to stop making such a racket...Either way, he was always a good sport.

Johan Krieck: Another Tennis great from South Africa and by far one of the most likeable, personable guys in the sport. Here we are at dinner. I was quoting Bob Dylan, but Johan reminded me that it was Mats Wilander, not him, who was the big Dylan fan. At that point all I could say was, "All you tennis guys look the same to me."

Jack Wagner: TV star, soap opera idol and singer, Jack is also an excellent golfer. I told him I thought I was a better actor than him. After all, I once did a 4 minute "Odd Couple" skit in Church, where I played Oscar Madison. I'm willing to admit he's the better golfer, but I'm not giving an inch on the acting thing!

LOOK WHO'S GOT THEIR COPY OF
DON'T BLOW IT WITH GOD

Chris Hammond: My brother in Christ and a great man of God, here's Chris doing some on field promo for my first book *Don't Blow It With God*. These days, Chris spends his time in Alabama raising his four children with his wife, Lynn, and running the Chris Hammond Youth foundation, which builds and maintains athletic facilities for kids in Alabama and is dedicated to helping youth and underprivileged families. Chris always says his most important job is spreading the gospel of Jesus Christ to a lost world. He is a true champion for Christ.

Tony Dungy: Champion NFL head coach and an on fire Christian. He was kind enough to show off my book. I am honored. Tony is a great Christian role model and speaks at many Christian events. When he and Lovie Smith were opposing each other in the 2007 Super Bowl (Colts vs. Bears) and a reporter asked him how it felt to be part of history where for the first time ever two black men were head coaches of opposing Super Bowl teams, Tony said the important thing was not that they were two black men coaching but that they were two Christian men coaching! What a great witness for Jesus!

Seth Joyner: Super Bowl champion linebacker with the Denver Broncos also played for the Philadelphia Eagles. Here is Seth holding up one book I hope is on the top of his favorites list. I can't help you be a champion football player, but I can help you be a champion for Christ. I believe *Don't Blow It With God* accomplishes that for its readers and I pray this book you have in your hands *Where the Rubber Meets The Road With God* will take you and all believers deep into the end zone for Christ.

Bart Starr: I grew up a Green Bay Packer fan living in NY, thanks to a huge influence from my older brother, Mike, so I was always a Bart Starr fan. Now Bart has my book *Don't Blow It With God*. He knows a thing or two about championship behavior. He has been a champion on and off the field for Jesus. Almost 80 years old in this picture, Bart is still scoring touchdowns for Jesus as he encourages believers to win souls for Christ. A thrill to have my boyhood hero reading my book. Man, life is good!

Kurt Warner: Here pictured with his wife Brenda, both of whom are superstars for Christ. Kurt is a Super Bowl champion quarterback, but has long told all who will listen, fans and foe alike, that he plays for Jesus, and his purpose is to live for Jesus. Kurt and Brenda give a great testimony about marriage, life and God. Man, did they inspire me. I hope I returned the favor here. You can see Brenda with her copy of Don't Blow It With God... In true Christian spirit, she said she would share her copy with Kurt.

Anthony Munoz: NFL Pro Football Hall of Fame lineman and sports broadcaster, his hand is bigger than my body, but not too big to clutch on to the precious truths of Jesus Christ. A wonderful loving man with a great testimony for the Lord, God is using him mightily as he speaks to thousands of people annually about Jesus. His Anthony Munoz Charitable Foundation works to impact America's youth. He's got my book; I told him I would not be upset if he quoted me on national TV. He told me it depends on how much he liked the book.

Michael Vick: Tremendous natural talent, this superstar NFL quarterback spent 21 months in jail in 2007 for his role in a dog fighting ring that he financed. Michael went bankrupt in 2008. After finishing his time in jail, he is now making his comeback. I like Michael and in this picture he has my book in his hand, which if he follows it, I believe is the roadmap to the ultimate Christian life. So here's hoping Michael has learned his lesson and will continue to learn God's lessons and will for his life. I'm rooting for you Michael.

Mike Jarvis: Here's NCAA basketball coach, Mike Jarvis, getting his autographed copy of *Don't Blow it With God*. Mike loves the Lord and he is a great inspiration to his players, and has shared the gospel with so many of them. I heard him give the keynote speech at a Fellowship of Christian Athletes conference once and he knocked my socks off with his testimony of how when his life fell apart, when he got fired from his head coaching job at St John's and was under tremendous financial stress, he completely trusted God, as God taught him that his life was truly in God's hands. A man today who truly has the peace of God and has given me great encouragement.

Howard Schnellenberger: Here I am with two wonderful Christian brothers, Howard Schnellenberger, one of the greatest football coaches of all time, and Carl Foster, my friend and well known radio and TV personality. We were at an FCA charity event, a mission that is dear to all of our hearts. Coach is holding his copy of my first book *Don't Blow It With God*. If you want to know what he thinks of *this* book, *Where The Rubber Meets The Road with God*, go back to the beginning of this book to see his comments. Both of these guys, with their careers and their lives, are true men of God who get to

influence so many people with the powerful, amazing, life saving message of the good news of Jesus Christ. I hope and pray my life and my books can do the same.

GLORY DAYS

Bruce Springsteen: Here's Bruce clutching my buddy Andy Brief and I to make sure "we are alive." In his dressing room after another unbelievable show, I don't think you will ever see 3 happier people in the world. It's a simple theory... if Bruce is happy, everybody is happy. That's why he's The Boss.

Clarence Clemons: Me and the "Big Man" have a lot in common, I wrote a book, he wrote a book. I like Bruce Springsteen, he likes Bruce Springsteen...the connection is obvious! A great guy and a man with a heart as big as gold, his charitable efforts on behalf of underprivileged kids are as legendary in South Florida as his performances with Bruce and The E Street Band!

"Miami Steve" Van Zandt: Television star of the Soprano's TV series, a true rock and roll pioneer, a really big hearted man and a true champion of the underdog. A strong political activist fighting for human rights and dignity throughout the world and the producer of "Underground Garage," a radio show giving young up-and-coming rock and roll bands advice and an outlet to get their music heard. Of course, one of rock and roll's great guitar players, "Little Steven," as he's often known, has played with Bruce Springsteen and The E Street Band since the beginning!

Southside Johnny: Here are my family and me back in 2002, hanging out at Boomers, a video arcade and go cart track in Boca Raton, Florida with Southside Johnny. My son Jackson was a baby, and we had just signed Southside up to host our new music show called "In Tune." Unfortunately, we could not secure enough sponsorship to make the show go, but we had a great day of pinball and bumper cars with Southside. We got to hear some great rock and roll stories and some personal insight on life, justice and the American way from Southside while at NY Prime steakhouse for dinner. Love his music, and have been a fan since I was a kid. Southside never achieved the fame and fortune of his friend, Bruce Springsteen, but among true rock and rollers, his musical star shines just as brightly. His live shows are amazing and I still enjoy them any time I can.

"Mighty Max" Weinberg: A great drummer, late night leader of the "Tonite Show" band with Conan O'Brien for years and, of course, continues to play with Bruce Springsteen and the legendary, heart stompin', soul rockin', awe inspiring, mighty E-Street Band!

8

You Be the Judge

In 2004, I took a trip up to New Jersey. It was great! My cousin Cliff owned a football team in the then new National Indoor Football League. He said, "Jack, come on up; you'll be my guest at my skybox—free food and a great view." How cool is that? I invited a friend of mine who God has placed on my heart in a big way and who I've witnessed to for a year and a half. My friend is about 35 years old and Jewish, but he goes to church, he gets it, and he understands. God had brought him to his knees, but my friend had yet to pull the trigger and bring Jesus into his life.

So, I invited him to come up with me to New Jersey for the game. I figured God is in New Jersey, too, we can go to church up there, and maybe then, it'll happen—maybe then, he'll bring Jesus into his life. I always love to visit churches in any city I go to, anyway, and my friend agreed to go with me. We woke up Sunday morning before the game. I looked in the directory to find a church, and we drove about 20 minutes to this beautiful church with nice people. Pastor Tony got up, and I was psyched. I thought, this is it, man; this is a divine appointment. This has nothing to do with football; this is my buddy's time to get saved! This is his time. God will speak to him, and he will be saved this day. I'm sure this is a divine moment coming. I'm thinking, come on, Pastor Tony; give it to him, baby.

Sure enough, Pastor Tony starts talking, and absolutely there was a divine appointment that day. It was amazing; I was blown away, except for one problem. The divine appointment wasn't for my friend. The divine appointment was for me. God showed up big, and He had a great surprise in store, but little did I know that that surprise was for me.

Sometimes, we're so concerned about what we think others need to do or how they need to change, as I was with my friend, that we don't see some of the same things in our lives, some missing basics. So, this divine appointment was for me, to refine me, mold me, shape me, and bring me closer to being the man God intended me to be. I was falling short, and I needed to see it for myself with Pastor Tony's help.

So, we were looking in John 13:12–17, Jesus at the Last Supper. They finished with supper; He knew He was getting ready to go to the Crucifixion; and He called His disciples together and began to wash their feet. No, no, no, said Peter; don't wash my feet. But Jesus said no, Peter, you don't understand. I have to wash your feet. They had to be thinking, man, what is going on here? It doesn't sound so shocking to us, but in that day, it was the worst task in the house, and only a servant did it. You can just imagine the look on the disciples' faces when Jesus told them to go do the same.

"Hey, guys, it's me, God, the Lord, descended from heaven. I'm your God, and this is what I do for you. I give up my life; I sacrifice for you. I'll gladly wash your feet because I love you. Here is what I want you to do. I want you to go and do the same for others."

So, here's the question for me and for you : How many feet have we washed lately? I know we don't really wash each other's feet, but we should do it, figuratively. We should live our lives as a reflection of Jesus Christ, as ambassadors of God and as children of God, obeying our Father. We should be like Christ, going out there, doing for others, and putting others before ourselves. Pastor Tony went on to John 13:34, "A new command I give you: Love one another. As I have loved you, so you must love one another." Pastor Tony looked up from the Bible he was reading and asked me, "Are you living a life of sacrifice, a life of service to God?" Well, I knew he was speaking to everyone in the church that morning, but don't you sometimes feel as if your pastor looks right into your heart when he asks a question like that? I did not even think about my friend that point; all I thought was how I would answer that question.

But why should we live a life of sacrifice? When Jesus tells us to do something, it's always for our benefit. In John 15:10, He says, "If you obey my commands, you will remain in my love, just as I have obeyed my father's commands and remain in His love." The Message Bible translates it this way: "If you keep my commands, you'll remain intimately at home in my love. That's what I've done—kept my Father's commands and made myself at home in His love."

Well, does that mean that if I don't obey your commands, you won't make your home with me? That's exactly what it means! Could God be any clearer? He says that the intimacy, the closeness, the joy of this relationship will be affected if I don't obey his commands. This is not about salvation, that one-time, irrevocable act between God and us; salvation can never be taken away from you if you genuinely believe and accept Christ in your heart. The passage talks about the quality of the believer's relationship with God and the joy coming from that. Carrying on in verse 11, "I have told you this so that my joy may be in you and that your joy may be complete." Do you want God's complete joy? Do you want everything God has to offer? Obey Him. And a primary example He gave is to wash some feet. You need to do what Jesus did. Wash some feet. Show some love for others and to others. Do something they don't expect.

Pastor Tony went on to talk about love, and he said, "God is love, and we need to sacrifice ourselves because that is what love does. When you love somebody, you sacrifice for them, just as God sacrificed for us." How can we tell how we're doing with this whole 'love others' thing? Let's first look at what love is, and then we'll look at sacrifice. There's a well-known Scripture passage about love and recognizing it. You're, no doubt, familiar with 1 Corinthians 13:4–8: "Love is patient, love is kind. It does not envy, it does not boast, it is not proud. It is not rude, it is not self seeking, it is not easily angered, it keeps no record of wrongs. Love does not delight in evil but rejoices with the truth. It always protects, always trusts, always hopes, always perseveres. Love never fails..."

Do you want proof that God is love? If you have any doubt that God is love, then there's a simple way to settle it. Just substitute Jesus' name for love and see if it fits: Jesus is patient; Jesus is kind. Jesus does not envy; Jesus does not boast; Jesus is not proud. Jesus is not rude; Jesus is not self-seeking; Jesus is not easily angered; Jesus keeps no record of wrongs (Psalm 103:12 confirms this: "As far as the east is from the west, so far has He removed our transgressions from us"). Jesus does not delight in evil, but rejoices with the truth. Jesus always protects; Jesus always trusts; Jesus always hopes; Jesus always perseveres. Jesus never fails.

Wow! That sounds like Jesus to me. Who *wouldn't* want to know a guy like that?

I thought we were done, but Pastor Tony said, no, no, one more step. Now, substitute your name.

Well, now my man Tony's getting really personal. Was he staring straight at me when he said that? I thought other people were in the room, but at that moment, it felt as if I was the only one in the place. "Put your name in there." My name? Uh oh.

Jack is patient (sometimes); Jack is kind (when everybody watches, and it's convenient for him to be). Jack does not envy (can we please not talk about that one?); Jack does not boast (I give myself that one); Jack is not proud (hmm, not so sure). Jack is not rude (unless I'm driving on I-95 or—oh, never mind); Jack is not self-seeking (I wish I were the humble man I strive to be); Jack is not easily angered (some days); Jack keeps no record of wrongs (will Pastor Tony ever shut up?). Jack does not delight in evil, but rejoices with the truth (got that one, usually). Jack always protects (I try);

Jack always trusts (no); Jack always hopes (no); Jack always perseveres (no). Jack never fails (uh, no, Jack fails a lot). Wow! That sounds like me. Who *would* want to know a guy like that? Thankfully, Jesus does.

As much as I disliked what I heard, I knew I had to see where I fell short, and I knew God had put me in that church in that town at that moment because it was time for me to start dealing with this stuff. And I'm not the only one. We all need to ask God to show us where we fall short. It's not to be mean. God is doing this like a baseball coach would, to encourage us to be better players, and that means fixing this _____ [fill in the blank with your issue]. It might hurt to hear what He says, but it's meant to help you improve and to build you up. Personally, I know I immediately need to work on whatever He shows me. I know God meant for me to be in New Jersey that morning. Likewise, I believe He means for you to read this today along this same line of seeing and tackling those things in your life that need to change. We have to. It's part of growing up and maturing, and God expects us to do that too.

In 1 Corinthians 2:6, Paul talks to believers, saying, "We do, however, speak a message of wisdom among the mature, but not the wisdom of this age or of the rulers of this age who are coming to nothing." What's that, Paul? You speak a message of wisdom among the mature?

Hey, believer! You are supposed to be mature if you spend some time with the Lord. Like if you went to school and went to first grade, second grade, third, and so on through high school, we would expect you to have learned something and not be sitting in 10th grade and have second-grade knowledge.

Hey, believer! That message of wisdom is not the wisdom of this age and not the wisdom of the world, and it comes not from this world's so-called rulers or authorities. That's right; this age's wisdom will get you nothing. The world's wisdom will get you nothing. Only spiritual wisdom will get you joy, peace, happiness, contentment, satisfaction, abundant life now, and a guaranteed place in heaven with eternal life forever, which sounds like a good deal to me.

Not only is it a good deal, but God also gives us the means to understand His wisdom and how it differs from the world. We live in a world, in a culture, where feelings or preconceived ideas can mislead us continually. We don't feel like going to church, or we think we understand an issue, but we don't spend any time getting informed. God says that's the world's way of living, and we are to do things differently. We are to test things to see if they are good, including what we read in Scripture. In 1 Corinthians 2:15, it says, "The spiritual man makes judgments about all things, but he himself is not subject to any man's judgment..." The spiritual man, the person who is saved, has the Spirit living in him to help him make right judgments about all things. If we test something, and it is good, we are to take it in; and if it is bad, we are to cast it aside.

Another side of this is that while the spiritual man judges all things, Scripture says that he himself is not subject to any man's judgment. Why aren't we subject to any man's judgment? Because we are subject to God's judgment. So, it's not what our feelings try to make us do, it's not what other people tell us about what's moral, ethical, or permissible, it's all about what God's Word says and if we'll obey. I must be careful to stop relying on what I feel or think, unless I have tested those feelings or thoughts against the Scriptures.

That means I must learn to judge myself. Paul encourages us to do so, saying in 1 Corinthians 11:31, "But if we judged ourselves, we would not come under judgment." Come on, would you rather see something ugly about yourself in the privacy of your own heart, or do you want God to have to point it out to you, often with others close enough to see or hear? It's like God saying, "Don't make me come down there. You know right from wrong. Live accordingly." And if I don't? I will come under God's judgment.

Do I know what God says is right and wrong? Do you? How can we?

Listen. I assume most of us have been in school. Do you remember what it felt like going in to take a test when you weren't sure of the answers? Man, it was sweat city and constant negotiating with God: Please Lord, how about a snow day, a bomb scare, anything, please! But you go in; you're shaking; you know you don't have this right; you know there is trouble ahead. You're full of anxiety; it's nerve wracking and just plain terrible.

Now, what's it like when you take the open book test? Ever take one of those? Yeah! We're singing in the rain; it's easy street—the open book test, the answers are in the book. Here are the questions, and I'm going to give you the answers right next to them. Your job is to open the book, find the answers, and have the very hard task (in case you're not sure, this is sarcasm) of writing them on your piece of paper. How hard is that? How lazy do you have to be to screw that up?

God has given us the Bible. He has given us all an open book test. Paul says if we judge ourselves, we won't come under judgment. So, let's judge ourselves. Let's open the book, see what we are supposed to do, and see what answers we don't have right. Then, let's fix them; make it right; put the right answer in our lives so that when we get to heaven, God won't say, "Hey, great to see you up here, but I don't have much of a prize for you. Your heavenly reward—that's based on your obedience to me while you were on earth and what you have done with the life I gave you to live."

Oops! What'll you say to that? Well, God, I wasn't sure, how could I have known what to do? How could you have known what to do? Look at the answers, right there in black and white.

Don't tell me you didn't know, because God will look at you and say, "Wait a minute, didn't I see you reading *Where the Rubber Meets the Road with God?*" What part of that chapter called "You Be the Judge" wasn't clear? You will not be able to say that you didn't know. It's your responsibility to see what God's Word (the Bible) says, and if something is wrong in your life, it is your responsibility to fix it. We are to act and make it right. And yeah, this will take a while. It's not some short relay we can run, and then be glad it's over. We're in a marathon down here, and God wants us to do it right. Paul reminds us of that in 1 Corinthians 9:24, "Do you not know that in a race all the runners run, but only one gets the prize? Run in such a way as to get the prize." We're supposed to work at it, ladies and gentlemen. Work at it!

Working at it means taking control of my heart, my mind, my thoughts, and my body. I'm in control, not my flesh. To do that, I have to stay in training. In 1 Corinthians 25–27, Paul continues, "Everyone who competes in the games goes into strict training. They do it to get a crown that will not last; but we do it to get a crown that will last forever. Therefore I do not run like a man running aimlessly; I do not fight like a man beating the air. No, I beat my body and make it my slave so that after I have preached to others, I myself will not be disqualified for the prize." Who's in control of your life—your feelings, appetites, cravings, or attitude?

Still, there are times we do all the right things and still feel as if God's presence is missing from our lives. What to do then? Go back to the beginning. You're saved, so trust God. Trust your salvation. You persevere in what you know about God, and you keep running the race, keep living the life He has given you, trusting His Word that says He is always there. If you think, "Jack, I don't feel the presence of God in my life," then I'd ask you to think about times in your life when you couldn't see, but you had to trust.

It's like being on autopilot. If I set the plane on autopilot, we take off, the weather starts to get bad and bumpy, and now, I can't see because it's dark, the plane shakes, and I'm not sure of where I am, I can still be sure of one thing. I set the plane on autopilot, and I can trust the autopilot mechanism to do its job and to take me safely where I need to go—even if I don't see it actually working. Now, maybe you don't feel God's presence, but that doesn't mean He's not there or that you won't again feel His presence. I can't tell you why God moves differently in different people's lives at different times. I was not one of those Christians who were saved, and the next day, every area of my life changed. God had to move me and change me slowly but surely, piece by piece, over the years.

So, here you are on autopilot; it's dark; the plane shakes; and you start to wonder if the autopilot works. You know you set it. You have a choice to make—trust the autopilot or not? If not, you will probably grab the controls and assume you'll be able to keep from crashing, but the chances are, if you grab the controls yourself, you will crash.

Or do you choose to trust the autopilot because you know you set it; you know it worked; and you know that even if the plane shakes, the autopilot can still do its job? Maybe God has chosen to test your faith. Will you pass the test? Maybe God has chosen to see if you will remain faithful even if you can't see Him or touch Him. Are you Thomas? Must Jesus come and let you put your hand in His side? I can imagine Jesus saying, "Jack, it's not enough for you that I died on the cross so you could live? That's not enough? You need more of a sacrifice?"

We can't rely on our eyes, feelings, or emotions, or else, we'll be tricked into giving up before the good stuff comes. Imagine sitting down to a meal and leaving after the appetizer because you didn't know more was coming. You would have missed the best part! Appetizers are good, but you know the meal, the filet mignon, the dessert—that's the best part. Spiritually, though, we so often get up and leave before we've gotten the best God has in store. He has promised He will do immeasurably more than we could ever ask or imagine, and here is what boggles my mind. We go to God for wisdom in one area. We're in trouble with a relationship, with money, with a job, with health, or whatever, and we go to God and say, "God, please help me with this," and God does. He helps you. Then, what? Then, we run for the hills, away from God, as if that one thing were the only thing He could do or would want to do for us.

It's absurd, really. How absurd? Imagine you wanted to be a car mechanic, and you went to a master mechanic and said, "Teach me."

He said, "Okay, come on in. Today, I will teach you how to change the oil."

You go and learn how to change the oil, and then, you head for the door and say, "Thanks, that's great." You go out into the world and announce that you're a master mechanic. Then, somebody asks you to fix his brakes, and you don't know how because you didn't learn it. You left too soon; you didn't let the teacher teach you about brakes; you only let him teach you about oil changes. Big mistake! Why didn't you let him teach you everything? Why didn't you let him equip you, give you the tools you need for greatness? Why wouldn't you have let the one who has all that knowledge, be it a master mechanic, Kung Fu teacher, or great baseball hitter, impart to you all his wisdom and knowledge?

We treat God that way all the time. We rely on our own judgment, and yet, we don't judge for ourselves what is good and right. So, here is God, the creator of the universe, your Father, who can give you, and wants to share with you, the keys to the kingdom and wants you to have knowledge. Here is the Holy Spirit inside you , teaching you. What do you say? "No, no, Spirit, sit down; shut up." That's the mistake.

Now, think if you were that teacher—that master mechanic, master Kung Fu guy or great baseball hitter. Think how sad you would feel when that student walked out the door, cockily thinking that he had learned what he needed. You'd shake your head, thinking, "Man, he was good. He could have been great, but he just wouldn't let me teach him. He ran away before I could give him more." I think that teacher would be pretty sad.

Take it one step further. Imagine it was your father. Or, if you are a parent, imagine that feeling if your son or daughter said, "Dad, Mom, I don't care; I don't want to learn what you have to teach me."

"What do you mean you don't want to learn? I lived this life already. I have all these things to teach you, so you can avoid all these mistakes, so you can move ahead quicker, so you can have the full benefit and blessing of everything I have to give you. Come here, Son, let me teach you."

"No, Dad."

I think that would be a very sad moment in a parent's life. I would shed tears. I think God sheds tears in heaven over every believer who just doesn't get it, who goes through his life living for himself, for his next meal, sporting event, or next raise. Hey, to be real about it, I like to eat; I like sports; and I would like to make more money, but it's God first. God says we are to sacrifice and to put Him first. Sometimes, we don't want to do those things.

I did things I didn't want to do. Years ago, when I had back pain, I did things I didn't want to do. I was in such agony and was so desperate to get well; I even tried acupuncture, though I hate needles. If you had asked me if I would ever try acupuncture, I would have said never in my life, never, that is, until I got desperate for relief from the pain. So, I tried it. Are you desperate enough for the full joy of God that you'll try anything to get it, anything He says? It's a battle between what He wants and what your self or your flesh, your old sin nature, wants. Do you remember Paul talking about controlling your mind, body, and soul?

Here's a strategy I use that helps me take control of my flesh. I have a board of directors meeting with myself. I know sin is a part of me. I can't get rid of sin until the day I die, so here's what I do. The board of directors meeting includes the Holy Spirit, my old nature, and me (the brand new creation I am in Christ). We think about stuff, and sin gets to speak at the meeting, mainly because he insists on attending. He speaks up and says, "Jack, Jack, Jack!"

And I say, "Yeah, sin?"

He says, "Here is what I want to do. I want to steal; I want to rob; I want to lust; I want to cheat, lie, and be self-seeking and self-serving. I want everything, Jack, everything."

I say, "Sin, is that all you have to say?"

"Yes."

"Thank you very much. Now, we'll take a vote." Sin shuts up because he knows he's lost the battle. See, even though he has a voice, sin has no vote. When it comes time to take the vote, he can't. He's not allowed. So, the Spirit and I, we vote. We vote yes to God and no to sin. I can't shut sin up, but he doesn't get any vote at that board of directors meeting.

So who do you invite to your board of directors meeting for your faith walk? Does sin get a vote? You be the judge. Don't wait for God to have to judge you. This is where the rubber meets the road with God, and it is a critical moment of truth for every believer and especially for you today.

9

Who Says You Haven't Got A Prayer?

I remember having another unusually tough week back in late 2003. In addition to other pressures, my father had just come out of the hospital after another heart surgery. Thank God, his recovery went well.

Next thing I knew, I was back in the hospital emergency room, this time with my son, Jackson, when he was just two years old. He climbed up his newborn sister's crib and fell. I raced to see what had happened as he screamed in pain. As my wife and I held ice on it, we could tell it wasn't getting better. Off to the emergency room for x-rays we went, and we found out he had broken his collarbone.

On top of that, I was preparing to preach five different sermons in seven days. Preaching is my passion, but with all the other stresses that bore down on me, life was more than a little crazy, and I confess that I was really down. Now, I know I'm not supposed to be down. I know I'm always supposed to be up and strong, and usually, I think I can handle anything. But I'll tell you what; this was a down week. I was uncertain about the future. I was uncertain about finances. My marriage was a little stressed; we had my dad's sudden surgery, Jackson's injury, and all the usual commitments and daily things to deal with. Most of you can relate to this, I'm sure; we all go through these times.

At 8 a.m., the next day, however, it all changed—even though nothing changed. None of my circumstances had changed. None of the responsibilities, challenges, finances, or issues had suddenly turned all peachy perfect. What changed was my spirit. At 8 a.m., my cell phone rang.

My friend Kathy said, "Jack, I need to tell you something."

I asked, "What's that?"

"I am bathing you in prayer this morning."

I blinked at the phone a couple of times. "What?"

"I am bathing you in prayer this morning. I want you to know that you've been bathed in prayer, and your father is bathed in prayer."

"Wow, that's so great. Thank you so much for calling me. I really appreciate it." I hung up the phone and continued driving, and I tell you what—I went from being seriously down in the dumps to feeling as if I walked on air.

I was just so psyched, so happy that she prayed for me. I'm

usually the one praying for others. I'm usually the guy calling people up too early in the morning to say, "Hey, I'm praying for you. I hope everything's going good." Now, I was the recipient, the one benefiting from someone else's intercession for me, and my reaction surprised me. My heart attitude and my mind's perspective about everything just changed. A sense of gratitude for Kathy's willingness to pray for me and for God placing me on her heart swept over me.

Now, listen, if she had chosen not to pray for me, then God would have raised up somebody else to do it because God's work will be done when God wills it. The thing is that Kathy would have missed the blessing she got from praying for me. I know, because I am blessed when I pray for other people, so I think I know how she felt.

What made her especially stand out is that I know the kind of suffering Kathy has experienced, and to know that she focused on someone else's life rather than her own is a testimony to her faith and an inspiration to me.

Let me tell you a little about Kathy. We became good friends when her husband went away to jail for a couple of years. (He was innocently caught up in some white-collar real estate mess.) She also has a son who is a friend of mine, a young man struggling terribly with drug addiction, and a grown daughter fighting that same battle. Back when she was adjusting to her husband being in jail, I'd call her a few times a week on my way to work to talk to her, pray with her, and try to lift her up and give her encouragement.

I watched her struggle, and I do mean struggle. She had to sell her house because she couldn't afford to keep it. I watched her sell her jewelry. I watched her sell her possessions. I watched her work three jobs to try to maintain the family, and she still volunteered in church.

Never once did she shrink from her responsibilities. Never once did the world see her pain and suffering. Oh, we all knew about it; her husband being in jail and her troubles with her kids using drugs weren't secrets in church, but all this woman did was praise the Lord. Like Job, she didn't like what she went through, and she would have traded it in a heartbeat if that had been possible, but she didn't turn bitter or resentful or walk away from God.

Instead, she just kept saying, "Lord, I trust you. I glorify you. I praise you. You must have a purpose, Lord. I stand on Romans 8:28, where you said, "In all things God works for the good of those who love Him…' I love you and I trust that all this stuff I'm going through will be for my good and your glory."

I was inspired. I was in awe of her faith, so I memorized God's promise to us in 1 Corinthians 10:13, "No temptation has seized you except what is common to man. And God is faithful; He will not let you be tempted beyond what you can bear. But when you are tempted, He will also provide a way out so that you can stand up under it."

So the Bible tells us that God is faithful, and if that's not enough to encourage us, He has also promised that He will bear our burdens. Psalm 68:19 says, "Praise be to the Lord, to God our Savior, who daily bears our burdens" and also Psalm 55:22, "Cast your burden on the Lord, and He shall sustain you; He shall never permit the righteous to be moved." Matthew 11:29–30 says, "Take my yoke upon you and learn from me, for I am gentle and humble in heart, and you will find rest for your souls. For my yoke is easy and my burden is light."

Are you worn out from living in this sinful world? Are you wondering why you're alive and why you were created? We all get that way when we don't know what purpose God has for our lives. God says, "Come to me. I'll show it to you. I'll reveal it to you. "

I didn't accept Jesus and get saved until I was 33 years old. My life before that was not great. It might have seemed great to you, but looks deceive. I had a great job. I had money. I had all the things the world had to offer; but I was empty inside. I had nothing. I didn't know why I was alive or what the purpose of my life was. But ever since I accepted Jesus Christ, my life has gotten better every single day because I know why I'm alive. Since I finally yielded full and total control of my life over to him three years later, at age 36, I have been the happiest man alive. I know what the purpose is because God's explained it to me (and that's to live a life that glorifies him and be filled with peace and joy as I bear lasting fruit for the kingdom of God).

So back to my friend, Kathy. She reflected Christ every step of the way. Her love for, and faith in, God were tested and tried continually for years. And you know what? She passed the test. Her reward in heaven will be unbelievable. Her faith was proved true, which should be the desire of every believer's heart, though it comes at a price. You don't *prove* your faith or anything else without putting it to the test.

Kathy knows what it means to have God carry her burdens and to connect with Him through prayer because she has been tried in the fire. She's not the only one who's been *tried*, or tested. Most of us get it on a regular basis. What do I mean by "tried in the fire?" That's how gold is refined. It's put into the fire, and when all the impurities are burned away from it, it comes out pure and valuable. God constantly refines us in the trials and tribulations of life to get rid of the useless, impure stuff that tarnishes us, and in the process, He makes us complete and mature, so we won't lack anything. In Hebrews Chapter 11, the Hall of Fame of Faith as it's so often called, it describes people who were tested and passed the test. By faith, through trouble, suffering, trials, and doubts, Noah built an ark; Abraham offered his son Isaac as a sacrifice to God; Moses refused to be known as Pharaoh's son; and the list goes on.

In James 1:2–4, God's Word says we should "Consider it pure joy, my brothers, whenever you face trials of many kinds, because you know that the testing of your faith develops perseverance. Perseverance must finish its work so that you may be mature and complete, not lacking anything."

We all know it's easy to praise God when things are going well and when there are no trials. It's like a bodyguard who's standing there guarding his client, looking all tough and mean, maybe even uttering some threats to anyone who gets too close. Big deal. Is he really as tough as he claims? We won't know until someone attacks his client. Then, we'll see if he's tough.

We'll see how the doctor handles pressure in the operating room, not while writing a prescription. We'll see how the lawyer does in the courtroom, not the boardroom. We'll see how tough the baseball player is when he's up at bat with bases loaded at the bottom of the ninth with two outs.

How about you? When you're under pressure, will you withstand the test? Or do you groan and mumble? Do you get discouraged and defeated? Do you sit out and refuse to play if things don't go your way? Do we abandon our principles and beliefs, the very things on which our lives and salvation are founded? Do we not trust God?

Kathy's response to the intense pressures of her everyday life was to lean on God's Word and to go to him in prayer, not just for herself, but also for others. As God prompted her to pray for various people, she obeyed. I know that her heavenly reward is secure and overflowing. I want to be like that. I want to be the one who is a blessing to other people, so I can be blessed.

Kathy has another quality more of us should seek for ourselves, and that is she is at peace with her lot in life (that doesn't mean, by the way, that she wouldn't want it to change for the better). None of us knows what we'll get in life. Maybe we won't be rich; maybe we won't always be poor. Maybe we'll be sick and maybe we'll be healthy. But God says that our focus should be on our rewards in heaven rather than on the creature comforts and things of this earth.

We need to examine our lives to see if we respond to God's will as Kathy did. Do we trust, praise, and stay faithful regardless of our circumstances, or do we question God's judgment and power? As I meditated on this, God taught me several things about prayer I want to share with you.

The first is that when God puts someone on your heart, you need to pray for them. Why? Because the Holy Spirit of God has pricked your heart, prompting you to pray for him or her, so it's a matter of your obedience. It's important. Kathy might never know what she did for me. Unless I go and tell her, how will she know? Before I hung up the phone, I told her, "Thank you very much. That was very sweet of you." It wasn't until later that the significance of what had happened hit me. I realized that if our prayers have no shot of working, then why bother? I wanted her to know that her prayers worked, and the next day, I called her again to tell her and thank her for the huge impact she had on me.

God promises us that our prayers work. Let's look at King Hezekiah, a great king of Israel (2 Kings 18:5), who got sick near the end of his life, "The prophet Isaiah son of Amoz went to him and said, 'This is what the Lord says: Put your house in order, because you are going to die; you will not recover'" (2 Kings 20:1). When God tells you that you won't recover, you had sure as heck better get your house in order. But watch what happens in verses 2 and 3: "Hezekiah turned his face to the wall and prayed to the Lord, 'Remember, O Lord, how I have walked before you faithfully and with wholehearted devotion and have done what is good in your eyes.' And Hezekiah wept bitterly." Hezekiah prayed that God would extend his life and God honored that prayer and extended his life another 15 years.

My friend Mel Stewart loves to quote Jeremiah 29:11, which he calls God's phone number. "'For I know the plans I have for you,' declares the Lord, 'plans to prosper you and not harm you; plans to give you a hope and a future.'" Can you get excited about that? I do! God's plan for you is not to hurt you. It's to prosper you and give you hope and a future, and then it goes on to say in verses 12 and 13, "Then you will call upon me and come and pray to me, and I will listen to you. You will seek me and find me when you seek me with all your heart." That's God talking, not me, saying clearly that when we pray, He will listen; when we seek Him with all our heart, we will find Him. I know I told you this already in a previous chapter, now I'm telling you again...because it's that important!

How about Abraham praying for Sodom and Gomorrah? God was going to destroy the cities; His mind was made up. "You're out of here, both of you. You failed. You're rotten. You're sinners. I'm taking you out." Yet, Abraham talked with God and prayed for them, and as a result of Abraham's genuine longing to find any righteous people left in the cities, God spared the few righteous people there were from total destruction (Genesis 18:16–19:29).

Some people don't think prayer is important. We have things mixed up. We say, "God, send me to Mississippi where I can help the people whose homes got destroyed in a hurricane. Send me on a mission trip. Anyone can sit around and pray, but I want you to give me an important assignment." Sound familiar? Uh oh, maybe that *feels* familiar. The implication that sitting around praying isn't important is false. Such attitudes discount prayer as being trivial and too little a thing to be bothered with and stand in stark contrast to Luke 16:10: "He who is faithful with little will be faithful with much."

If God has placed someone on your heart to pray for and you don't pray for them, you're not being faithful to this assignment; you're being disobedient. In effect, God has asked you to pray for someone, and you brush Him off because you decide it's not important enough to do. If that's the case, what makes you think you'll get a bigger assignment next time? Your action reveals that you believe the ability to impact someone's life through prayer is unimportant. The opportunity to make a sick person well is too small a task for you? The chance to bring a lost person to the Lord isn't worth a few minutes of your time? The joy of encouraging someone who is down isn't worth it, and neither is the potential to influence God to provide for a brother or sister in need? That's not important? Are you nuts?

Our willingness to obey a prompting to pray indicates that we value the power of prayer. What else does Scripture say about prayer?

Philippians 4:6–7 says, "Do not be anxious about anything, but in everything, by prayer and petition, with thanksgiving, present your requests to God. And the peace of God, which transcends all understanding, will guard your hearts and your minds in Christ Jesus." We should bring everything to God in prayer. If you do not have a prayer life communicating to God, you blow it.

We get things backward at times, wondering, "Why should I bring all my prayers and requests to God when He already knows what I think?" God says, "Bring them to me because you're my child and I love you and I want to bless you" (Luke 12:32).

"I know that, but you're God. You created everything. You know exactly what I will pray about and what I think, so why should I have to actually pray to you?"

The reason is simply that prayer is about *our* getting into God's mindset, not the other way around. Prayer helps us draw near to God and strengthen the love relationship He wants to have with us. God delights and takes joy in communicating with us the same way I am delighted and joyful when my kids come to me with what's on their minds and their hearts. I love listening to them and talking to them.

Why? Because I love them, I want to bless them in every way I can, and if they come to me with a request I can give them, then I will do so, unless of course, it's not in their best interests.

If my 17-year-old son wants to go out and get in a car with a drunk driver, I will say no. If my 3-year-old son wants to ride a bicycle without a helmet, I will say no. Why? Because I love them too much to let them hurt themselves. God loves us too much to let us hurt ourselves. He will say no when our prayer is not aligned with His will, but He will always say yes when it is aligned with His will. John 14:13–14 says, "And I will do whatever you ask in my name, so that the Son may bring glory to the Father. You may ask me for anything in my name, and I will do it." John 15:16 says, "You did not choose me, but I chose you and appointed you to go and bear fruit— fruit that will last. Then the Father will give you whatever you ask in my name." And John 16:24 says, "Until now you have not asked for anything in my name. Ask and you will receive, and your joy will be complete." This is not a blank check for all our wishes; this is a promise that when we ask for the things Jesus himself would have asked for (hence, asking in His name) that God will say yes. The *yes* might include a waiting period, but we are to be steadfast in asking and waiting.

One request God will certainly answer is a request for wisdom: Look at what God's word says in James Chapter 1 verse 5 says "If any of you lacks wisdom, he should ask God, who gives generously to all without finding fault, and it will be given to him". Do you want wisdom? Ask God. How do you ask God? You pray. That's how you communicate with God.

How can we be sure that our prayers are effective? It depends on our relationship with God. James 5:16 says, "The prayer of a righteous man is powerful and effective." It's the prayer of a righteous man, not a spiritually slothful, lazy bum, that's effective! It begins with having a right relationship with God through Jesus. Do you? Have you committed your life to Christ? When you come to God in prayer, *confess* your sins to Him, so you can clean out anything that might separate you from God. Then, pray with reckless abandon. I love that verse because God tells me that when it's used properly, prayer always works, as long as it is aligned with God's will.

Well, you say, maybe that was true for those Old Testament stars such as Elijah and Moses, but I don't believe that's still true today—for me. Really? Look at James 5:17, in which Paul talks about Elijah: "Elijah was a man just like us." What do you mean he was a man just like us? He was a prophet, Jack, and I'm not a prophet.

Oh, you of little faith! Yes, Elijah was a prophet, but Paul assures us that this prophet was just like us, no better or worse; but catch this—Elijah was obedient. He was righteous and, therefore, his prayers were effective. If we respond to God with the same obedience, we will see answers to our prayers. Look at the verses themselves (James 5:17–18): "Elijah was a man just like us. He prayed earnestly that it would not rain, and it did not rain on the land for three and a half years. Again he prayed, and the heavens gave rain, and the earth produced its crops."

Elijah prayed and saw results. Like him, my friend Kathy prays faithfully for others, and we need to do the same thing. Ephesians 6:18 says, "And pray in the Spirit on all occasions with all kinds of prayers and requests. With this in mind, be alert and always keep on praying for all the saints." Who are all the saints? You and I, all the believers in Jesus Christ—we're the saints of God, the family of believers. Kathy was being obedient to God by praying on all occasions for the saints—for her brothers and sisters in the faith. And her prayers, her intercession with God on my behalf, were effective.

Let's look at an example of intercessory prayer involving the disciples. In Acts 12, Peter was held in prison because of his faith. Did the church say, "Good luck, buddy? We'll see you in a couple of years. Call us when you get out and we'll help you?" No, it says, "... but the church was earnestly praying to God for him" (Acts 12:5). They did the most important thing of all—they relied on God's power, not their own, and committed themselves to intercede for Peter. Scripture doesn't spell it out for us, but it's apparent by what happened that they had prayed for his release and deliverance from Herod's murderous intentions. It's a really cool story, and I encourage you to read all of Acts 12 to see how God can do anything He wants to answer prayer and save His people.

In Psalms 66:17–19, David cries out to God. "I cried out to Him with my mouth; His praise was on my tongue. If I had cherished sin in my heart, the Lord would not have listened; but God has surely listened and heard my voice in prayer." If you know anything about David, you know he had many warts and blemishes on his record, yet he celebrated his prayer life. Why? Because his repentance before God was true. His own sin overwhelmed him when he realized it.

Godly repenting is when you really mean that you're sorry about what you did and you turn away from that behavior and turn toward

God. If you have confessed your sin, God will never withhold His love from you. Then, there's just one more *little* thing (just kidding... it's a huge thing!) we need to do before our prayers can matter. Mark 11:24–25 says, "Therefore I tell you, whatever you ask for in prayer, believe that you have received it, and it will be yours. And when you stand praying, if you hold anything against anyone, forgive him, so that your Father in heaven may forgive you your sins."

Forgiveness is a requirement for effective prayer. It's not negotiable. If you have a grudge in your heart against somebody you haven't forgiven, God will not hear your prayer. That sounds kind of harsh, but it's not my rule; it's God's rule. If we hold on to a grudge, it's a sin, and we have to not just confess the sin, but also address the forgiveness issue, so we can be righteous before God.

Once those two things are taken care of (confessing your sins and forgiving others), God will always hear your prayers. But remember, if what you seek in prayer isn't in your best interest, then it's not part of His will, and in those instances God will say no. He alone knows what is in our true, eternal best interest because He alone has that true, eternal perspective. Paul tells us in 1 John 5:14, "This is the confidence we have in approaching God: that if we ask anything according to His will, He hears us."

We can go before God with confidence: "Father, I love you so much. You are an awesome God. Here are the prayers of my heart today."

What if His answer to your prayer is no, what do you say then? I'm at the point in my life, and I hope you are at the point in your life, where our response is "Thank you, Lord."

You might be ready to throw this book across the room right now as you scream, "What do you mean 'Thank you, Lord?' You have no idea what I'm going through."

I might not know your exact circumstance, but with God's grace and mercy (and I'm sure some help from the intercessory prayers of believers who loved me) I have been saved from the gutter of addiction and have learned to thank God that He knows what's best, and I don't. I lived into my thirties thinking that my idea of what's best for me would work out before I crashed my car through a fence during a drug-induced blackout. That was the day, I abandoned my idea of what's best and abandoned myself to God's will for my life. Things have gotten better every day since.

So yes, I mean it when I say that, in the midst of what we would normally call lousy, rotten answers to prayers (meaning *we* didn't get what *we* wanted), I honestly thank God. I have never said, "Thank you, Lord, for taking away someone I loved." But I have said, "Thank you, Lord, that you know what is eternally best for that person; maybe your timing has spared that person some immense trial or suffering down the road. Lord, obviously, it was that person's time, and even though I grieve, and it's not what I wanted, Lord, you are God, and I trust you. You're God, and you're in charge of everything." For those reasons, I can thank God. For me, it has been a turning point in my prayer life. I'm learning a lot. I'm not interested in dodging the hard places in life. Yes, I've fallen hard on my butt in those places, but God has grown my faith through them every time.

Learning to pray involves learning to confess our sins and learning to let go of our will and wishes and trust those of God. Is there anything else we need to know about prayer?

In fact, Jesus gives us a warning about what not to do, in Matthew 6:5–6: "And when you pray, do not be like the hypocrites, for they love to pray standing in the synagogues and on the street corners to be seen by men. I tell you the truth, they have received their reward in full. But when you pray, go into your room, close the door and pray to your Father, who is unseen. Then your Father, who sees what is done in secret, will reward you."

Prayer is private between you and God. Now, my earthly father, Jerry, he's a great guy. I hit the all-time jackpot of life with my dad and mom. My dad has said to me ever since I was a little kid, "Son, I'm the only guy who will ever be behind you 100 percent in your life. No matter what you do, good or bad, I'm behind you. You can always count on me." And you know what? I really put him to the test on that. Lucky for me, he's lived it and proved it to me all my life.

Maybe you weren't as blessed in the earthly parent cards you were dealt, but count on this—we are equally blessed with our heavenly Father, God. I pray Kathy's adult children learn that truth for themselves, as they watch their mother trusting God to provide for her. Each one of us has the same heavenly Father, so we have no excuse for not going to Him. There are things that my earthly father knows about me that nobody else in the world knows because he has given me the confidence that I can come to him and talk to him. But my heavenly Father knows stuff that even my earthly father doesn't know, and right now, you have that same potential relationship with your heavenly Father. It's private. It's about what happens when you shut the world out. It's about taking that time and making prayer with God the first priority in your life. That doesn't mean you pray for 20 hours a day. It just means that God needs to be the priority of your life. You need to show Him that He's number one.

How do you do that? First, you need to show up regularly and consistently spending time with God, not just once a week, for church. Amazing and lasting growth in the Lord comes when it's you and God alone, with the Bible opened up and the Holy Spirit teaching you. John 14:26 reminds us of the Spirit's job: "...the Holy Spirit, whom the Father will send in my name, will teach you all things and will remind you of everything I have said to you." I have a great teacher, but I have to be there if I want to learn anything. I have to show up.

So, besides warning us about praying publicly to get attention, does Jesus teach us anything else about prayer? Yes, but this time it's a warning about our flesh's ability to impact our prayer life. In Matthew 26:41, He says, "Watch and pray so that you will not fall into temptation. The spirit is willing, but the body is weak."

How do I avoid falling into temptation, Lord? Say, I have a problem with drugs, gambling, alcohol, or sex. What should I do? God says, "Watch and pray." The body is weak; it is prone to giving into temptations, and so we are to use prayer as a weapon to fend off temptation.

Most people in Kathy's shoes will be tempted to give up, complain, withdraw, and become bitter. Kathy stayed close to Jesus, and in doing so, she experienced a peace and joy that is satisfying and rewarding and does not yield to any temptation Satan throws at her to quit in life and give up on her God.

And prayer is also a weapon against our enemy, Satan. Ephesians 6:18, "And pray in the Spirit on all occasions with all kinds of prayers and requests. With this in mind, be alert and always keep on praying for all the saints!"

How often should we pray? That's another good question. Always? Just during a morning quiet time? Does prayer during a commute *count* with God? In 1 Thessalonians 5:17, we are told to "pray continually." All the time. While our spiritual growth develops best with committing specific time to studying the Word and praying (which many people like to do in a quiet time in the mornings), we can pray continually and even abruptly. Arrow prayers, as they are sometimes called, are those prayers you shoot up to heaven when the boss calls you in on the carpet, for example. And yes, they count. Study Nehemiah 2:4–5; Nehemiah had prayed diligently in chapter 1 about the condition of Jerusalem, and in chapter 2, when he is before the king, he suddenly has an opportunity to speak what's on his mind: "The king said to me, 'What is it you want?' *Then I prayed to the God of heaven,* and I answered the king, 'If it pleases the king and if your servant has found favor in his sight, let him send me to the city in Judah where my fathers are buried so that I can rebuild it'"(*emphasis mine*). Nehemiah shot up an arrow prayer before he answered the king, and often, we should do likewise before we open our mouths to speak.

What else can we do to make our prayer life more effective? I think Kathy really lives this one out. "Devote yourselves to prayer, being watchful and thankful" (Col. 4:2). When you devote yourself to something, you focus on it. Tell me something that you're devoted to, and I'll tell you that's something you're focused on. God wants you to devote yourself to prayer, so He can communicate with you and bless you, and so you can affect the future and influence lives for the kingdom of Jesus Christ.

Prayer is two-way communication with God. He speaks to us through Scripture, sermons, music, and through all kinds of means. We can sing songs about Him, but prayer is our time to speak to God and communicate with God, and He even invites us to be persistent in our prayers. In the parable of the persistent widow in Luke 18, a woman goes to an unjust judge's door and asks for help against her adversaries, but the judge brushes her off. She returns a second time, and she is sent away again; but she persists, and finally, the judge figures that he'll never get rid of her unless he helps her, so he does.

In telling this parable, Jesus teaches His followers that devotion and persistence in our prayers are encouraged. If an unjust judge, who cared nothing about dealing with this woman's adversaries, could do the right thing, how much more will God, who loves His children and has their good in mind at all times, respond to our fervent prayers for help? God wants you, His child, to keep coming to Him with your prayers, all the while remembering that His timing is not necessarily the same as yours. We have our watches tuned to drive-through speed, but God doesn't work that way, so just trust His timing. It's hard to do, but as I've watched Kathy trust God's timing to provide for her needs and to deal with her problems, I have been encouraged to do the same thing.

One last thing God revealed to me about prayer is that Jesus himself prays for me and for you. That should knock our socks off!

Jesus prayed all the time while He was on earth, and He still prays for us in heaven. Look at God's word in Roman's 8:34 "Christ

Jesus, who died—more than that, who was raised to life—is at the right hand of God and is also interceding for us." In Hebrews, it says, "For Christ did not enter a man-made sanctuary that was only a copy of the true one; He entered heaven itself, now to appear for us in God's presence" (Hebrews 9:24). The phrase "appear for us in God's presence" means that He pleads our case before God; He intercedes for us. Can you imagine? Jesus is up in heaven sitting with God and praying for me, Jack, and for you. How cool is that?

Just as Jesus prayed for Peter in Luke 22:31–32, "...Satan has asked to sift you as wheat. But I have prayed for you..." Jesus prays for you and me as well. How lucky and fortunate we are to be sons of God.

Jesus also prays for us when we don't know what to say. When I'm down and out, and I can't pray for myself, Jesus, through the Holy Spirit, prays for me, according to Romans 8:26: "We do not know what we ought to pray for, but the Spirit himself intercedes for us with groans that words cannot express."

Jesus is our attorney, our representative, our defender. We're Christ's ambassadors here on earth, but he is our ambassador in heaven. You can't buy that no matter how much money or fame you have. It's no accident that you are reading this, either. God is speaking straight to you about your prayer life. Are you listening closely?

Imagine if God wrote you a letter. Here's what I think it would look like. See if God touches your heart right now as you read it.

Hello, my child,

I know that sometimes it's hard to figure out how to communicate with someone you can't see or touch, so maybe these will help guide you along the way, so we can talk more before you come home.

When my Holy Spirit prompts you to pray for one of my kids, for one of your brothers or sisters, stop and do it; I have my reasons for asking you.

If you cherish sin in your heart or if you harbor a grudge, confess those things and forgive that person so that I'll be able to hear and pay attention to your prayers.

Remember that prayer is about doing my will and not about convincing me to indulge your preference.

Pray anytime, anywhere, about anything, but I also really like to spend some quality Father-child time together.

I know what I do and why, so trust that my timing will bring about the right outcome to every situation.

Don't pray simply to get attention or praises from other people because then you do it for the wrong reason.

Your flesh is weak and easily tempted, so use prayer to help you overcome those times when you are at risk for caving in to your own weaknesses. You know what they are.

Prayer will thwart your enemy's attacks, so stay in touch with me.

When you are so overwhelmed that you don't even know what to pray, I'll still hear you because my Holy Spirit that lives within you will do all the praying you need.

And take heart, because your brother, Jesus, is up here making sure you are taken care of.

Talk to you soon.

Love,

Dad

10

It Happened To Me

Is God a liar? Or are you?

God says, "My word... will not return to me empty, but will accomplish what I desire and achieve the purpose for which I sent it" (Isaiah 55:11).

God says, "For the word of God is living and active. Sharper than any double-edged sword, it penetrates even to dividing soul and spirit, joint and marrow; it judges the thoughts and attitudes of the heart. Nothing in all creation is hidden from God's sight. Everything is uncovered and laid bare before the eyes of Him to whom we must give account. Therefore, since we have a great high priest who has gone through the heavens, Jesus the Son of God, let us hold firmly to the faith we profess" (Hebrews 4:12–14).

God tells us over and over that His Word is real; it has a purpose; nothing will stand in its way; and nothing is hidden from Him—no thought, no action, no inclination of your heart or mine can hide from Him.

That's a good reason to hold firmly to the faith we profess and not wander off, back to our old habits that linger in the sin nature, thinking we have things under control.

Not a problem, you say? Maybe. But probably, ultimately, you lie. I know, because it happened to me.

We all have some areas God wants to remove, but we won't give them to Him, and they end up getting between God and us. Isaiah 59:1–2 says, "Surely the arm of the Lord is not too short to save, nor His ear too dull to hear. But your iniquities have separated you from your God; your sins have hidden His face from you, so that He will not hear." Our sins separate us from God and cause Him not to hear our prayers.

I was just like the people the psalmist talked about in Psalm 106, verses 8, 12, and 13, in which it says, "Yet He saved them for His name's sake, to make His mighty power known... Then they believed His promises and sang His praise." Sounds like me. Got saved, believed His promises, sang His praise, and then verse 13 says, "But they soon forgot what He had done and did not wait for His counsel." And Psalm 106:24b says, "...they did not believe His promise." Unfortunately, verses 13 and 24b also sound like me. How about you? Do you believe God's promise? Do you believe God always, or only when it's convenient? Maybe you read Scripture and say, "Oh, well, God, I believe some verses, but really some other verses just don't work for me."

What do you mean it doesn't work for you? You didn't make the rules. God did. Imagine going to work and doing only three of the ten things your boss told you. You'd be fired so fast your head would spin. If you did nine out of the ten, you'd probably still be let go. You have to follow the rules to get your paycheck.

It was always me who strayed from God; God never strayed from me. God never left me; God never walked away from me. I walked away, but just as He did with the Israelites, God rescued me. You see, God allows His children to wander off only so far because He loves us too much to let us waste our lives.

So yes, God rescues us, but what does it cost us? What blessings do we miss, what joy do we forego? We often skip God's Word and His plan for us, which would bring righteousness, peace, and joy, and instead, pursue those things we think will bring peace, joy, and so much more... and usually, they don't. We have things backward.

John 6:63 says, "The words I have spoken to you are spirit and they are life." What's the value of the Word God has spoken to us? God says they are life! It's what you use to grow your faith. Don't say, "Lord, increase my faith" and ignore the tools He's given you to do it. That's like going to Michael Jordan for advice on basketball, and when he tells you what to do, you say, "See you later, Michael; I won't do it." Or you go to Warren Buffett for financial advice and ignore what he says. Why? Michael Jordan and Warren Buffett have so much more knowledge about those subjects than you do. And so does God. So, why wouldn't you listen to God?

Back to my story. I felt as if the enemy had kidnapped me, yet I knew I unlocked the door and invited Satan in. I caused myself to be held captive. Listen to what James 1:13 says about sin and see if it doesn't apply to your own life: "When tempted, no one should say, 'God is tempting me.' For God cannot be tempted by evil, nor does He tempt anyone; but each one is tempted when, by his own evil desire, he is dragged away and enticed. Then, after desire has conceived, it gives birth to sin; and sin, when it is full-grown, gives birth to death." It happened to me.

God didn't do it. It wasn't a test. I knew it was wrong, I knew where it could lead, and I did it, anyway. I fell into the trap of believing that I was strong enough this time to know where to draw the line. I believed I could invite Satan in, and then order him to leave when I wanted him to. I'd tell him when to go, and he'd say, "Okay, Jack," but I was wrong. I depended on my strength and my power to control Satan and to control that sin that so easily entangles. This would be a good time to get out a pen, cross out the word I, and write in your own name, along with the name of the sin that so easily entangles you (I'm purposely not telling you what my particular sin was this time...it doesn't matter does it? All that matters is it was sin). I was not using God's power, nor was I capable of doing so because I was too ashamed and embarrassed at the time even to bring this to God because I knew it was wrong. Of course, I knew God knew. I wasn't hiding it from him, but I wasn't taking it to him for forgiveness and deliverance, either. And things got worse.

It happened to me. Does it happen to you? Do you do the same with something in your life? Is there something coming between you and God, something that you know you're not supposed to do? You know it's wrong, but you do it, anyway, and you give God one excuse after another.

"I was brought up this way, Lord, you understand." "It's just how my father was. I have it in me, Lord, you understand." "It's my temper, Lord, you understand. It's the way I was born." "It's just how I'm wired, Lord, you understand." "I always drink like this, Lord, you understand." And God says, "No, I don't understand."

Let me translate that phrase, "you understand," into point-blank English: you and I want God to pat us on the head and say, "Oh, that's okay, I love you, anyway." We want God to accept and even approve what we do, even though it clearly goes against His Word, because quite frankly, we like that thing, we're comfortable with that thing, and we don't want anyone telling us it's wrong.

God, on the other hand, says, "Yes, I understand—that you're a sinner and can do nothing on your own to earn my love. I love you how you are, but I love you enough not to leave you how you are. I have better things for you, and that (fill in your sin) needs to go."

God knows all your thoughts. And more than that, His ways and His thoughts are higher than ours are (Isaiah 55:9). When God showed me that verse, I had to come clean. Ezra 9:6 describes my feelings: "Oh my God, I'm too ashamed and disgraced to lift up my face to you my God, because our sins are higher than our heads, and our guilt has reached to the heavens." That's how I felt. Have you ever felt that way? Do you feel that way now?

See, I figured I had brought it on myself. I knowingly crossed the line into sin; I got myself into it first by pushing God out of my decision-making process. Big mistake number one. I just didn't ask God about what I would do. Why? Because I knew it was wrong, and I simply didn't want to hear His answer. Then, I figured, okay,

Jack, you got yourself in this mess; you'll have to get yourself out the same way, without God. Big mistake number two. Sometimes, I'm so dense... if my son were in trouble, would I ignore him? No. My oldest son has been in trouble, and I have been there for him. I have seen the blessings in my own life of submitting to God's authority, yet I forget that I am God's son, and He will not ignore me. He wants to help me, but I won't go to Him.

Like the Prodigal Son, we can always turn back to God, and yet I didn't. And I can tell you this: once Satan had me in his grips, I really felt trapped, as if I couldn't turn back to God. Satan delighted in seeing me squirm and suffer, knowing he had succeeded in separating me from my Father by guilt and shame. I got an inkling of what Adam must have felt when he hid from God in the Garden of Eden.

Adam and Eve were in the Garden, having a great time fellowshipping with God, and then Satan came in and tempted them. They ate from the tree they weren't supposed to, and the first thing Adam did was run away from God. Of course, he ran. He knew he had sinned. Now, think about what Adam thought. He didn't even know what he was doing. He just went to hide, figuring, "Hey, I have to make a plan; what will I tell my Father? Oh man, this is bad. I'm in trouble."

And we're in trouble, too, because we're descended from Adam, and yeah, we sometimes do the same thing. We run away from God, thinking we have to make a plan. I know because I hung back from God, trying to figure out how to make this right, and anytime I thought I heard God calling me, I ran away, just as Adam did, until I realized I was too far gone. I realized that I was lost and stripped of the shadow of God's protective power, and if I didn't change direction, things would continue downhill. Psalm 91:1 says, "He who dwells in the shelter of the Most High will rest in the shadow of the Almighty." When I had been abiding under the shadow, I was fine, but when I chose my own way, when I chose not to ask God because I didn't want to hear what He had to say. I ran away from the shadow; I left my father's side; and I was no longer protected by Him. I knew I needed to get back under His protection.

My God, my Savior, was faithful to me, and He's faithful to you today. The same love God had for sinners when Jesus Christ died on the cross and rose again so that we could be in heaven forever is the same love God has for you and me today. Jesus paid the penalty for our sin, which is death (Romans. 6:23). That's the penalty; that's what we deserve, but Jesus paid it once and for all so that we who believe can count on Him to protect us today. Psalm 91:3 says, "Surely He will save you from the fowler's snare..." Surely! Not maybe, not once in a while, but "surely" He will deliver you and me from the snare of the fowler, from our enemies, and from even ourselves when we wander away. I know because it happened to me.

Now, listen to this, my status with God had not changed in God's eyes. Satan tricked me, and I thought that my status with God had changed, but it only changed in my mind and my heart, not with God. In my thinking, I was diminished; I was worthless to God because I had failed him and failed myself. Oh, foolish ignorant Christian that I am, questioning the one absolute certainty in my life, and that's God's unconditional love for me, proven multitudes of times, but most convincingly by Jesus' death for me on the cross.

This is the most important part of this whole chapter: God says, "So, if you think you are standing firm, be careful that you don't fall! No temptation has seized you, except what is common to man. God is faithful; he will not let you be tempted beyond what you can bear. But when you are tempted, he will also provide a way out so that you can stand up under it" (1 Corinthians 10:12–13). How often do we think we can wander along the sidelines of an old behavior or thought without being drawn into the game? Our former team, Satan and his cohorts, wants us back on the field and in the dirt with them. The best strategy is to avoid that team's playing field altogether, but we often fail when temptation sets in.

God always provides a way out of everything. Always, every time, no matter what you go through in your life, I don't care what it is. Alcohol? Drugs? Pornography? Do you have rage, anger, malice, jealousy, greed? Don't tell me God hasn't provided a way out. That's a cop out, what you are really saying is "Look, God, I won't take your way out because I don't like it."

That is the issue. God gives us the choice as to whether to take the way out or not. If you're an alcoholic, there's Alcoholics Anonymous. If you have anger problems, there's counseling. There's always an escape route. I know because it happened to me; I had to look at my own life; and I had to confess: "God, you did provide the way out, and I just wouldn't take it. I wanted my way out." Then sometimes, if we are honest we'll admit it, we don't want the way out; we just want to keep indulging the sin. I've been there too. I knew there was a way out. God had given it to me, but I was just too stubborn to take it.

God won't force it on us. Just like salvation, it's a gift, but you must take it. There's always an action required on our part, and I'll prove it to you. If you were dying of thirst in the desert, I came up, and I said, here's the water, you must still take it and swallow it. Even though it's right in front of you, if you don't take it and swallow it, you don't benefit from it.

We see this clearly in Mark 3:1–5, in which the Pharisees again tested Jesus, as usual, trying to find a reason to accuse Him. I paraphrase the passage to make it sound like something we'd hear today. The Pharisees said, "Can you heal on the Sabbath?" A man with a shriveled hand stood there while they asked Jesus that question. They taunted Him, "Well, will you heal Him?"

Jesus looked at them, and the Bible tells us He was angry at their stubborn hearts. He told the man to stretch out his hand, and He healed it. But why did the man have to stretch out his hand? Jesus is God. He could have just said, "You're healed." No, He said, "Stretch out your hand" because whatever little we can do, God wants us to do. Just as with the paralytic who was lowered down through the roof and lying there on the mat. Jesus told him to get up, take his mat, and go (Matthew 9, Mark 2, Luke 5, John 5). God's Word tells us, "So I say to you: Ask and it will be given to you; seek and you will find; knock and the door will be opened to you" (Luke 11:9). There's always an action required on our part (ask, seek, knock). We do what we are capable of and God does the rest. He steps in supernaturally and does everything else after we've done our part.

I know because it happened to me, and I want to share with you that I feel now how Adam must have felt when he walked with God before he sinned. I don't mean I feel as if I'm some super perfect person, but I feel restored to my full relationship with God. With peace in my heart, I can honestly stand before God and say, "Lord, right now I know of nothing between us."

So, who's the liar? Is it God, whose Word consistently reveals His love for you, who knows you will be tempted, and who provides a way out? Or is it you, who insists you're okay with God even while you hold on to something separating you from His best, you who denies that you even need a way out?

Oh, Lord, you've promised that your Word penetrates between joint and marrow, and that nothing is hidden from you, God, so show me what I hide from myself. Lord, today, I give to you what I have not given to you before. I see the way out that you have provided, and I will take it today, this very day.

11

Struggles with Sin

I sold my TV production company in 2002. A year later, I still believed that God called me to do something ministry-related, but restlessness crept in. As time went by, my mind switched back into corporate mode with thoughts like "Maybe I'll get back into business because the preaching thing isn't happening so quickly." I never take money for preaching so it wasn't about dollars, it was about being occupied doing something productive. Thanks to my pastor, Truman Herring, and his recommendations, I had a couple of preaching gigs—oops, I don't know if you are supposed to call them gigs in the pulpit world, but I do. At that point, it averaged just one a month and, even for an optimistic guy like me, that was not enough to keep me busy for real.

So, I figured that maybe I'd do something else. That idea seemed to get a confirmation one night when I took my son, Ricky, to his girlfriend's church. It was a Wednesday night, so I dropped him off at 6:30 and sat out in the parking lot for a minute. I could sense God's spirit nudging me to go into the service.

I said, "Actually, God, what I'd really like to do is go to the batting cages. Our softball team is in the playoffs trying to win a championship, and I need the practice."

God said, "No, Jack, you need to go into church."

"But I don't want to." And like a stubborn child, I stayed outside and called a friend about something totally unimportant. Ten minutes passed. "Okay, God, I'm leaving."

God's nudge turned into more of a mental shove. I don't hear him audibly or feel him physically; it's just a way of saying that I really sensed his Spirit telling me to go inside. Oh, fine. Can you just hear the heavy sigh as I slam the car door? I went inside, and it turned out that the pastor of that church was a guy who had worked for me as an actor when I had owned the TV production company. I couldn't believe it! I had wondered where he was for years.

What desperate, maniacal guy named Jack Levine, looking to justify his own behaviors and desires, wouldn't take that as a confirming sign from God that I was supposed to get back into the business? Was I just delusional? Or perhaps looking to twist and fit every circumstance into justifying my own way of thinking so I could have what I want and call it God's idea. (Of course you would never think of doing that in your life – you are squirming now, I hope!) I thought surely, God had led me to this guy, someone from my past in TV production who was now in ministry, to connect the dots and confirm my desire to go back into business. My idea was to stick with what I knew by opening a very small television production company, not a big one like the one I used to have, maybe eight or ten guys. We'd keep it casual, glorify God first, and our second priority would be to make a few bucks. I'd glorify God because I'd still get to preach on Sundays.

It all seemed to make sense in my mind until I examined my heart and asked myself, "Jack, do you really have the desire to do that?" The answer was no, I really didn't want to do it.

Not long after that realization, I had breakfast with my friend Richard, and we talked about it. He was in a similar boat, trying to think about what he would do with his future, and we began talking about the Israelites wandering in the desert, grumbling and complaining as God called them forward, called them to some place new, and they just wanted to go back to where they'd been. They wanted to go back to bondage, back to Egypt, and that attitude cost them 40 years. They didn't get to where they were supposed to go in the time they were supposed to go there.

I just want to trust God and not shortcut Him. I know God is right. Bruce Springsteen once wrote, "I pity the man who doubts what he's sure of." I didn't want to be that man!

So, where did that leave me? I have learned that trying to give up the things of the flesh is very difficult and that those things don't go away so quickly. Here's just one example, and it's very telling about the spiritual condition of my heart at that time. When I sold the business in 2002, there was a provision that if it kept going and succeeded, I'd get some residual income from it. That seemed like a reasonably good deal. Honestly, I wasn't sure if the company would survive. Obviously, there were many advantages for me to see it succeed, the biggest one was I would be paid, yet there was this part of my brain that wasn't so sure I wanted it to succeed. Sounds crazy, right? Yet, I had this craving to be right, to be considered a genius for selling out at the top.

Where did such a thought come from? Why wouldn't I want it to succeed, especially since it's success would give me an income that might carry me through for a little while? How ridiculous that I'd trade that income stream just to be proved right. Yet, this wasn't just a fleeting thought. It rolled around my mind for a while, and I had to push it out of my head to get rid of it. I was rather disgusted with myself because it was really just a nasty, evil thought that showed me for what I was—still a sinner, still dealing with many struggles such as jealousy, anger, and a desire for stuff that comes from the world.

Here are some other things God has shown me. In James 1:19–21, it says, "My dear brothers, take note of this: Everyone should be quick to listen, slow to speak and slow to become angry, for man's anger does not bring about the righteous life that God desires. Therefore, get rid of all moral filth and the evil that is so prevalent and humbly accept the word planted in you, which can save you."

Every believer is supposed to be quick to listen, slow to speak, and slow to become angry. Why? Because our anger doesn't produce the righteous life that God desires. Notice that God didn't say that we won't have anger; He didn't say that we won't have moral filth or evil, so we shouldn't be surprised when that stuff creeps into our bodies, minds, and hearts. We're supposed to get rid of them and to accept humbly the Word of God. Accept the love, peace, and Word, and they will help us get rid of the nasty stuff. Remember that nasty thought I had about the business failing so I could look like a genius businessman? The Word commanded me to get rid of that and to focus on what God had to say in Scripture.

Look at James 3:13–18: "Who is wise and understanding among you? Let him show it by his good life, by deeds done in the humility that comes from wisdom. But if you harbor bitter envy and selfish ambition in your hearts, do not boast about it or deny the truth. Such 'wisdom' does not come down from heaven but is earthly, unspiritual, of the devil. For where you have envy and selfish ambition, there you find disorder and every evil practice. But the wisdom that comes from heaven is first pure; then peace loving, considerate, submissive, full of mercy and good fruit, impartial and sincere. Peacemakers who sow in peace raise a harvest of righteousness."

God says if you are wise and you understand who you are in God's sight, then you will show it by your good deeds done out of humility, humility that comes from wisdom. What is wisdom? Wisdom is knowledge coupled with understanding, applied to life. First, you acquire knowledge by studying and learning; with that comes understanding, and then when you combine the two, you have the wisdom to know how to use the knowledge you have.

When it comes to our Christian life, we need wisdom to know how to live. We start with the instruction manual, the Bible, to gain the knowledge of what God has to say about how we should live. Then, we need to think about how those instructions apply to our relationships, our jobs, our neighborhoods, and so forth. As we do that, we gain understanding, and as we apply our knowledge and understanding, we develop wisdom.

James goes on to say, "But if you harbor bitter envy and selfish ambition in your heart [remember the example I gave about not wanting the company to succeed?] do not boast about it or deny the truth." If there is somebody you resent, if there is envy, jealousy, anger, malice, rage, other sinful thoughts or sins, God is very clear—get rid of it.

Sometimes, we don't even realize we are in denial. I was guilty of this. We are so busy living our lives that we don't acknowledge the resentment, the envy, or the whatever. We pretend or even convince ourselves that we don't have these issues in our heart. Most people are so busy being a husband, father, wife, mother, worker, employee, neighbor, volunteer, and so forth that they don't have time to see those things in themselves, and so they never stop to look at them. God says that whatever you do, don't boast about it, and don't deny the truth.

God's word goes on to say in Matthew 10:35-38, "For where you have envy and selfish ambition you will find disorder and every evil practice." What's envy? Envy is wanting something somebody else has. It's also being mad at a guy for having it. What amazes me is that I only envy people I know. I couldn't care less about anybody living on the beach in North Carolina. Why? Because I don't know anybody in North Carolina, but I do have a couple of friends down here in south Florida that live on the beach, and I envy them sometimes (except when hurricane season rolls around). It doesn't matter what you have; it seems you can always envy the next guy who has more than you do.

The wisdom from God illustrates the characteristics we are to have toward people. We are to be sincere, considerate, peace loving, and pure. If we have those things in our hearts, then we love other people rather than wanting to see something taken away from those who have it. Or how about those times when you're so mad at someone, you wouldn't be upset if something bad happened to him or her? We've all had those times, so what should we do with them?

Work at being a peacemaker instead. The passage in James concludes with this observation: "Peacemakers who sow in peace raise a harvest of righteousness." Can you imagine standing before God on Judgment Day, and God says, "Wow, Jack, look at this harvest of righteousness you did! Good work, well done, good and faithful servant." Isn't that what we all want to hear at the end? What will your harvest look like from heaven's standpoint? I can tell you that every choice we make down here to do things God's way will affect how bountiful a harvest we have.

God reveals something else, and that is my struggle with covetousness versus contentment. In 1 Timothy 6:6–12, it says, "But godliness with contentment is great gain. For we brought nothing into the world, and we can take nothing out of it. But if we have food and clothing, we will be content with that. People who want to get rich fall into temptation and a trap and into many foolish and harmful desires that plunge men into ruin and destruction. For the love of money is a root of all kinds of evil. Some people, eager for money, have wandered from the faith and pierced themselves with many griefs."

If I live according to God's Word, I will be content with what He chooses to give me. Then, I'm not envious; I'm not jealous; I don't act with malice or slander others; and I'm certainly not angry. Have you seen contented people in your life? Have you seen the peace and love of God in the content person? That's what God talks about. Whatever I have, it's because God has given it to me, and if I am truly content with that, God calls that great gain.

What about the connection between money and evil? Money is neither evil nor holy; it is simply an object. The warning about money, then, is about how we view it and what priority we give it in our lives. If we make it the top priority, then Scripture says it can lead to ruin and destruction. As I write this, the mortgage crisis has sunk so far that the whole economy of the United States is tanking and dragging the world down with it. The crisis has its root in financially "creative" actions in the name of profit... and it has plunged nations into serious economic harm. Instead of pursuing the temptation to get rich, Scripture advises us, "But you, man of God, flee from all this, and pursue righteousness, godliness, faith, love, endurance and gentleness. Fight the good fight of the faith" (1 Timothy 6:11–12a).

It was very tempting for me to return to what I knew and try to "Christianize" it, so I can say it's for God, when really doing that would be all about what's comfortable for me. Just because I slap a "Christian" label on it doesn't mean it's what God asked me to do. God asked me to commit to trusting Him; He made a commitment to me in His Word that He will provide all my needs if I will put Him first (Matthew 6:33). And putting Him first means committing that He's more important than what's comfortable or convenient for me.

For you and me and for every believer, choosing to make that commitment is exactly where the rubber meets the road with God.

So now is your moment of truth —you have to choose. The envelope,
please!

12

Are You Ready?

That little dash between the date you were born and the date you die is your life. Boom— that's it. My dash started in 1958. When it ends is up to God, and that same truth applies to everyone, everywhere, for all time. Birth and death are universal, as is this question: What will we do with our dash?

David, the psalmist, considered this question thousands of years ago as well and wrote in Psalm 39:4, "Show me, O Lord, my life's end and the number of my days; let me know how fleeting is my life." If you knew what day you would die, you'd have a much finer appreciation for the days of your life because it would be a finite number.

Without knowing that date, we often take for granted our life and the amount of time we actually have. Psalm 39 continues in verse 5,

"You have made my days a mere handbreadth; the span of my years is as nothing before you. Each man's life is but a breath." Have you noticed how you can see your breath on a cold morning, but just for a moment? Poof. An exhale, a white puff, and then it's gone, and God says that's exactly how our lives are here on earth. The older I get, the easier it is to believe that analogy.

Verse 6 goes on to say "'Man is a mere phantom as he goes to and fro: He bustles about, but only in vain; he heaps up wealth, not knowing who will get it.'" A phantom is someone who doesn't even exist. God says your life is so quick that you're like a phantom and a busy one at that, on the go, hustling here and there, and worrying about how to get all the stuff done that seems so important, but you do it in vain.

In vain? In vain, when it's done apart from God. In Ecclesiastes, King Solomon searches for the meaning of life through pleasures, intellect, and labor. The bottom-line conclusion of all his research is that it all comes down to vanity—fleeting things with no value, because the only things that matter are loving God with all your heart and enjoying what you do each day as you serve the Lord. All our rushing is for nothing. And what about the wealth we spend our lives accumulating? We don't always know who will get it, or how they will spend it. All we can do is prepare the best we can. Are you ready for your dying day? Sounds grim, but it's a legitimate question from both a practical and, especially, a spiritual standpoint.

Middle age is upon me, at least according to the AARP, and I am in the process of planning for my family's future if I'm not around. This is fresh on my mind because a friend of mine just died. He had planned for his family's future, but it turns out he made some mistakes in his estate planning, and now, there's a fight between his kids and his second wife (not the birth mother of his children). You know what? The money will not go where he wanted it to go. In fact, the lawyers will probably eat it all up. He planned in vain, because once you've breathed your last breath, there are no second chances to make things right, either with the lawyers or with God.

No second chances. Scripture says we die, and we face judgment (Hebrews 9:27), so we need to get things right while we're alive. How can we do that? We can ask God like the psalmist did in Psalm 119:34, "Give me understanding, and I will keep your law and obey it with all my heart." Isn't that our prayer? It should be. God is basically saying you can have all the understanding you want. Now that you have understanding, go and do what you understand that you should do. It's not hard to understand what God wants us to do.

Psalm 119:35 says, "Direct me in the path of your commands, for there I find delight." Do I ask God to do that? Do I open His Word and read, study, and find delight in it? I do now, but I didn't used to. Like Solomon, I searched for joy and delight in the world, searched every conceivable way I could think to get it. I certainly didn't have the same resources as Solomon, so my *research* involved seeking drugs, women, gambling, wealth, jobs, relationships, and sex, but none of them brought me the delight the world promised. In fact, I'm sure if you've searched in your own way, you've gotten the same result, which is a lack of joy.

Where does the joy that we desire and search for come from? The psalmist had it right; it comes only from the Lord, and he goes on in 119:36–37 to say, "Turn my heart toward your statutes and not toward selfish gain. Turn my eyes away from worthless things;

preserve my life according to your word." Turn my eyes from worthless things, the things that seem as if they'll give me joy, but don't. Help me focus on the real treasure, God and His Word. I love how God's Word always confirms God's Word. Matthew 6:21 says, "Where your treasure is, there your heart will be also."

God's Word continually assures us that our joy and our delight come from God and not the stuff of the world. We can pray and ask God to help us change our focus—to turn our eyes away from the mall displays, sales flyers, and sports teams and to turn our eyes toward Him and His Word. The stuff of the world promises freedom and excitement, but honestly, when was the last time you looked at your overstuffed closets, garages, attics, and storage units and jumped up and down for joy, shouting about the freedom that all that stuff brought you? If you're like me, those closets and storage units are full of things that excited you for a moment or a day, perhaps a bit longer, but now they simply represent obligations, burdens, and frustration. We had to work and work some more to buy those things, maintain and clean them, insure them, pack and move them, and of course, store them. Instead of hearing freedom's bells, I hear alarm bells!

Did the psalmist deal with this quest for freedom? Yes, he goes on in 119:44–45 to say, "I will always obey your law, for ever and ever. I will walk about in freedom, for I have sought out your instruction." Freedom doesn't come from having more stuff; freedom from the burdens of life comes from following God's instruction. He will show us what's important to hold on to and what's not. He will show us how to make choices that will build us up rather than tear us down, and He will show us how to let go of things weighing us down and keeping us from being ready for the joy and blessings He wants to give us. If we seek out His instruction, He will show them to us. They are right there in the Bible for us to read (and confirmed by the Holy Spirit in your heart), and God will teach us how to apply them to our lives if we will seek Him out.

Verse 46 goes on to say, "I will speak of your statutes before kings and will not be put to shame, for I delight in your commands because I love them." Do you delight in the commands of the Lord? Do you love them? If you do, they are not a burden to live under, but a joy to live by.

I'm a serious baseball fan, and if someone told me I could be second baseman for the New York Yankees, believe me, I would not complain about batting practice at 10:00 a.m., wearing a uniform like everybody else, or abiding by a curfew the night before a game. I'd be the happiest man in the world. Those rules would not be a burden to live under, but a joy to live by because I love baseball so much. And when I live by those rules, then and only then, am I allowed to participate, play on the team and get the most out of the sport.

The love of the Lord *should* be the exact same thing. If you find the Lord's commands burdensome in your life, you need to communicate with Him and ask yourself what you delight in, because obviously, it's not the Lord. Loving the Lord makes living by His commands a joy and helps you be ready to get the most blessings possible in life.

If you're married, think about the love you have for your spouse. You can't wait to do things for him or her. It's not a chore to pick up your bride at 8:00; it's a joy, and you can't wait to get there. (Okay, I know some of you might be single or are well past that starry-eyed beginning of your relationship with your spouse, but you get the picture. When we love someone, it is a joy to serve them and be with them, and when we love God, it's the same way.)

Sometimes, our thoughts and our focus affect our ability to delight in the commands of the Lord. In Psalm 119:48, it says, "I lift up my hands to your commands, which I love, and I meditate on your decrees." What do you meditate on during the day? Is it pornography? Is it gambling? Drugs, work, money, lust, or anger? Is there somebody you haven't forgiven? When your mind is full of such thoughts, you cannot develop your love for God and His Word. They are in opposition to one another.

To change that, start by deliberately changing your thoughts. It helps to read the Bible, so why not go to Psalm 119 and hang out for a while? The more time you spend in God's Word, the more you'll be able to rely on it for help and hope to let go of the porn, the gambling, the whatever-it-is that wants to make you think that God's Word is a burden.

Sometimes, a period of suffering we weren't ready for affects our delight in the Lord. In those times, too, we can turn to God's Word. "Remember your word to your servant, for you have given me hope. My comfort in my suffering is this: Your promise preserves my life" (Psalm 119:49–50). It's that hope, comfort, and certainty in Jesus Christ that is the entire basis for our faith. Jesus gives us eternal life in the future, but He also preserves us through times of suffering. Knowing Jesus and His Word will help you be ready for those times as well.

You say, "Jack, I'm not ready for any more suffering. Aren't Christians supposed to have it easy?"

No. The Bible never promises the easy life. It speaks of trials and tribulations that we *will* have (not *might* have). (See James 1:2–4, John 16:33, and 1 Peter.) God allows us to go through trials and tribulations so He can mold us and shape us into the men and women He wants us to be, so He can use us for the purpose for which He created us.

Along with trials and tribulations, there will also be conflict, something that catches many people, believers and not, off guard. The Bible does not guarantee peace everywhere. "Do not suppose that I have come to bring peace to the earth" (Matthew 10:34a). Are you ready for the conflicts that will come your way?

You say, "Wait a minute. God says He's a God of peace. If I believe in God, why would I have conflicts?" The peace God offers is peace with Him. Before we are saved, we are God's enemies, and we are in conflict with all that He is; once we are rightly connected to God through Jesus, we are no longer in conflict with Him, but rather, we have peace with Him. That peace means we will spend eternity with Him in heaven. The peace God promises is between man and God, not peace on earth. The verse continues, "I did not come to bring peace, but a sword. For I have come to turn 'a man against his father, a daughter against her mother, a daughter-in-law against her mother-in-law--a man's enemies will be the members of his own household.' Anyone who loves his father or mother more than Me is not worthy of Me; anyone who loves his son or daughter more than Me is not worthy of Me..."

I love my wife. I love my kids certainly more than I love myself. Now that I have kids, I understand even more how much Jesus loves me and why He sacrificed his life and died on the cross for you and me. I understand how you could love your child so much that, of course, you would die for that child. I'd take any suffering I could if it would prevent my children from suffering. So Lord, why can't I love my kids and my wife more than you?

God didn't say you shouldn't love them. Of course, He wants us to love our wives and our families; Scripture commands us to love them and provide for them. What God said is that we cannot love them more than we love Him. He said we can't put anything in the world ahead of Him, and so strongly did He want to illustrate this point that He named the things He knew would mean the most to us—spouse and family.

Your wife, your kids, the people you love the most—if you love them more than God, you're not worthy of God. That's a heavy-duty statement. Our reaction is often something like this: Lord, I accepted you into my life. Aren't I worthy? I did what I was supposed to do. Salvation is a one-time irrevocable transaction between you and me. I confessed and invited God into my heart, I'm saved; I will go to heaven. So, how can I not be worthy?

God says you're not to put anything in this world before Him.

Who do you love most on this earth? Would you die for your wife? Your kids? Your friends? I bet you would, but would you die for God? We think that's just martyrdom from the old days, but what about Cassie Bernall in 1999? Newspaper reports said she was the girl in Columbine High School who refused to deny being a Christian, even though she knew she'd be shot for her faith. What would you have said if you had been in her shoes? What did you say last week when someone got on your case about Christianity?

Are you ready to live out what you say you believe, every day? "Anyone who does not take up his cross and follow me is not worthy of me. Whoever finds his life will lose it and whoever loses his life for My sake will find it" (Matthew 10:38–39). The Message translates the passage this way: "'If you don't go all the way with Me, through thick and thin, you don't deserve Me. If your first concern is to look after yourself, you'll never find yourself. But if you forget about yourself and look to Me, you'll find both yourself and Me.'"

Have you taken up Christ's cross, or have you taken up the cross of the world and self? This is where your faith comes in. This is where you find out what it's all about, and it's a daily choice.

God is basically saying, "If you will lose your life for Me, if you will abandon your selfish worldly desires and put Me first, you will have a bigger life than you can ever imagine. But if you don't do that, if instead you put the things of the world first, not only will you not have Me, but you will also lose your life (you'll have fewer blessings, less peace, and eternity in hell)."

Let's see what prevents us from putting the Lord first and serving the way we should. Jesus speaks in Matthew 13:3–12. It's a very familiar parable, The Parable of the Sower.

Then He told them many things in parables, saying: "A farmer went out to sow his seed. As he was scattering the seed, some fell along the path, and the birds came and ate it up. Some fell on rocky places, where it did not have much soil. It sprang up quickly, because the soil was shallow. But when the sun came up, the plants were scorched, and they withered because they had no root. Other seed fell among thorns, which grew up and choked the plants. Still other seed fell on good soil, where it produced a crop—a hundred, sixty or thirty times what was sown. He who has ears, let him hear."

So, what prevents us from putting God first and serving Him as we should is the depth to which His Word has taken root in our lives. The parable presents four different responses to the Word that is made available to us. Which person are you? We pick up the passage in Matthew 13:18:

Listen then to what the parable of the sower means: When anyone hears the message about the kingdom and does not understand it, the evil one comes and snatches away what was sown in his heart. This is the seed sown along the path. The one who received the seed that fell on rocky places is the man who hears the word and at once receives it with joy. But since he has no root, he lasts only a short time. When trouble or persecution comes because of the word, he quickly falls away. The one who received the seed that fell among the thorns is the man who hears the word, but the worries of this life and the deceitfulness of wealth choke it, making it unfruitful. But the one who received the seed that fell on good soil is the man who hears the word and understands it. He produces a crop, yielding a hundred, sixty or thirty times what was sown.

That third one sent a shiver down my spine when I read it years ago because I realized that was me. Sure, I knew we all fell into one of the four categories: first, the guy who hears the Word, but just doesn't believe it. Second, the guy who hears the Word and thinks, "This is great," but the minute the troubles of the world come along, he's gone. He had no real root. He really didn't get it. Third, this is me, the guy who hears the Word, who claims to love the Lord, but the worries of life and deceit of riches choke him and make him unfruitful. Ouch. I needed to hear that, but I sure didn't like to hear that. What I really want to be is the fourth guy, who is the one God desires, the one who hears, understands, and produces a crop above and beyond what was sown. That's what God intends for each of us, that we multiply 30, 60, or 100 fold.

What's your number? I was Guy Number Three wanting to be Guy Number Four, realizing that I love God, but the world—status, wealth, image—was a major focus for me. God revealed this to me years ago. He said "Jack, there's one thing you must do. Just one thing, and that's die to self. If you don't want to be the guy choked by the riches and worries of the world, then you just need to die to yourself. Then, you'll be good soil, and then you'll be ready to produce a good crop."

I'm no farmer, and I don't come from a rural background. I'm a city boy turned suburbanite, through and through, so it makes me feel a little better to see that even the disciples didn't quite get what Jesus said. They finally asked Him why He spoke to the people in parables, and "He replied, 'The knowledge of the secrets of the kingdom of heaven has been given to you, but not to them. Whoever has will be given more, and he will have an abundance. Whoever does not have, even what he has will be taken from him'" (Matthew 13:11–12).

When we became believers, we became children of God, adopted into His kingdom. The Holy Spirit of God came to live inside of us. According to Jesus, we know the secrets of the kingdom of heaven, and in fact, we will be given more (Matthew 13:12). So, what do we have? We've been given the keys to the kingdom of heaven(Matthew 16:19), an inheritance that can never perish or fade (1 Peter 1:4), access to God's throne of grace (Hebrews 4:6), the knowledge of the secrets of the kingdom of heaven (Matthew 13:11), and that little thing (being sarcastic, of course, I mean *huge* thing!) about my sin debt that would have caused me to burn for all eternity in hell has been paid. It has been wiped away and cast aside forever.

Scripture says whoever has will be given more; it's there for the asking. Do I want what the world offers, or do I ask for what the Holy Spirit offers? Do I seek after and apply the knowledge of God or the knowledge of the world? Does God add to me spiritually, or does God take away? The answers to those questions help me see whether or not I am ready to produce that good crop God mentioned earlier.

How about you? Are you ready to produce that crop God calls you to, a crop of peaceful relationships, of gratitude, of joy, contentment, and blessings? A crop that makes others look at you and say, "Whatever you've got, I want—who is this Jesus?" Are you ready? You will be if you seek Him, study His Word, and apply that Word to your daily life.

Jesus was on a roll, so He gave another farming example for those who didn't get the one about the sower. It comes right after the Sower, and it's called the Parable of the Weeds, starting in verse 24: The kingdom of heaven is like a man who sowed good seed in his field. But while everyone was sleeping, his enemy came and sowed weeds among the wheat, and went away. When the wheat sprouted and formed heads, then the weeds also appeared. The owner's servants came to him and said, "Sir, didn't you sow good seed in your field? Where then did the weeds come from?" "An enemy did this," he replied. The servants asked him, "Do you want us to go and pull them up?" "No," he answered, "because while you are pulling the weeds, you may root up the wheat with them. Let both grow together until the harvest. At that time I will tell the harvesters: First collect the weeds and tie them in bundles to be burned; then gather the wheat and bring it into my barn."

Burning the weeds—that's what happens to people who reject God. God lets them walk on this earth with you and me, maybe even in our own homes. They might be a brother, sister, mother, or father. They might be our employers, our friends, or our enemies, but God is very clear. If you reject Him, you will have this life to live, but at the end, on Judgment Day, you will be gathered up, burned, and spend eternity in hell.

A lot of people are of the opinion that hell isn't real. Well, most of us should know by now that opinion does not equal fact. I can have an opinion about the existence of the tooth fairy, but my opinion will not affect the facts about the existence of the tooth fairy. What we think doesn't necessarily have any bearing on what's real. For example, say I place two glasses on a table in front of you, and both are filled with clear liquid. Would you think there's water in both these glasses? Or would you think there's water in one and something different in the other? With all due respect, what you think is in them doesn't change what's in them, does it? In this example, one glass has water, and the other has rubbing alcohol. If you drank one, you'd be fine, while the other one would send you to the hospital, even though you thought it was safe to drink.

The same holds for Scripture, which states that hell is a real place. Either the Bible is all true, or it's not true, but it's not half true. It's not true for the parts that I find to be convenient and false for the parts that I don't like. God does not offer us a salad-bar theology. His Word is very clear. You are either part of his kingdom or not. And you can only become part of his kingdom and have the benefits of his kingdom and his promises if you believe in Christ. If not, when you die and face judgment, you will be outside of his kingdom, separated from God, and in the end, that means hell forever. No second chances.

Will it be God's barn, or will it be burning with the weeds? Are you ready to choose?

"Are You Ready?" is also the name of a song Bob Dylan wrote after he got saved, and the lyrics include this verse: "When destruction comes swiftly and there's no time to say fare thee well, have you decided if you want to be in heaven or in hell? Are you ready? Have you got some unfinished business? Is there something holding you back? Are you thinking for yourself or are you following the pack? Are you ready to meet Jesus? Are you where you want to be? Will he know you when he sees you or will he say 'depart from me'?"

The thing we should do to make sure we are ready is to live our lives to please God, and when we do that, we will have joy, peace, and abundance (don't confuse that term with money). At this point, some of us need to face the things in our lives that make us view God's ways as a burden and that prevent us from living the abundant life. We each probably have an area of our life we need to turn over to Jesus in order to experience true freedom, but we've hesitated, holding on. Why not do that now? Are you ready? If so, you can say a prayer such as this: "Oh, Father, I bring to you my addictions, my abuses, my greed, my issue. I admit those things and lay them before you. And Lord, I finally bring the worst possible thing I could, and that's myself, just as I am. Thank you for loving me, just as I am." Name the issues you deal with and picture yourself laying them at the foot of the cross for God to deal with.

Finally, as believers, we should ask ourselves if we are ready to receive our heavenly rewards. Rewards, you ask? Like bonus points on your credit card? Well, sort of, in a much holier way, and these points are good forever! God not only promises that we can live an abundant life on earth (John 10:10), but also that we will receive rewards in heaven for what we do on earth. God says it clearly in Jeremiah 17:10, "I the Lord search the heart and examine the mind to reward a man according to his conduct, according to what his deeds deserve." The topic of eternal rewards could fill a completely different book, so I encourage you to study the following verses for yourself and to seek God's heart on how they apply to you: 2 Corinthians 5:10, "For we all must appear before the judgment seat of Christ, that each one may receive what is due Him for the things done while in the body, whether good or bad"; Revelation 22:12, "Behold I am coming soon! My reward is with me, and I will give to everyone according to what He has done"; and Matthew 5:12, "Rejoice and be glad because great is your reward in heaven."

So, do you remember your dash, that little line after your birth date? That itty-bitty line is your life, and it's how long you have to prepare for eternity. I hope you're getting ready to spend yours in heaven because I look forward to meeting you there.

Are you ready for your dash? You know your birth date and birthplace. Now, think about the other side of the dash. There are no second chances. Only God can fill in that date, whenever He decides your time on earth is up, but you can determine and control for sure the rewards and blessings you'll receive by living in complete obedience to God. So, remember, in that regard, you control your own fate and destiny. Truly a moment of truth for every believer... *where the rubber meets the road with God!*

13

Rules for Holy Living

Do those three little words, "Some assembly required," send you into the stress zone? Your fingers shake, and your palms start sweating because you don't know till you open the package whether the instructions will even be there or not. Will they be in plain English? Will they be easy? Did the product designer know what he was doing? A friend I know bought a desk from Office Depot, and there were no assembly directions; instead, there were a few pictures on the box. It kept her and her two sons busy for quite a few hours putting it together.

What's all that have to do with Rules for Holy Living? Well, we can't live a holy life if we don't have the instructions, and unlike that time my friend bought the desk, they don't come stamped on our backsides when we're born. We assemble our lives as we grow, and much of it depends on the instructions we get along the way and who those instructions come from. In my case, I got little religious training at all (it was offered; I was just too stupid as a kid to take it), so as I assembled my "life pieces" over the years, I screwed up a bunch of times.

All that sounds kind of funny, maybe, until we realize perhaps we put ourselves together wrong. When I did that, it made me squirm in my seat. Too many people assume they are right with God because they went to Sunday school a few times or confirmation class, or they hit the Easter and Christmas services. Maybe even you. Some think they did the "right thing" at a church service by walking up the isle. Maybe they did it for their grandmother's sake? Maybe that's why you did it. Did your father pay you to go, so your mother would be happy? Maybe you just wanted to be able to say yes, I was confirmed, dedicated, or baptized. All that external stuff doesn't get you a personal relationship with God, and it sure doesn't fool God. I can guarantee you that.

When we do something visibly religious for the sake of what some other human will think or say, we've missed the point. All we should care about is what God would say. He makes it clear He's not all about whether we go through the visible motions of being religious. In 1 Samuel 16:7, God tells the prophet Samuel, "...The Lord does not look at the things man looks at. Man looks at the outward appearance, but the Lord looks at the heart."

If that's what God wants to look at when He looks at us, then we need to do the same. We need to look at our heart's motivation and desire and see if what we want is what He wants for us, and that is to become more and more like Christ. So, I've made a habit over the years of praying for my desires and goals to line up with what God wants for me, rather than making my prayers all about what I want and what I prefer. I will not make my Christian life center around me. I truly want to submit myself humbly to God's love. I want to humble myself before Him and turn from my wicked ways, and I want to see His face.

I remember back in 2002 one particular instance of what we Christian's like to jokingly (or sarcastically... take your pick) call an "Opportunity for Spiritual Growth," or in regular English, a trial, problem, or issue. This one played itself out as I tried to make what seemed to be a difficult decision about the future of my television production business.

I founded the company with a partner in 1994 in Pompano Beach, Florida. He was a Christian guy. We were fifty/fifty partners. The business was great. God blessed it; my life was turning around; and we witnessed to people through the business and watched people come to Christ. I mean it was just a terrific ride, up until the September 11, 2001, terrorist attack on the World Trade Center Towers in New York City, which delivered a crippling blow to our economy. Shortly after that, things started changing for the economy and then for us. Business dropped off. We started pouring money back into the company each month, and I remember sitting there talking to God: "OK, God, either we go out of business because the economy will knock us out of business, or the company will turn around and be profitable again, either way then I'll leave and do ministry work."

I really figured it would be one of those two things. I felt God had worked on my heart and drawn me closer to Him and wanted me in ministry. My partner was 10 years younger than I was, so it seemed like a great idea to turn the business over to him, hopefully while it was on top of its game, which would be a nice way to go out. You know, leave while you're the champion. Maybe get some dollars out of it, or we go out of business, and if that's God's will, so be it. This mental pendulum swung back and forth for eight months. The whole time, I prayed constantly, but there was no change in the business whatsoever. For eight months, we poured money back in, just enough to stay afloat with just enough business coming in to keep us there— just enough that we went further under each month. You probably know how that feels, whether it's in your business or your home finances. Not a fun place to hang out for any length of time, and we endured close to a whole year of this.

I'd prayed about it constantly, and one night, God woke me up and said, "Jack, I'm not going to make this decision for you. The company will not go bankrupt, and it won't turn around until you make a decision. It is going to stay just like it is. If you want to come follow me, then you have to choose to come and follow me."

That day, I decided. It was in May of 2002. I sold my interest out to my partner, and I said, "All right, God, I'm following you. And where we are going, I don't know."

Preaching is my real desire. However, all along, my prayer has been that I would do what God wants and not what I want. "Lord, if preaching isn't your plan for me, then show me the ministry you would have me in." I continue to humble myself before Him and seek His direction. Over time, I realized that my prayers were often along the lines of "God, I want to be more holy. I want to be like you.

I love you and want to be just like you. Please, please, please, make me more holy and then I can do better and be a better guy."

God, in His infinite wisdom and way, pointed me to the Scripture and said "Jack, I won't do this for you. I won't make you more holy, but you can be more holy if you want to. I'll show you how, but you have to do it."

And I realized it is often that way in our lives. I heard my own words: "and then I'll leave and do ministry work," "and then I can do better and be a better guy." *And then...* two little words full of irresponsibility because I tried to put a condition on what I would do for God: "I'll do this for you, God, *after* you do something for me."

Man, that revelation hurt. And we all do the same thing. We ask God to do something for us that we can do ourselves, and then we blame God when it isn't done, and we are not how we want to be. What happens is that God will take care of the impossible, but He wants us to do certain things. We are the ones who have to act in faith. Once I realized the ball was in my court to act, it was a little scary. After all, I had no spiritual training when I was growing up, no understanding of what it meant to be holy or, especially, how to become holy. All I knew from my childhood was you could bribe your way through some ceremonies to get the desired appearance of holiness to benefit others.

How would I move beyond that and understand how to become holier in God's sight? God showed me how in Scripture. I went through this same prayer theme with God one morning praying to be more holy. I opened my NIV Bible, and I had to laugh. Imagine praying to God to make you more holy, then waking up one morning, having your quiet time, and opening the Bible to Colossians 3 where the NIV headline for that section states "Rules for Holy Living." Sometimes, God cracks me up. I had the *rulebook* all along and didn't see it!

"Okay, God," I said aloud. "Let's see what the rules are."

The first one is clear. Chapter 3, verses 1 and 2, "Since, then, you have been raised with Christ, set your hearts on things above, where Christ is seated at the right hand of God. Set your minds on things above, not on earthly things."

I stopped right there and asked myself, what is the focus of my life? I ask you the same thing. What is the focus of your life? Is it your job? Money? A girlfriend, boyfriend, husband, or wife? Maybe it's sports. Or is it pleasing yourself? Is the purpose of your life, as mine was for a long time, just to get as much pleasure as you can? Media multi-millionaire Ted Turner (the founder of CNN news and a pioneer of the cable television industry) once said that, after age 15, life is a repeat. I matured late, so I guess I'm a little different from Ted, but I certainly will say that after age 21, you just do the same stuff. Doesn't that get dull?

Who is the focus of your life? Is it you, or is it Christ? Is church a one-hour-per-week obligation to fulfill, a requirement you do to stay on God's good side? Hey, give that up. God looks at the heart, remember? If that's where you are, then apply that same thinking to other relationships. Would you be a good husband if you saw your wife one hour a week? Would you be a good father if you saw your kids one hour a week?

I don't think so. God very specifically says to set your mind on things above, and you can't really get that mindset continually by being in church one hour a week. So, if you want to be holy, the first step is to set your mind on things above, like God, Jesus and heaven. When we do that, the things of earth, career, status, titles, and the stress of trying to keep those things up for the sake of appearances will fade in importance.

God goes on to say, in 3:5–8, "Put to death, therefore, whatever belongs to your earthly nature: sexual immorality, impurity, lust, evil desires and greed, which is idolatry. Because of these, the wrath of God is coming. You used to walk in these ways, in the life you once lived. But now you must rid yourselves of all such things as these: anger, rage, malice, slander, and filthy language from your lips." Ridding yourself of these things means throwing them out—you get rid of them, so they are gone forever.

In case we wonder what things belong to our earthly nature, God is kind enough to be very specific. Sexual immorality, impurity, lust, evil desires, and greed, which is idolatry. God did not say that we wouldn't have these things; as a matter of fact, I interpret this passage very specifically to mean we would have all these desires. I'm going to have sexual, immoral thoughts; I'll be impure; and I'll lust, have evil desires, and be greedy. And I know I'm not the only one. If you're a human being, you'll have the same desires.

But I also now have the desire to be holy. I want to have God's full blessing on my life; I want to know Him and walk with Him; and when I get to heaven, I want Him to pat me on the back and say well done, good and faithful servant. You're reading this book, so I assume that you desire the same thing. God says if you want that, then put those other things to death. That means to kill them; that means destroy them, eliminate them, so they don't exist anymore.

Next, in verses 9 and 10, he tells us, "Do not lie to each other, since you have taken off your old self with its practices and have put on the new self." You're on God's team now, and things will be different. If you were on the Boston Red Sox last week, you used to play your games at Fenway Park, and if you were traded to the New York Yankees this week, you would no longer show up at Fenway Park to play your game. You would now go to Yankee Stadium. You would no longer put on a Red Sox uniform; you would now put on your Yankee uniform. As a believer, you're on God's team now, and God says, don't lie. Let your yes be a yes and your no be a no. Everyone can know a tree by its fruit, so if we claim to be a Christian, then people should be able to look at our lives and see evidence of Christianity all through it.

God goes on to say, "...there is no Greek or Jew, circumcised or uncircumcised, barbarian, Scythian, slave or free, but Christ is all, and is in all." No labels, other than we are all brothers and sisters in Christ. People come up to me and say, "Hey, you're Jewish; are you a 'Jew for Jesus'?" I say no. I know it's an organization, but I don't belong to it. I tell them that, in my mind, there are only two categories of people in the world, saved and unsaved. I don't know any other categories, but I am definitely in the saved category, regardless of what categories or labels others apply to me.

I had to go through this with my father. He said to me, "So, you're not Jewish anymore."

I said, "No, Dad, I'm still Jewish. I'm as Jewish as I am white. I was born that way; I could not be more Jewish if I wanted to be.

I'm privileged and glad to be Jewish, but Jesus Christ is the Lord of my life, and that's by far the most important thing to me. I'm saved and that makes me a Christian." When God tells us "...no Greek or Jew, circumcised or uncircumcised...," he means we are all brothers in Christ. That's it. We are all together.

And the next verse goes on to say, "Therefore as God's chosen people, holy and dearly loved, clothe you with compassion, kindness, humility, gentleness and patience." Clothe yourself? I try to imagine I am getting dressed in the morning, and I put on these signs as if they were big badges: compassion, kindness, humility, gentleness, and patience. They cover my clothes, and I walk the street wearing these signs. Do you believe that the actions of my life, or your life if you were to wear that clothing, would be as they are today? I think I would live to reflect what my sign says. I think I would check myself a little more than I would if I didn't have the God signs hanging on my clothes. God is very specific. We are to clothe ourselves with these things. We are to put them on so that everybody can see them. Doing this will help us toward a more holy life.

Then, he says (Colossians 3:13), "Bear with each other and forgive whatever grievances you may have against one another. Forgive as the Lord forgave you." Oh, man, don't tell me we are talking about forgiveness again! I already told you a few chapters ago I have a problem with that one. I just don't want to forgive some people! However, God believes that forgiveness is important. In fact, and God reminds me as He reminds you, it is so important that we need to talk about it again. When the disciples came to Jesus and asked Him how they should pray, He included instructions about the need to forgive others: "...and forgive us our trespasses as we forgive those who trespass against us" (Matthew 6:14–15 and Luke 11:4).

Jesus told them, how you forgive others is how God will forgive you. Our natural mind wants to hold a grudge, stay angry, get revenge, and not trust God to repay as He promised He would on Judgment Day. When we don't forgive, it shows we don't trust God to judge according to His own timing. We are basically saying, "God, I don't believe you will take care of that guy on Judgment Day, and even if you do, I don't want to wait. I have to take care of him my way."

God says, "No you don't. I'll take care of him, but if you don't forgive him, I won't forgive you."

Obviously, forgiving others is both mandatory and crucial to holy living. There's no getting around it. If you want to be holy in God's eyes, then you have to practice forgiveness. Not just say it, but practice it; do it.

Forgiveness. Not lying. Putting to death lots of lousy behaviors. It's hard to do it all at once. Is there one that's more important? God continues, in Colossians 3:14, "And over all these virtues put on love, which binds them all together in perfect unity."

Love? Yeah, love. Consider what God says in 1 Corinthians 13:1–3, "If I speak in the tongues of men and of angels, but have not love, I am only a resounding gong or a clanging cymbal." Can you just imagine that pounding in your ear? Gee, that's pleasurable! Not! God lets us know that no matter what talent we have, no matter what else we have, if we don't have love, that's what we sound like to Him. If you don't have godly love for your brother, then you have nothing. He goes on, "If I have the gift of prophecy and can fathom all mysteries and all knowledge, and if I have a faith that can move mountains, but have not love, I am nothing." Again, God says that is what you are without love, all the good things that you think you do, that you count on to score points, they all mean nothing without love. Can he get any clearer? He takes it even further by saying, "If I give all I possess to the poor and surrender my body to the flames, but have not love, I gain nothing."

The kind of love I need to show others is the love that comes from God himself. I can't drum it up whenever I want. It doesn't come from me. If it could, I wouldn't need God. In 1 John 4:12, it says, "No one has ever seen God; but if we love one another, God lives in us and His love is made complete in us." The reverse of that is, if we don't love one another, God doesn't live in us, and His love is not made complete in us. Do you want God's complete love or incomplete love? Would you want your new car delivered before they put in the engine and steering wheel? Do you want your home built with no roof? Who would want to live without God's complete love? Our lives get so much easier when we have all God's complete blessings.

In Colossians 3:15, we get more rules for holy living: "Let the peace of Christ rule in your hearts, since as members of one body you were called to peace. And be thankful." There's a condition there, in order to let the peace of God rule in your heart, you have to *have* the peace of God, which can only come from a love relationship with God through Jesus.

Then, it says, "Be thankful." I love that one. I am to love and be thankful. How do you show it? How do you show your gratitude to

God? It's hard to really imagine how to do that unless we understand how much He's done for us.

Try thinking of it this way. Say a murderer kidnapped your baby and held a knife to your baby's throat. Then imagine I came up from behind, knocked down that murderer, saved your baby, just when you thought your baby was a goner. I think about how much I love my own kids, so this is just the most horrible scenario I can think of.

I saved your baby. Would you just say, "Hey, thanks, Jack!" and forget it ever happened? I doubt it. I believe you would shower me with gifts and season tickets to every Miami Dolphins football game for the rest of my life. You would love me and talk about me for the rest of my life, not because I am the greatest guy, but because I gave you something you loved dearly, something you would have lost forever unless I got it back for you. You'd be so grateful that you would talk about me forever.

That's a far-fetched scenario for most folks, but really, that's what Christ did for every believer. He saved us from hell. He bought us not just eternal life in heaven, but abundant life here and now, and He says, "Be thankful." Where is my thankfulness? Where is yours?

Colossians 3 goes on, "Let the word of Christ dwell in you richly as you teach and admonish one another with all wisdom, and as you sing psalms, hymns and spiritual songs with gratitude in your hearts to God." Do I want the Word of Christ to dwell in me richly? If I do, I need to know it, and to know it, I have to know the Bible because that **is** the Word of God. If I'm serious about becoming more holy, I have to be serious about reading and studying God's Word. There is no excuse for not knowing it. Now, I am not a Bible scholar. I sit with some at church, and I know they can ace any Bible trivia test out there, and they can tell you addresses of most every verse.

I can't. But I'm not intimidated. I love God. I think I know Scripture, and it's okay that I'm behind those guys in Bible theology. This is not a memorization contest. Still, every believer is responsible for knowing God's Word as much as they can, just as sure as anyone driving a car is responsible for reading the road signs and obeying them.

The next thing Colossians 3 says is, "And whatever you do, whether in word or deed, do it all in the name of the Lord Jesus, giving thanks to God the Father through Him." Now, can you imagine? Every day, we wake up, and before we speak or do anything, we say, "I do this in the name of the Lord Jesus Christ. I speak these words in the name of Jesus Christ. I do this action in the name of Jesus Christ." Would my behavior be different? Oh, yeah. Absolutely. I'm sure your behavior and your speech would change if you did the same thing. Try it for a day, a week. I dare you. Then, e-mail me and tell me what happened, what changed, who noticed. I can't wait to hear from you (e-mail me at jack@dontblowitwithgod.com).

That's the end of the section of Colossians my NIV calls Rules for Holy Living, but I can guarantee those aren't the only ones. I want to share some others.

Backing up a little to Colossians 2:6–7, it says "So then, just as you received Christ Jesus as Lord, continue to live in him, rooted and built up in him, strengthened in the faith as you were taught, and overflowing with thankfulness." Just as I received Christ as Lord... do you remember when you were saved? For me, it was March 10,

1991. Oh, man, has my life changed for the better. I know the drugs didn't go right away, but eventually God gave me the strength to overcome that. But believe me; God was in me. I was a fired-up guy because I had this new relationship with God. It was like when I first met my wife, and I was just the happiest guy in the world when I first got to know her. It was unbelievable. I ask you, is your relationship with God as exciting today as when you first were saved? God says we are to continue to live in him, rooted and built up in him, and be strengthened in the faith, as we were taught. And in 1 Thessalonians 5:15–22, we are told:

"Make sure that nobody pays back wrong for wrong, but always try to be kind to each other and to everyone else. Be joyful always; pray continually; give thanks in all circumstances, for this is God's will for you in Christ Jesus. Do not put out the Spirit's fire; do not treat prophecies with contempt. Test everything. Hold on to the good. Avoid every kind of evil. "

It's as if Paul says that the secret for being happy is to rejoice in the Lord no matter what goes on and to give thanks in all circumstances.

In all circumstances? How can I be thankful if my father is sick? How can I be thankful if I lose my job? How can I be thankful if I have no money? What's the deal with that?

The deal is that God promises to use everything to work for our good, eventually, ultimately, even if it makes no sense now. I'm talking about Romans 8:28, "And we know that in all things God works for the good of those who love Him..." You can race to the airport, but not make it on time and miss your flight. You say that's a tragedy, day ruined, appointments missed, and it's not fair. After all, you left your house on time; traffic and long lines at airport security were not your fault.

What if you would have died in a car crash that day had you made that flight? What if missing that flight saved your life. Or maybe God wanted to use you as a witness through this circumstance or remind you to trust Him in all circumstances (Proverbs 3:6). I don't know, but God does. We wonder why God allows us to go through the fire when really, God is using that fire to refine us like gold and make us pure, make us complete, and help us along the path to becoming more holy.

Here is another rule for holy living, found in both Matthew 4:7 and Luke 4:12—"Do not put the Lord your God to the test."

I have a good friend I was out driving with not long ago. I'll call him Al. He started talking to me.

"Jack," he said, "I'm having a problem with women."

I said, "What kind of problem?"

He said, "What do I pray to God before I go out to the bar so that God will protect me from evil women?"

I pulled off the road, so I could look him in the eye. "There is a problem with your logic, Al."

"What's that?"

"You are testing God by asking Him to protect you while you are doing things He is telling you not to." He looked surprised, but I kept going. "Al, I have a cocaine addiction, among other drugs. So, let me tell you what I'm not doing. I'm not going out, hanging with guys who do cocaine, and then asking God to protect me from the cocaine. I think I could say no a couple of times, but by the fifth or sixth night, I'm going down."

"So, what do you expect me to do?"

"Just don't go to the bar."

You can change the names, you can change the addiction or the temptation, but the principle for holy living remains. Al knew that going to the bar would cause him to drink, and that drinking would lead him to be with women he shouldn't be with. So, the solution was simple—I didn't say easy; I said simple—don't go to the bar. For Jack Levine, I know that hanging with guys who do cocaine will lead me to do cocaine, so I don't hang out with any of them. To do so and then ask God to protect me is ridiculous, hypocritical thinking and will not enable me to pursue my desire to become more holy.

Take a good, honest look at your choices and ask God to show you if there is a problem with your logic, if there is something in your life that needs this simple, just-don't-go-there solution. I ask you to do that because I know that Al and I aren't the only ones who find themselves tempted to test God in this way.

Why should we want to live holy lives? Does it matter?

It matters to God. All the way back in Leviticus 11:45, He instructed His people to "...be holy because I am holy." A holy, pure God cannot allow sin in His presence. He wants us in His presence and wants us in a close relationship with Him. To do that, though, we first need Christ to cleanse us from all our sins, but we also need to obey His instructions because they are for our good in the long run. When we commit ourselves to learning how to live holy lives, the natural outcome is that we stop doing those things that bring us trouble, pain, and sorrow.

Does that mean we stop doing anything that's fun? No. We live in the shadow of a myth about Christianity, and that myth is that we can't have any fun. We can't do this or that and what we are allowed to do is eternally boring.

The real myth is that the junk we think is fun, by the world's standards, is the stuff that causes so much grief. *They* say you deserve to live the fun life, and you can do it by loading up on the credit cards. Do you have fun working double shifts to pay for those toys? Is it fun to make a fool of yourself when you're too drunk to stand up? Is it fun to face the judge for a DUI or the parents of a child you killed when you swerved on your way home? Of course, the answer is a big, fat **no**. And the list could go on.

God gives us rules for holy living, guidelines to follow to keep us from harming ourselves and to enable us to live life to the fullest. Think about it this way: Would it be more fun to play football on a field with no sidelines, no end zones, and no rules? That wouldn't be a game; that would be chaos. The sport is possible *because* of the boundaries and rules. Within those, the players have all kinds of opportunities for creative and exciting plays. Without boundaries and rules, people—players and spectators alike—get hurt.

I am so glad that I have the instructions so I won't miss the fullness of life God wants to give me. I'm so thankful that God didn't give me a box full of stuff and say, "Here's a life; try and put it together." God gave us his Word in the Bible (and His Holy Spirit in our hearts to confirm it), the directions to make everything fit together, and if we follow the directions, the rules for holy living, we can have the life He designed for us. It will be better than we could ever imagine because God put it together. Listen to what God promises us in 2nd

Peter Chapter 1 verse 3 "His divine power has given us everything we need for life and godliness through our knowledge of Him who called us by His own glory and goodness"

If you're breathing right now, then you're alive, and that means your life is still being assembled, even if it looks like it's falling apart. We all have "Some Assembly Required" stamped on our souls when we are born. The question is, will we, will you and I, trust **God** (our Creator/Designer) enough to follow His directions to put our life together properly, so it looks and functions as He intended it to be?

14

Is Less More?

It was in 2003 that I wanted to "intern" as a pastor, to understand whether I was headed for full-time ministry or not. A pastor at a church in Hallandale Beach, Florida, was kind enough to invite me to spend a month or more with him so he could teach me things about being in the ministry and give me a firsthand glimpse of a pastor's life.

As good an offer as it was, I still remember getting in the car, driving back from that meeting, and talking to God, saying, "Thanks, but I won't go down to Hallandale. It's an hour each way back and forth from where we live; this is ridiculous. It's too far!"

God said to me very clearly, and I mean there was no doubt. I got a direct word, and a sarcastic one at that, "Jack, I understand that this is way too much of an inconvenience for you to drive an hour back and forth. After all, my only son only died on the cross for you."

"Okay, God, Hallandale it is."

Do you ever wonder about this in your life, ever wonder what the *real* reason is for God putting you where you are?

Again, God's Spirit spoke to me and said very specifically, "What if the only purpose I have for you being in Hallandale is because I wanted to see if you would obey me?"

"Okay, God, not my will, but yours, be done."

God said, "How can I trust you with bigger things later if you won't obey me now with little things?"

John the Baptist put it so simply in John 2:29-30. Listen to his words: "The bride belongs to the bridegroom. The friend who attends the bridegroom waits and listens for him, and is full of joy when he hears the bridegroom's voice. That joy is mine, and it is now complete. He must become greater; I must become less." Some translations finish the verse with "he must increase and I must decrease."

Up to this point, Jesus hadn't become a public figure, and John the Baptist was center stage in the wilderness talking about the coming Messiah. So, when Jesus finally began His work, John the Baptist's role began to change.

Humanly speaking, this is when jealousy over the new kid on the block got rolling, but not in God's plan. John reacted with humility, recognizing that his role was to *point* to the coming of Christ, and now that the Christ had come, his role was no longer needed. Did he pout? Heck no, he celebrated!

So, let's look at this concept. Just in case any of you have never been a best man at a wedding, this is an actual role and not just a title. The role is to take care of the groom and make sure all his needs are met and that the groom has no worries or concerns because the best man takes care of everything for him. The best man does advance work, prepares for the groom's big day, and is the first to toast the groom and his new bride. From the time you are labeled "best man" to the end of the big day, you exist to do everything and anything the groom needs. This day is not about you, what you look like, what you'll eat, what others think of you. Your only focus and concern is making your friend's very important day even better. That's the attitude of the bridegroom's friend.

In this passage, John the Baptist talked about his relationship with Jesus and explained that he looked at Jesus how the closest friend of the groom, the best man, looks at the groom. John had prepared himself and others for this day, and now that it was here, he wanted to do anything he could to make sure all the attention and glory belonged to Jesus; fading into the background as Jesus moved to the forefront made his joy complete and full.

That's an example of how you and I should be in our lives today. Our attitude toward Christ should be the very same. We take the focus off ourselves and place it on Christ. What can we do to glorify you, Lord? What in my life must fade to the background, so you can shine in the spotlight?

John summarized this whole concept by saying that Christ must increase, and he, John, must decrease. The scale needed to tip in favor of Christ. I picture those old scales with the two flat dishes.

You'd put stuff on each dish and try to weigh something out or bring something into balance. Our spiritual scale should have Jesus outweighing everything, and our side of the scale should be empty.

So, how does that look in your life? Who weighs in the most on the scale? You say, "Jack, what if I do 50 percent for me and 50 percent for Christ? Fifty-fifty sounds fair, doesn't it?"

No, John is very specific. Christ must increase, and we must decrease. It's continual. Christ continually increases in our lives, and we, our natural, sinful selves, continually decrease. The best human example of this is in the life of Paul. He was sold out to Christ, so much so that he said, "To live is Christ" (Philippians 1:21). What's life about? According to Paul, it's all about Christ. Paul believed his own life was worthless apart from Christ. In essence, he was saying he was lower than the floor, that's how low he described himself, because Christ was so high up in his life—Paul decreased; Christ increased. And what of it?

Just look at the miracles God accomplished in his life. God can do the same in my life and yours. Absolutely, He can do the same, but He'll do it in people where Christ has increased, and they have decreased. Our natural reaction to that is how unfair it seems. Truth be told, I think I speak for many of us who would like to ask Jesus why we both can't increase. That sounds like a much better deal, like an investment in which everybody gets a 50 percent return. What's wrong with that?

It all boils down to this. Do you believe God or not? You say, "Eternity is all well and good, but what about now? What about the abundant life God promises? I don't have the car I want, the house I want, the job I want, the wife I want."

It's only when we are finally willing to exercise our free will and replace the "I want" with "what God wants" that things will change, because then we choose to *decrease* while asking Christ to increase in our lives. Things will change, but you may not get a new car, house, job, or wife. Your heart's attitude toward those things will change, as you submit to God and understand that he molds you, shapes you, and refines you.

I've had several opportunities to learn that lesson, times when I've been at the end of the line and wondered if things could get any worse. One of them was back in 1990 when I was out of work for a year. I literally had no money; I'd gone through every nickel I had, and I truly would have been out on the street homeless if not for the fact that my parents were willing to send me rent money every month. I remember lying in my bed thinking, "This is it; I could be homeless." I finally understood how somebody can go from being a professional or having a job to being unemployed and homeless. By God's grace, I didn't stay in that situation, but it was one of the building blocks He used to help me see the futility of living life my way. As long as I lived life on my terms, there was no room for God. When I eventually turned my life over to God, things changed. But what if God had chosen homelessness for me? What if I hadn't had parents willing to keep a roof over my head? What if...?

Maybe you are at a point in your life where you suffer, suffer emotionally, physically, financially, spiritually, maybe with relationships, maybe with God. You feel as if you are abandoned at the bottom of the pit.

I've been there, more than once. I say no, you're not abandoned;

you're not alone. If you are a believer, you know God's hand is on you, and regardless of what you suffer on this earth, God waits for you to give him room in your life to work.

I have to ask you, does "I want" still echo through your mind as you consider your circumstances? What if you were a baseball player? Would you dare say to the coach, "No, don't make me bunt for the good of the team. I don't care if you want to sacrifice the runner ahead, so we can win the game. I want to swing away. I want... I want... I want." How selfish could you be?

I know the answer to that because I also talk to myself about myself. I look at my own life. God says, "...from the one who has been entrusted with much, much more will be asked" (Luke 12:48). As believers, we have been given much, and we are expected not just to handle it well, but also to handle more. The difficulty for us is that the "more" we want, usually in the form of material blessings, isn't always the "more" God has in mind. God wants us to glorify his name even more as we grow up spiritually, and sometimes, that means we will suffer and feel helpless. Paul said it best in 2 Corinthians 12:9, in which he explained why God would not remove the thorn in his flesh. "But he said to me, 'My grace is sufficient for you, for my power is made perfect in weakness.' Therefore I will boast all the more gladly about my weaknesses, so that Christ's power may rest on me." Paul didn't want to suffer, but he was willing to, and absolutely, he suffered that the power and the glory of Christ would be seen in his life.

Think about it. If we are sick, we go to the doctor. The doctor says, "Yeah, I can fix you, but I am going to have to operate." What happens? Some of us run away. "No thanks, I don't want the pain of surgery or recovery. I'm scared of surgery, so, Doc, can't you just fix me magically while I play tennis or maybe while I'm out to dinner? Or how about this, I'll listen to a bunch of preaching on TV; will that do it? Can't you just heal me miraculously?"

God says, "I could, but that's not the point. I need to perform some surgery on you to make you a better person, so this is actually going to be more about spiritual surgery."

Have you ever known anyone with a serious back problem? It's a debilitating condition. You can't run or play ball. You often can't drive. Your back hurts you so much that you are not as effective as a person, and guess what? In order to fix that back, you have to go to the doctor; sometimes you have to have surgery. Then, the doctor removes the problem, and though it does hurt, and you are sore, you eventually get better than you ever were. I understand there are some surgeries that don't work, but I talk generalities here in order to make a point. The same idea applies spiritually. We are all sinners. We have blind spots. When the time comes to deal with those blind spots, it often surprises us. It often means we will suffer while God does his surgery because he wants us to understand that a chronic, debilitating problem is in our faith walk that keeps us from being as effective as he wants us to be, or else it limits what he can and is willing do through us. He operates to remove those things (decrease them) so that Christ can increase.

But you say, "Hey, Jack, I thought God promised me an abundant life, what's with the pain?" The pain comes from forgetting who gets to define *abundance*. God does. It's His world; He created it!

When you agree with God about the definition, He is willing to do great things in your life. He can, and He will do exceedingly and abundantly more than you expect, just as He promised, but it's as *He* sees fit for your life, not as *you* announce all your personal wants. I look back at the suffering I've experienced, and I can imagine God said, though I didn't listen, "Jack, trust me. I need to operate on you, and yeah, it will hurt, and yeah, you will be a little sore, but hey, Jack, the things hurting you in your life *interrupt* your life right now. Those things have to come out, so I can move forward in your life and do better things in you."

Part of what He needs to do in each one of us is do a "self-reduction" procedure so that we decrease, and Christ has room to increase. So, you know what? I should run to the operating table right now, submitting to God's hand, asking Him to please perform spiritual surgery on me. Make me better, mold me, and shape me, because I know without a doubt that my joy, happiness, and peace, everything I have, comes from God. I know for sure that when I lived life on my terms, I never had joy, happiness, and peace. What I did have in abundance was agony, misery, and pain. If that is what you want—agony, misery, and pain—just keep living for the world. Even Christians have that option: you can just show up to church for an hour on Sunday and live like everyone else the rest of the week. In other words, you can be a Christian, but not allow Christ to increase in you.

If that's what you are doing, then you are not growing spiritually. If you are not hearing from God directly, and if you don't feel God leading you and talking to you, then you are absolutely doing something wrong. You need to decrease the emphasis on *you* and increase the emphasis on *God*. God is the great physician, and He looks to repair you, restore you, and refine you. You need to come to His spiritual operating table and stay put. After all, how can you expect a surgeon to fix your back if you won't show up in the operating room?

I want to share with you a couple of great observations from a pastor friend of mine named Weldon Stockwell. His input has helped me better understand this new math God has that requires decreasing in order to increase. I don't know if his explanations are original, but he talked about two of the Beatitudes.

Matthew 5:3 reads, "Blessed are the poor in spirit, for theirs is the kingdom of heaven." For a long time, I didn't understand what that meant. Weldon shared with me a slightly different translation, and it reads, "Blessed are those of a broken and contrite spirit." That makes more sense to me. The publican had that spirit when he cried for mercy on himself, a poor sinner. Jesus says that the humble and broken in spirit are blessed because they recognize they need God. That's where you want to be because then the kingdom of heaven is yours. If you're full of your own spirit (self), then you keep God's spirit out—you do not decrease, and God does not increase, and what you have is a frustrating, spiritual stalemate.

In the next beatitude, Matthew 5:4, it says, "Blessed are they who mourn for they will be comforted." I really didn't understand that one, either, until Weldon explained that it is not about mourning the death of a loved one or sorrow over loss, but rather it is the mourning over our sins. It's the kind of mourning that breaks our heart when we see how short we fall compared to the glory of God. I compare myself to Christ, and I can see just how much of a sinner I am and just why Christ had to die on the cross for me. When I see that, I understand the reason I must decrease, and He must increase. That's mourning, and when we do that, God shall comfort us. I want to have that spirit. I hope you want to have that spirit.

Some people think I'm nuts, but I confess that I find Romans 16:1–16 rather exciting. Your first reaction is probably along the lines of, "Yes, Jack, you are nuts. If this gets you excited, then the book of Leviticus must really get you excited." Hang with me. This is Paul's personal greeting at the beginning of a letter:

> I commend to you our sister Phoebe, a servant of the church in Cenchrea. I ask you to receive her in the Lord in a way worthy of the saints and to give her any help she may need from you, for she has been a great help to many people, including me. Greet Priscilla and Aquila, my fellow workers in Christ Jesus. They risked their lives for me. Not only I but all the churches of the Gentiles are grateful to them. Greet also the church that meets at their house. Greet my dear friend Epenetus, who was the first convert to Christ in the province of Asia. Greet Mary, who worked very hard for you. Greet Andronicus and Junias, my relatives who have been in prison with me. They are outstanding among the apostles, and they were in Christ before I was. Greet Ampliatus, whom I love in the Lord. Greet Urbanus, our fellow worker in Christ, and my dear friend Stachys. Greet Apelles, tested and approved in Christ. Greet those who belong to the household of Aristobulus. Greet Herodion, my relative. Greet those in the household of Narcissus who are in the Lord. Greet Tryphena and Tryphosa, those women who work hard in the Lord. Greet my dear friend Persis, another woman who has worked very hard in the Lord. Greet Rufus, chosen in the Lord, and his mother, who has been a mother to me, too. Greet Asyncritus, Phlegon, Hermes, Patrobas, Hermas and the

brothers with them. Greet Philologus, Julia, Nereus and his sister, and Olympas and all the saints with them. Greet one another with a holy kiss. All the churches of Christ send greetings.

Is that boring or what? I used to think so. I would skip over this every time. But everything in the Bible is there for a reason because God wants us to know about it. So, one time when I read this section, God got me thinking about history, because this is about history for us, but you see, when Paul wrote it, it was current for him. It involved people he knew and worked with.

Then, I started wondering about the future, 50 or 100 years from now; what sports names and politicians' names will be in the history books my grandkids will study? I thought about how that history is being lived out right now and will be based on people we are alive with today, just as when Paul wrote this letter and commended these people, the saints of the church in his day. Paul named them and said, look at this one, working hard for the Lord, look at this one who helped me here, and look at that one who helped me there. And I start thinking, hey, I want that written about me! Don't you want that written about you?

Let's not confuse what I am getting at with the one-time act of being saved. The question is what will that book of life say about you? What did you do? Imagine for a moment that a Bible was being written today (and I understand that no one can add to or take away from the Bible, but imagine God is recording an account of our lives, and that is what we will be rewarded for). Would your name be remembered in that Bible describing the time in which you lived and you're accomplishments for God's Kingdom? Would someone like Paul lift you up, commending you for loving others, for working hard, for persevering? How do you feel when you hear someone bragging about you to others? I want to hear that about my spiritual walk. I want to hear that I do good work for the Lord. The gratitude that you and I have for God and what we give back in return for that gratitude is reflected in the actions we take, and all those things are recorded by God today and will be rewarded by God when we get to heaven. The question I must ask myself is whether the record will show less and less of me and more and more of Christ. And you, as a believer, must ask yourself the same thing.

It doesn't mean we won't make mistakes, and mistakes don't mean we've done permanent damage to the journey we are on to have Christ increase while we decrease. The good news is that God gives us new mercy every single day, every morning. Each day is like a new beginning. Look at it this way. Say you're an athlete, and you made an error in yesterday's game. Today, there's a new game. You would be an idiot to sit there thinking about yesterday's error because it would affect your performance today. You need to focus on the task at hand *today*. So if you sinned, if you screwed up that whole "I decrease/you increase" bit yesterday, what do you do?

You confess. Every time we sin, we are to confess our sins to God and repent, and repent means we have Godly sorrow. We are sorry *not* because we were caught, but sorry because we know we have offended God. When we do that, God promises to purify us from that sin and forgive us (1 John 1:9).

What about when you suffer? Do you serve a purpose in God's kingdom? What if the entire purpose of your life was that you suffer, so God could be glorified in you and in your life? What is the purpose of that? What if you were like Job? What if you were like the man born blind in John 9, or Lazarus raised from the dead (John 11:4), or the twins born to Rebekah (Romans 9), or Pharaoh, all of them used for and purposed by God to accomplish His will, under circumstances that certainly were not chosen by them or seemed pleasurable or beneficial at the time. What if God wanted you to be physically sick or for you to be dirt poor? What if He wants you to have problems so that when the rest of the world looks at you, they can see God through you? Whichever of those circumstances or others apply to you individually, do you understand that the rest of the world watches to see how you, God's kid, **the Christian**, responds? Will we let God use us as a lighthouse to the rest of the world, meaning that *we* decrease so that the light of Christ can *increase* in us?

Ephesians 2:10 tells us, "For we are God's workmanship, created in Christ Jesus to do good works, which God prepared in advance for us to do." Would you like to know why you are alive? Here it is! God created you to do good works, and He already knows what He wants you to do. Ask Him. Explore His Word to see what He wants His children to do to bring honor and glory to His name.

It's so simple. Not easy, but simple. Christ must increase; we must decrease, requiring us to change what we do. It is one thing to hear those instructions, and it's another thing to act on them. Where do you start?

If you do not feel that inexpressible and glorious joy in your life, I challenge you to pray right now. It's between God and you. Just say, "Lord, I've done this wrong. I need to change the scale. Lord, not both of us increase, but you increase Lord, and I decrease." That prayer my friend, is clearly the place where the rubber meets the road with God and a moment of truth for every believer! So are you saying it or not?

15

Dead Man Walking

I spent three full days of study in preparation for a sermon in late 2005, finally deciding on which section of Scripture I wanted to focus. Then, the Lord and I had an interesting conversation about my plan. I said to God, "This is what I'm going to preach on."

And God said, "No, Jack, we have to talk more about stuff that is going on in your life."

"I'm tired of exposing myself," I said. "The last couple of times I got up to preach I bared my soul; I just ripped myself open. Can't you just close me up, and go on to somebody else?"

"No."

"Then, can't we just take a verse of Scripture and stand on that?"

"No, Jack. By the way, other people are going through what you go through. They need to know what you go through and what you learn from it. It's not about you. It's about them."

For years, I've basically been saying, "God, I want to follow you. I've lived my life for me long enough, and I'm ready to live it for you. What do you want to do in the second half of my life?"

God said, "Okay, Jack. We can do that. There's just one last thing you need to do."

"Anything, God, just tell me." It was a very simple revelation, so simple that I can't believe it took me 14 years of being a Christian to see it.

God said, "You don't have to do this, but you told me that you want to be my guy, you want to serve me, that you want this unbelievable walk with me that you see others have. So, all you have to do is die to yourself."

"I thought I had."

"Only in certain places, Jack. You've held some things back from me, so that limits what I can do in your life. I've done the best I can with the portion you've given me, but if you want this relationship you keep talking about, then this is non-negotiable. You need to completely die to yourself." Wait a minute, Lord; last chapter, you told me, 'you must increase and I must decrease"; now, you tell me I must die to myself. This gets harder by the minute! God said, "Yes, it does. I never said it would be easy. It is hard, but the rewards are out of this world... literally!"

We all have choices. We can choose to stay in our comfort zone until we die. We can satisfy our flesh instead of growing our spirit. We can refuse to yield to God or let Him have His way because we think we're in charge, and we decide what gets done around here. That's called living for self, which is where we all are before we enter a relationship with Jesus Christ. After we do that, God says, "No more of that garbage." That way just leads to death. Once we accept Christ, God says it's time to die to self and live for Him. This is very much the opposite of what the world will tell you. If *world* seems too vague a term, then try *neighbor, coworker,* the self-help gurus on TV, the magazine covers at the checkout line, and even family members.

The phrase "dying to self" probably sounds odd to those unfamiliar with the Bible, so let me tell you a story that might get the point across. When I was a kid, my nickname was Hawk. I used to think of myself as Jack "Hawk" Levine. (This is a secret, so it goes no further than this page.) In fact, I was so enthralled with this alter ego that I painted a big fat H (for Hawk) in the stickball box in Yonkers, New York, where I lived. My father came home one night and asked if I'd painted it, and I said, "No way, it wasn't me. It was Hawk." I'm pretty sure my dad knew who H was.

As I got older, Hawk would do the things that Jack wouldn't do. Then, years later, when my drug problem got the best of me, I put my car through a fence in a blackout and nearly died. It's only by the grace of God that I lived to tell about it, but when I came to my senses, I *killed* Hawk. I stopped living for him and faced up to the fact that I was just Jack, and when I did that, I buried that alter ego. More years have passed. I've grown up some as a Christian, and now, God has brought me to this next level of commitment where He tells me it's time for Jack to spiritually die and join Hawk so that He, God, can live through me. So, that's it; that's dying to self, getting rid of my fleshly selfishness, pride, and greed and simply saying yes to God.

Let me tell you, scripturally, why God says we should all do that. In 1 Peter 2:24, it says, "He himself bore our sins in His body on the tree, so that we might die to sins and live for righteousness..." We are all born of sin; we are sinners. Christ died so that we could "die to sin," meaning that we could break the hold that sin has on our lives. We have His power living in us, a power that can break us out of bad habits, addictions, or destructive behaviors. If we are in a relationship with Christ, we have a responsibility to die to sin and live for righteousness. Righteousness lives God's way.

Romans 14:7–8 says, "For none of us lives through himself alone and none of us dies to himself alone. If we live, we live for the Lord and if we die, we die for the Lord." Paul was the classic example of dying to self. He began life as Saul and grew to prominence in the Jewish culture, where he became zealous about stamping out Christianity. At one point, he condoned the killing of a Christian teacher named Stephen, then proceeded on a journey to Damascus to round up more Christians and throw them in jail. But his journey was divinely interrupted on that road when Jesus spoke very clearly to him and changed the purpose of his life—from trying to annihilate Christianity altogether to becoming one of its most significant teachers in the world. Saul became Paul. He died to his old life completely, meaning that everything he had lived for up to that point became unimportant and worthless. The only thing that mattered from that point on was living for the Lord, doing what God wanted—nothing more, nothing less. Because of that, Paul got the benefit of that walk with Christ for the rest of his life, and we get the benefit of his faith today.

Paul uses a different example in Galatians 2:20–21, in which he says, "I have been crucified with Christ and I no longer live, but Christ lives in me." Could he be any clearer about dying to himself? The verse continues, "The life I live in the body, I live by faith in the son of God, who loved me and gave himself for me." Paul gave up his life—his *self*, his desires of the flesh, his pride, and selfishness—to live Christ's life.

I want to do the same thing. I challenge you to do the same thing if you truly want to experience God's full blessing, but it's a choice we each have to make, a choice to either follow Him or go back to the world, to the things we are used to. My pastor recently preached about not going back to comfortable things and not longing for familiar things, but that means moving forward with God, and that can seem risky. As Christians, however, how could we not be willing to take risks for God?

Many people pray to God only after they realize their situation is hopeless. So, at that critical point of hopelessness, despair, and desperation, they reach out to God hoping and praying for a miracle. It shouldn't be like that. Instead, we should trust God enough to give Him our life and let Him mold it and shape it, as He sees fit.

I was unwilling to do that. I was saved at 33, but for three more years, I continued to write my own plan for continuing with the things I knew, the lifestyle I knew, and the plans I was used to. As a result, part of my salvation testimony had me in the gutter.

Let me tell you, a trip to the gutter changes your perspective. It makes you realize that your way doesn't work. I had known for a long time that my plans didn't move me forward; eventually, I was willing to admit that my plans were actually holding me back, but it wasn't until they nearly killed me that things changed. That's when I chose to turn it all over to God. While my testimony includes a gutter, it doesn't conclude with one. I don't want the rest of my Christian life story to be that God had to knock the crap out of me every step of the way just to get me to do what He wanted me to do. I don't want that to be my life. I understand that God had to bring me to my knees to get my attention and get me to change direction and follow Him, and I am grateful He did. I truly am.

What's your story? I hope it is more about walking with God and receiving His blessings than being in the gutter and wondering if you'll live to tell about it, but you have to make that choice. When you're ready to let go of your plans and reach out to God, He'll be there.

Gods wants all of you, not some of you. God tells us to be hot or cold but not lukewarm (Revelation 3:16). God hates that. We should be so hot that we are on fire for the Lord. Our surrender to God must be without limit. Have you tried to make deals with God? Do you try to claim control? That's what I tried to do, but not anymore. God made it clear that not only was that unacceptable, but it also wouldn't get me where I want to be, and it would actually have the opposite effect in my life and make me miserable. I don't know why we complain at the thought of turning over all control to God. After all, we know that we have to turn control of our bodies over to the surgeon when he operates on us and to the pilot when he flies the plane on which we are a passenger. So, we do give up control many times in our lives, but only for certain instances and certain periods of time. We're always anxious to get back into the controller's seat, aren't we?

Pastor Erwin McManus, in his book titled *Uprising*, talked about the subject this way: "You can't escape who you are, you will be forever stuck inside your skin, but you can become someone else. You can leave the person you have grown to despise and become the person you admire. How? There's no magician on earth that can pull that off; such a change requires no one less than Jesus Christ. It is no illusion, no magic, and no sleight of hand. Jesus sets you free through the power of change; He is the gift of transformation." McManus has such a great way of putting things. I recommend you read my favorite book of his *Seizing Your Divine Moment* (after this one, of course).

Do you want to get rid of the person you've become and become the person you admire? God can do it. God can take the person (the self) that we are not satisfied with and that we judge guilty of not doing enough, and He can transform us, but it is all about His doing it and not us. That can be a scary thing because you truly have to trust God with each step in your life. I can remember being at the scariest point in my life. There was no safety net. I had no clue what would happen next, and God spoke to my spirit and said to me, "Jack, you're exactly right, you have no clue, now you understand. For the first time in your life at age 46, you finally understand that's exactly where I want you, with no safety net, just trusting me."

Jesus himself said it best; Jesus talked about dying to self and living spiritually. In Luke 9:23, He said, "If anyone would come after me, He must deny himself and take up his cross daily and follow me."

We must lose our life daily, from the little things to the huge ones. It amazes me the struggle I have. I raced harness horses as a hobby. It was a lot of fun, but in 2004, when my wife was pregnant with our third child (Talia), God laid on my heart that He wanted me to take a break from it.

"Come on, God," I said, "it's summertime, all the good drivers are going away. There will be four times as many amateur races for me to drive in, and I need to get more experience."

And God said, "No, I don't want you to drive now."

Hey, when God tells you clearly not to do something, you'd better listen. I learned that the hard way in the past, and I didn't want to have to learn it again, so I set the racing aside. It didn't mean I could never do it again, it just meant leaving it alone for a while.

Then, God used that to show me how foolish I am about what I'll trust Him with. God wants me to trust Him with everything, to die to self, and that includes trusting Him with my future, career, and finances. And I keep resisting. I'm a husband and a father, and I have a God-given responsibility to provide for my family, but I want to do it my way, and my way has always been to be in business. But God says, "Jack, I want you to trust me with your future. I want you to trust me with your finances and with your life." My response? "Whoa, God! My future? My finances? The big things? No, I'll handle those. I have to take care of all that stuff. I have to make sure that I provide for my family. I have to plot the course for the future." Then, God showed my how ironic my thinking was.

I trust God with something that is not critically important to me—harness racing (a hobby)—a place where I don't really see the need for His power and sovereignty. It's fun, but I give it right to God when He asks for it. But when something is important, when something is so big it demands God's power and sovereignty, what do I do? I keep it. I hang on to it, refusing to give it to God. Why? Because it means dying to self and doing it God's way instead of mine.

If I can be blunt about it, and I think others feel the same way, we think that dying to self and doing things God's way, which is a form of worship, will be a chore. Silly me. And silly you. Let me amend that—stupid me and stupid you! God isn't about boring. He's about doing the unexpected and the impossible and giving us joy as a result. I didn't expect to crash my car through a fence in a drug-induced blackout nearly killing myself, but God used that to get me to change direction so that I could experience what I'd thought was impossible: a joy-filled life of purpose and love. I don't recommend that approach to everyone, only to those who need that kind of hard knock to switch gears.

And it's worth it. For the first time in my life, I truly see God as the quarterback, and I'm the guy on the team whose only job is to execute the play He designs. That's all I have to do. Execute the plan; run the route I'm told to run. I'm not the coach. I'm not the owner. I'm not the quarterback. God is. Worshipping God by dying to self isn't a chore. I see how glorious and holy He is and how much He loves me. It's a pleasure to worship Him, to get to know Him.

How do you do that? Read the Word and see how it describes God. One day, I read in John and in Revelation, and I saw a few names God used to describe himself that helped me understand the true difference between God and me. I always thought of myself as the boss, the guy who signed the paychecks, chairman of the board, man in charge, decision maker, majority shareholder, CEO, president, the man, and head of the household. All those names reinforced my self-image of being in charge and being in control. Yet, as I read the Scriptures, I saw how God was described: the true vine, the gate, the resurrection and the life, the alpha and the omega, the bread of life, the good shepherd, the door, living bread, the truth, the way, the light of the world, I Am, Almighty God. It was obvious to me that God's titles carried a little (okay, much) more weight than mine—and yours. It's easy to see why we should worship God, but it's hard to refocus our priorities. And what should those priorities be?

We were created to give glory to God, to worship God. Look at Galatians 1:3–5, "Grace and peace to you from God our Father and the Lord Jesus Christ, who gave himself for our sins to rescue us from the present evil age, according to the will of our God and Father, to whom be glory for ever and ever." Glory forever. We are saved by Jesus Christ, to whom we should give glory forever, but we don't. We give glory—the praise, the credit, the power—to ourselves. We give glory to God, sometimes. As long as there is something we have not given over to God, some limit we put on our life with God, then we cannot give Him the glory, the credit, the attention, and honor He is due.

But that's what we're supposed to do. In 2nd Peter 2:9 God tells us "you are a chosen people, a royal priesthood, a holy nation, a people belonging to God, that you may declare the praises of Him who called you out of darkness into His wonderful light." We're told in 2 Corinthians 3:18, "And we, [that's us] who with unveiled faces all reflect the Lord's glory, are being transformed into His likeness with ever-increasing glory, which comes from the Lord, who is the Spirit." An unveiled face means we do not hide anything from God. With an unveiled face, we reflect the glory of God; we are transformed into His likeness more and more. But if we hide something from God, then we are not transformed into His likeness, and we are not transformed into His glory.

I know that on the Day of Judgment we will all be transformed, but what about now? What about this life? Here, Paul tells us that, with unveiled faces, we can reflect the Lord's glory and be transformed into His likeness while we are on this earth. That's what I want. I want to be transformed into His likeness—made to look like Him in my actions and in my love for others—and I would hope and pray that is what you want for yourself. To reflect something is to mirror it, and that's what we are supposed to do. We are supposed to mirror God, so the world will see God reflected in us.

Jesus' life reflected the Father's glory. What does your life reflect? What does my life reflect? God? Or self? This isn't about "doing church" on Sunday morning. I just assume that, unless you are an idiot, you will not come to church and misbehave, so we take that as a given. So what do you do outside church? This applies to me as well. Do we leave church and "return to our normal lives" or do we "take God with us," as we go and live our lives in such a way that others see Him and not us?

I'm reminded of the story in Luke 17:11, where Jesus healed 10 lepers as He traveled along the border between Samaria and Galilee.

He told them to show themselves to the priest, and as they went to do so, they were cleansed. One of them immediately came back, threw himself at Jesus' feet, thanked Him, and praised God in a loud voice.

Jesus took note that while all 10 were cleansed, only this one, a foreigner at that, gave thanks and praised God. Why did the other nine head off into the sunset? Because as soon as they were healed, they must have been grateful for a minute, but they immediately went back and focused on what their life was about and what they had to do. They didn't focus on God; they focused on the rest of their lives. They didn't die to self; they lived for self.

What about us? Most of us, me included, are as guilty and ungrateful as the nine who fled. We are happy the instant God does something special for us, but then we go right back to life as usual, instead of being like the grateful fellow whose attitude set him apart for eternity. Our gratitude for what our God has done for us should show in how we live our lives.

Let's look at Christ's attitude; it was much different from ours. In Philippians 2:5–7, God's Word tells us, "Your attitude should be the same as Christ Jesus: Who, being in very nature God, did not consider equality with God something to be grasped, but made himself nothing, taking the very nature of a servant..." Then, in John 13:15–17, Jesus said, "I have set you an example that you should do as I have done for you. I tell you the truth, no servant is greater than his master, nor is a messenger greater than the one who sent him. Now that you know these things, you will be blessed if you do them."

The reverse of that is if you know these things, and you don't do them, you won't be blessed. God is very specific. He wants us to live

wholeheartedly devoted to Him. Why? Because there are blessings
we can't even imagine waiting for us. Listen to what Paul has to
say. This line blows me away; it's Romans 1:9–10: "God, whom I
serve with my whole heart in preaching the gospel of His Son, is my
witness how constantly I remember you in my prayers at all times...."
Paul feels compelled to explain that wholehearted devotion drives
him to do what he does. I wish I could look you in the eye and say
that I serve God with my whole heart, but you know what? I don't.
It is a goal, something I'm striving for, because I want what Paul had.

Do you serve God with your whole heart, or do you just give
Him a little portion of it? Maybe you're like me, giving God some of
my heart, but holding back (not dying to self), so I can divvy it up as
I choose—there's that living for myself selfishness again. "Hey, God,
it's me. Here is a little bit of my heart. You have it on Sunday, then
I'll serve you Sunday night, and the other six days of the week, I'll
delegate the rest of my heart as I see fit." Does that sound like a real
commitment to you?

That thought scares me because it suggests that I do not worship
God how I should. Worship goes beyond Sunday morning. It's the
place, the prominence, we give God in our daily lives, and I don't
think I worship Him how He wants. That realization has brought
me to God with sorrow and repentance because the thought that my
worship is counterfeit scares me to death. It suggests that I don't love
God with my whole heart, and if that's true, then I'm back to loving
myself rather than dying to self.

In the book of John, Jesus says, "I don't speak my own words but
that which the Father has given me. I come to do the Father's will not

my own." We are to do the same. If we do our will rather than our Father's, we simply reject God's purpose for our lives, which means we reject God. You can try to justify it or rationalize it any way you want, and believe me, I have, but I can assure you that God will not put up with that behavior from His children forever.

Sometimes, God's purpose can leave us confused. We sense a call to a specific career or ministry but cannot find the route to get there. I've been in that mode before for months at a time, and I confess it can be very frustrating. What helps is seeking the counsel and wisdom of others. Back in 2004, I was blessed with an invitation to a pastors' conference in Miami. One hundred seventy pastors were there, and Dr. Johnny Hunt, a preacher from Atlanta with a 15,000-member congregation, led it. This guy was so fired up for the Lord, even after doing it for more than 30 years, and I remember thinking that whatever I do in my life, I had to have his kind of passion and desire for it.

Johnny Hunt relayed a quote he had heard, and I don't know who he attributed it to, but this is the quote: "We have all eternity to enjoy our victories but only one lifetime to earn them." I find a lot of inspiration in that. When asked how he kept his fire alive for ministry for so long, he replied, "It's not my work—it's my life; it's my passion; it's what I do."

Are we passionate about the Lord? Is Jesus Christ your passion? Wherever you are, whoever you are, wherever God has placed you at this point in your life, is Jesus Christ a priority? Does it show through so that everybody around you knows it? There is no middle ground, there is no maybe—it's your whole heart, or it's nothing.

Either you've died to self or you haven't. When you live that way, you do things differently; you decide differently.

I realized I'd been focused on what I couldn't do rather than on what God could do. It turned my thinking upside down—or maybe I should say right side up because, now, I concentrated on God's power, God's ability, and God's resources, and I lived on full alert for examples of God on the move.

Apparently, I needed one more kick in the pants to get the point, and it came from a pastor friend of mine who looked me in the eye and said, "God does not call the equipped. If you're equipped, you probably wouldn't be called. God calls the unequipped and then He equips them." Why? So that all the glory, all the praise, all the credit goes to God.

As I let that sink in, I couldn't help but think about Abraham, who trusted God for everything. Most of you, I'm sure, know the story of Abraham offering up his son Isaac to God as a sacrifice and God providing the ram instead. But in Romans 4:18, it points out something else Abraham did, and it always blows me away. It says, "Against all hope, Abraham in hope believed and so became the father of many nations...." God had promised a child to Abraham and Sarah when they were beyond elderly; they were exceedingly old. If having a baby in their fertile youth hadn't happened, how in the world could it happen when their bodies were as good as dead? Yet, we are told that Abraham believed God against all hope. Hope was lost; it was gone. He was ancient. Sarah was way past the age of giving birth, much less conceiving. How in the world would it happen? It wouldn't happen in the world's way, in the natural way, but it would happen God's way. That was the promise from God and, in spite of everything to the contrary, Abraham believed.

Would you believe God against all hope? If your army was wiped out, and the enemy's army charged at you, would you believe God against all hope? If you were financially ruined and had nothing, would you believe God against all hope? If you were between careers, with no income and no funding for your ministry, would you believe God against all hope? That was my challenge.

But Abraham, when there was no more hope, believed in God. And, of course, God was and is faithful. Abraham knew that God was greater and more powerful than any understanding or comprehension of hope he could have. He knew anything was possible with God, and if God said it, it was good enough for him.

What about us? We talked about dying to self. Is it really such a hard decision? Let's consider the situation.

Jesus (God's son):

Lived a perfect life.

Never made a single mistake.

His plans will always work for the eternal good, even if it includes some pain in the near term.

He sees the eternal scope of things.

Us (You and Me):

Can barely get to the office or the grocery store without sinning in deed or thought.

Often make mistakes and don't want to admit them.

Our plans (if we have any) often fail because our power is limited, and imperfect people cannot make perfect plans.

We can't even see what's around the corner. Heck, some of us can't even see the corner.

Almost funny, isn't it? When it's laid out so plainly, refusing to die to self—refusing to let go of myself and my desires and live for God through a relationship with Jesus Christ seems kind of foolish and self-destructive.

I challenge you to spend some time with God talking about what you've held back from Him. Ask Him if you've fully died to self and live for Him, and He'll show you specific places and issues you need to deal with.

That's a great place to start asking God to help get rid of yourself and to start filling you with Him. Now that, my friends, is your ultimate moment of truth. So are you going to ask Him to do it or not?

And that decision is the exact place *Where the Rubber Meets the Road with God*!

Ending Thoughts

So there you have it. Now, you know everything I know, at least for today (smile!). What really matters now is what you do with what you know. How much of what you have will you use? And what are you going to use it on? You only have a certain amount of time to live here on earth; it's your freedom of choice to use it as you will. I want to make the best of my time on behalf of the Lord, as a show of my eternal gratitude for the salvation and new life I have been given and the love I continue to receive from Jesus every day. I am so grateful. Thank you, Jesus.

I hope I have helped you establish some guidelines and to clearly focus on what it takes to get to the finish line for Christ—to win the race and to have lived as a champion for God.

God wants you to be a winner for His kingdom, and He has already given you His spirit to insure you have the tools and guidance you need. Now, the only question is whether you have the desire.

I hope so. The real secret is to realize that the actual life you live everyday is "where the rubber meets the road," and you will be rewarded by how you performed in those days you lived.

So now, you have read my personal operating manual. Nothing left to do but get back in there and win the race. See you at the feast at the Master's table! I will be the one clapping and shouting the loudest for you when you get your reward!

Keep the faith!

Love,

Jack

Acknowledgments

In *Don't Blow It With God*, my first book, I think I thanked everyone in the world. So I'll keep it short and to the point this time.

I continue to thank my God, Jesus Christ, each and every day for the wonderful gift of life he has given me. I want to again thank my wife, Beth; we just celebrated our 10 year wedding anniversary. Best 10 years of my life. Honey, now that the introductory 10 year trail period of our marriage is over, I want to sign up for the lifetime membership! Thanks from my heart to my three wonderful, special, loving children, Ricky, Jackson and Talia, for continually bringing joy and love into my life. The love of my wife and children is as close to the pure love of God as I have ever seen and I am so grateful for it. Thanks to my mom

(Marcia), dad (Jerry) and brother, Mike and my sister-in-law Leslie, and Zac and Dylan (the greatest nephews in the world). A special thanks to all my family and friends, each one of you who makes being alive such a joy and so interesting and exciting! Thanks for loving me.

I want to thank Pastor Don Karpinen who, with one of the greatest sermons I have ever heard preached, planted the seed in me for "The Devil's Credit Card" chapter of this book. His inspiration brought this chapter to life.

To all my Pastor friends who have inspired, encouraged, loved me, and trusted me to share the gospel with their people... thank you from the bottom of my heart.

To Shaun and Maria Smith, whose trust in God, even when they could not see his provision or understand his timing, has proven to be a great witness and testimony to God's sovereign knowledge and perfect timing as he brought them together in marriage. Today, they lovingly reflect the model of a Christian marriage, so grateful to God for the gift of each other and nourishing it and not taking it for granted. I know, Shaun, you weren't certain God would give you a godly woman to love you, but you were faithful, and that is always the requirement to see God pay off in huge ways. You deserve it. I am glad to have been a part of your life when you needed to hear reassuring words from God himself, and it was my pleasure to be used by God in some small way to influence you in a positive way. I pray all God's blessings upon you and your marriage for all your days.

To Dennis and LeeAnn D'Agosta—you guys endured it all and with faith that could not be shaken by Satan himself, and he tried (Lord knows he tried). Through thick and thin, trouble of all kinds—financial, physical, relational, spiritual, health, job, finance—you managed to glorify God in all you did, praise his name, and stand on his great promises and live the life of glorified saints in the Lord, even when the world attempted to beat the snot out of you. You guys are my heroes. The impact you have had on others and me is mind-boggling. Rest assured that God has used you mightily to influence others. Even though it seems you have paid the price with earthly suffering, your reward in heaven will be so great. I hope you remember to share some with me up there. For now, remember God's promise to Job and, I believe, to you both—the second half of your life will be better than the first.

To my friend Pete Rodriguez, thanks for all your passionate prayers on my behalf. Your friendship, encouragement and unconditional support have blessed me tremendously. I know God's light will continue to shine through you.

To Jeff Lee, Jose Rodriguez and Wayne Gill, my Thursday morning prayer partners. Thank you guys. You will never know this side of heaven just how much your friendship and prayers mean to me.

To Tom Damberger and Steve O'Brien. Thank you both for devoting your energy and time to my projects. If God's only reason for having me involved in the solar industry was to meet you guys, then it was well worth it. You have blessed me with your loyalty, friendship, advice and expertise. I pray I have blessed you back by reflecting God properly in all our dealings.

I also want to thank Lee Owen of Writepoint Media who played such an important part in this book as coach and editor, and blessed me tremendously, just as she did in my first book.

With my deepest thanks to Bob Zuccaro and Carl Foster who helped proofread and Sean Lagasse who also proofread and had the toughest job of all, "keeping Jack focused," as I sought to finish this book.

A special thanks to Allen D'Angelo and Kim Leonard for their hard work and publishing expertise.

I also want to thank Bob Dylan who, a long time ago, taught me one of life's great lessons, which is "You shouldn't let other people get your kicks for you."

I am happy to say I didn't.

FREE INSIDE-THE-BOOK EXCLUSIVE OFFER!

The *Where the Rubber Meets the Road with God* Messages

FREE- 3 different audios of Jack Alan Levine's relevant and dynamic messages. Each one will teach you first hand another principle of "Where the Rubber Meets the Road with God"

You can download for free by logging into our website
www.DontBlowItWithGod.com

or have all 3 CD's mailed directly to you for just a total of $2.95 for shipping and handling.

| Download and listen from your computer... | ...which works with Apple iPod, iPhone and most other MP3 devices... | ...or, order a CD and have it shipped right to your door! |

GO NOW TO: DontBlowItWithGod.com

www.DontBlowItWithGod.com